T0368373

THE POWER AND WEAKNESS WITHIN

THE ART OF CHANGE AND SELF-THERAPY

DAVID S. ARNOLD, M.D.

authorHOUSE'

AuthorHouse™
1663 Liberty Drive
Bloomington, IN 47403
www.authorhouse.com
Phone: 833-262-8899

Published by AuthorHouse   10/23/2024

ISBN: 979-8-8230-3629-0 (sc)
ISBN: 979-8-8230-3628-3 (e)

Library of Congress Control Number: 2024922180

Dedication

I dedicate this book to my mother Dorothy Sinclair Arnold. For without her care, love, and presence I would not be the person I am today. Quite simply, without her, I would not exist at all. I wish to thank my other family members and friends, my current and former patients, and my publisher for their precious contributions and undying support. A special thanks to Edward H. Adelson, Professor of Vision Science at MIT for his very gracious permission to use his diagram as presented in chapter nine of this work.

To my readers: You are truly unique in our universe. Understanding yourself and others in this ever increasingly complex world is not easy. It is not a subject matter to be taken lightly. This is a critical task for all to embrace. For those who choose to take this topic lightly often suffer the dire consequences of their inattention and all too frequent coincident misdirected action. I have written this book for all of those vital people who seek truth and desire life-long personal growth and change. Those who wish to free themselves from systemic dynamic imprisonment.

Self-change can be difficult but can be very rewarding. It is a process of personal growth and development that enables us to become the person we want to be. Self-change is a journey of self-discovery and growth. It involves challenging our beliefs and developing new ones. It is a process of transformation and growth that can help us to become more successful and happier in life.

Self-change involves challenging our beliefs and developing new ones. By challenging our beliefs and looking at them in a different light, we can learn how to change our attitudes and behaviors. For example, if we believe that we are not capable of achieving success, we can challenge this belief and look at ways to become successful. By doing this, we can begin to see the potential within ourselves and take the necessary steps to achieve success.

We speak of freedom. But if you are working a job that you hate, are in a relationship that you feel is unhealthy for you but feel stuck, if you find yourself rigidly doing things because that's the way you've always done them or were always told to do things that way, and you find yourself mostly inflexible. Then you my friend are not free! True freedom requires the flexibility to adapt to constant change resulting in personal growth. Living life on one's own terms. Those who are inflexible will predictably find it exceedingly difficult to grow both emotionally and intellectually. True freedom and happiness will always elude them.

This book, which has gone through several revisions, examines how people and systems operate. At first glance this writing may appear to be somewhat academic in its approach. However, by its conclusion the true efficacy that this book may offer the reader through its direct practical application will hopefully become abundantly apparent and realized. This writing attempts to present a mental model that reveals the core "glue" which holds together individuals, families, systems, and indeed entire nations.

Above, I have placed a picture of my son Alex. It was taken during one of our summer vacations at a local beach. He was eleven years old at that time. Behind him stand the beautiful waves of the Mighty Atlantic Ocean; with all of their magnificent ebbs and flows. Some of those waves created loud crashes as they met the shoreline, while some were nearly silent as they softly merged with the sand. Symbolically, the waves are meant to represent the ebbs and flows of our unconscious minds. As we go through life our thoughts, feelings, emotions, and behaviors tend to either softly or moderately merge with, or sometimes violently crash with, our immediate environment. In pursuit of understanding our true nature and the true nature of our world this book explores the structure and power of our unconscious and conscious minds. A model is presented that clarifies how we are constructed as people.

I chose to use a photonegative of my son's picture to highlight the fact that we all typically sit in absolute darkness. We are most often totally blind to our true natures and to our world as we choose who to be at any given moment. I promise you that both the cover and the analogies I have used will make much clearer sense once you have read this book. The fundamental insights provided by this writing will hopefully provide some of the keys you can use to unlock your inner awareness and vision, your mental and emotional power, and your path toward change and self-creation. This book will show you the fundamentals of how to consciously transform yourself. I wish you all the very best on your personal journey!

Best regards,
David

Contents

1

Introduction

FOR MANY CENTURIES, SEVERAL REPETITIVE QUESTIONS REGARDING our existence have arisen:

Who am I?

Why do I feel the way I do?

Why do I think and behave the way I do?

Why do other people think and behave the way they do?

What really controls a person's life?

Is it our thoughts, our feelings, or our desires?

Is it our behavior?

Is it our environment?

Is it our genetic make-up?

Is it the way we were raised?

Is it the laws set by society that one feels compelled to follow?

Why are people and systems so frequently resistant to new ideas and so resistant and slow to change?

What if I need to make changes in my life?

Am I really happy with my life?

Can I really change myself or others?

How can I make change happen?

Can things really ever change at all?

The list goes on and on...

Attempting to find answers to these questions many people have searched for the right 'way' or 'path' to follow. This in the hope of finding their true nature and place in our universe. In response to this identified need, many ways and paths have been created, developed, taught, and instilled throughout the ages. Historically, the developers of those ways and paths have most often used the platforms of philosophy, religion, psychology, therapy, and politics to spread to the masses their various 'answers' to life. Many of those answers, right or wrong, have come in the form of beliefs, myths, prose, and doctrines regarding life's most challenging questions.

Quite often those teaching the various paths have claimed to have the superior path to follow. This of course is quite absurd. The truth is that there is no one right way or path to follow. There are many paths to many ends. The presence of many paths to follow often leads to the inherent confusion and confounding nature of our life's journey. In truth life is specific to each of us as individuals based on our own personal desires, needs, circumstances, and experiences. Therefore, this book does not attempt to place any one path, philosophy, system of belief, or end above another. Which path to follow must ultimately be chosen by the individual to meet their own particular needs and desires within the context of their life circumstance.

One's chosen path is often best woven and crafted within the context of one's own set of evolving circumstances and personal vision of their desired future. By examining the core of who we are, using a structured model, the aim of this book is to teach a powerful perspective and provide several tools that can be used to obtain deeper self-enlightenment, personal growth, and inner change. It reveals a method that can be used to overcome the many obstacles that hinder our ability to develop greater mental flexibility and emotional stability. If for some reason one feels compelled to refer to this method as a way or path, as you will soon see, the way of the flexible gyroscope would suffice. For insight, flexibility, and emotional stability lie at the heart of our ability to adapt and change.

Using a simple unified model, this book also attempts to explain the behavior and interactions of individuals, groups, and systems. It presents a unique model and method that can be applied to the psychotherapeutic process. It provides a powerful tool therapists can use to deliver psychotherapy in a clear, competent, and comprehensive fashion. The core gyroscopic theory presented here can serve as a model upon which all schools of psychotherapy and analysis can be superimposed. It can be used as a central amalgamated unifying point of reference for examining and performing the art of psychotherapy and of self-therapy. The model and methods presented can be used to examine, analyze, understand, and to teach about individual human behavior and about the behavior of systems. However, for the individual, the long-term goal is continuous *personal* growth and change.

During the latter chapters of this book, for the purpose of illustration, I have provided several brief case studies from my own work. Each case study presented has been condensed from several real psychotherapy cases and therefore none of them represent any specific individual. They are intended to help solidify and enhance the reader's understanding of the application of the concepts and therapeutic methods illustrated in this writing from a clinical perspective.

To be completely successful in psychotherapy it is my firm belief that each individual leaving psychotherapy should for the most part be able to effectively serve as their own active therapist going forward. To pursue continuous emotional growth and enlightenment going forward by seeking a deeper understanding of themselves and others. Thus, for the reader, the model and methods presented here are ultimately intended to be used to obtain greater mental flexibility, power, and stability.

As you proceed with employing the model and methods described you will gain a deeper understanding of your own innate ability to change. You will better understand yourself and others, our world, the therapeutic process, and your ability to heal yourself and others. Your power for self-creation will be examined. You will gain new tools you can use when dealing with the people and the systems that surround and impact you. You can use these tools to teach others about your own personal nature, perspectives, and goals. You can also use them to teach others about their own particular natures and perspectives as well.

As we attempt to analyze and understand our thoughts, feelings and behaviors things can quickly become confused and corrupted in our mind's constantly shifting eye. In order to avoid such a state, it would help us greatly to have a structured model or framework in mind that we can use as a point of reference. It can help to anchor us as we attempt to sort through, in an orderly fashion, our multitude of thoughts and feelings. To help keep us fully focused and anchored as we proceed with our self-analysis and mental work. Structured models can provide us with a highly useful roadmap of the human experience. They can also provide us with familiar points of reference and perspectives from which we can further expand our knowledge base and gain a deeper understanding of ourselves.

Such models can provide us with a clear structure that lends itself to greater clarification of our own personal observations, thoughts, feelings, emotions, behaviors, and conclusions. They can also be used to test our ideas, beliefs, assumptions, and hypotheses. Ideally, our chosen model should prompt us to remain objectively focused when we stray off-course. Serving as theoretical guiderails on the highway of self-exploration. It is my hope that individuals and therapists will both find this model and method to be of great utility. Firstly, by providing for some of the structure and guideposts that can be used to create the foundation for a highly productive therapeutic experience. Secondly, by providing a model that opens the door to a whole new world of experiential exploration.

Many theories and models have been proposed in an attempt to understand and explain both the human mind (psyche) and human behavior. After close clinical and scientific scrutiny some models of mental functioning and human behavior have been accepted as being more valid and relevant than others. One such model was Dr. Sigmund Freud's tripartite model. There he described three basic components of our psyche. Namely: the id, the ego, and the superego. His many observations and theories continue to sit at the center of modern-day psychoanalytic practice.

He also described the initial sets of our Ego Defense Mechanisms: which were then further expanded by the great works of his daughter, Anna Freud, and by others as well. I present a small portion of their monumental works in Chapters 2 and 3 of this book. I have done so to provide a greater supportive foundation for my own gyroscopic model, which I present in Chapter 7 of this book. As I will demonstrate, these and other models can be superimposed on my gyroscopic model to get a richer appreciation of the workings of our minds. Most models of the mind use a basic theoretical premise or core concept for their foundation. My model follows such a paradigm. It states that all people and all systems are "gyroscopic", which I will fully explain in a moment.

During my third year of training as a psychiatry resident, while sitting in the hospital cafeteria with several of my fellow residents, I asked one of my mentors Dr. Robert Wenger to describe what psychotherapy is. He was a psychoanalyst and began to describe for us the process of psychotherapy by likening it to the manipulation of a Rubik's cube. In that the therapeutic process involved slowly making sense of things by gently manipulating information and insights to get a clearer perspective of a person's symptoms, problems, and situation. That by putting things back in order one could arrive at a healing experience.

As I sat there, I wondered if there might be one unifying theory that would transcend all forms of therapy and would unite them. There was the Freudian model, but I had a feeling there was some underlying intangible force that must exist. That some form of energy and universal order served as the platform for our mental life. At that moment, while thinking about forces and balance and equilibrium, a picture of a gyroscope came to mind. That was the answer! All things are gyroscopic! That day occurred some 36 years ago and this book derives from the work and the observations I have made since my original conceptualization.

What I mean by the term gyroscopic will be explained more fully in a later chapter. But briefly, gyroscopes are devices that have an inner wheel that spins freely at high speeds. Gyroscopes resist any attempts that are made to change their axis of rotation. People, like gyroscopes, also have an 'inner wheel'. And like gyroscopes, we all cling to our own central axis for a sense of stability. Driven by our own powerful inner wheels, we are all by our very nature mostly inflexible. Thus, we all tend to remain set in our own ways and perspectives as we move through life. We are inherently resistant to change by natural law. In fact, I propose that not only people but all systems resist change as a matter of natural law. Unfortunately, this can sometimes result in us remaining mostly blind to the world around us. It can sabotage our potential for a happier and more fulfilling life.

I propose that the gyroscopic model I will present is rooted in the natural laws of the universe, much like any other phenomena such as gravity or inertia. As such, I consider this model to be an indelible part of our daily existence and a world-wide universal fact. As you proceed forward, with the new knowledge you gain here, you will begin to see the gyroscopic force in operation in many areas of your life. It is truly a powerful force. I refer to

David S. Arnold, M.D.

this universal phenomenon, which leads to our growth and to our innate resistance to change as gyrotropism. I use the term gyrotropism to keep consistent with the general scientific nomenclature used to describe other natural phenomena. For example, when we use the term geotropism to describe the effect of gravity on plant movement and the term phototropism to describe the effect of light on plant movement. What lies at the core of gyrotropism is key to all that we are or may become. We will examine our inner power and our inner weakness. However, the major purpose of this book is mental exploration, personal growth, and self-therapy and it begins with you in mind. Enjoy!

2

Sigmund Freud's
Tripartite Model

I WILL START WITH SOME BASICS AND THEN MOVE ON TO DISCUSS MY model in Chapter 7. Let's start by looking at one theory of how our minds are thought to be constructed. One of the most powerful models of the human psyche ever developed was Sigmund Freud's tripartite (three part) model.[1] With his tripartite model Freud described three basic parts of the human psyche: the "id", the "ego", and the "superego". A full discussion of his many findings and theories is not possible here. A full appreciation of his many contributions would require the careful study of numerous volumes of his written works over many years. That having been said, and in keeping with the goals of this book, let's start with some important basic concepts, terms, and definitions that deal with the workings of our minds. It is hoped that these specifics will provide for a clearer understanding of what this book hopes to provide to its readers.

Freud's initial discovery of the preconscious and the unconscious mind eventually led him to develop his theories of how our minds operate. Our preconscious mind is associated with a part of the mind below the level of immediate conscious awareness, from which memories and emotions that have not been repressed can be recalled. The unconscious mind is like a hidden part of your brain that holds all kinds of thoughts, memories, and feelings that you are not aware of. It affects your thinking, feelings, behavior, and decisions without you knowing it. It is important to keep in mind that our unconscious mental world is completely hidden from us. So, it was quite extraordinary for Freud to discover it.

He was able to show that our conscious behaviors are directed by unconscious activity and directives. That our unconscious mind can reveal itself; even through our seemingly misspoken words. He found that our words often hold a deeper meaning and significance that what appears on the surface of our conversations. These are frequently referred to as 'Freudian slips' (of the tongue). There is an old joke that goes: A Freudian slip is when you say one thing, but you mean your mother.

Here again I will get a little creative with visualization. The unconscious mind can be likened to a boiling pot of vegetable soup with bits of carrot, potato, celery, peas, meat, etc. that are in a constant state of flux. Those bits and pieces of food can be seen to represent our ideas, thoughts, beliefs, perspectives, feelings, wishes, desires, hopes, fears, impulses, memories, fantasies, past experiences, etc. This core state of our mental being has been termed primary thought process. Of note, the unconscious mind has no need for logic. Right can be left, and left can be up, and down can be left, or right, or both, or neither, or an elephant eating ice cream while holding an umbrella in the sunset. It simply doesn't matter if it makes sense to the conscious mind!

Our primary thought process stands in contrast to our secondary thought process. Secondary thought process operates at a conscious level and is where we put our thoughts into their proper 'logical' context. It is where we attempt to make sense of our thoughts. Freud's model laid the foundation for the field of psychoanalysis; which attempts to uncover and make sense of our unconscious thoughts and motivations.[2] I will now present several basic definitions related to Sigmund Freud's tripartite model.

ID is a term used to describe that place in our mind that holds the energy source for our two most basic instinctual drives: our sexual and aggressive drives. Put crudely, the Id creates and powers our drive to have our basic needs met. Several psychoanalysts have expressed the concern that the terms sexual and aggressive can be somewhat misleading. When we use the term 'sexual drive' (originally termed libido) it is not meant to be taken in the modern sense of the term 'sexual' (i.e., 'adult sexuality'), but instead is better described as our drive (need) to create. Likewise, the term 'aggressive' is not meant to represent the more common view of the term aggressive (i.e., 'violent'). Rather, it is meant to represent our drive (need) to dismantle (undo) the things around us.

Some have proposed using the terms construdo (the constructive force) and destrudo (the destructive force) in place of the former terms to clarify things. Thus, construdo is an energy that arises from our Id's Eros: our 'life drive'. It is the source of our need to create and to procreate. Destrudo arises from our Id's 'thanatos': our 'death drive'. It is the source our need to undo and dismantle things. The id does serve as the main energy source fueling our aggression. It is important to bear in mind that these id forces (construdo and destrudo) always co-exist in all of us. That they are unconscious: and never operate in isolation from each other. And, that they are always present together in every thought and action of ours.

The unconscious mind fully accepts both the constructive and destructive drives as being equally valid, acceptable, and necessary. So powerful are these unconscious forces that the term psychic determinism has been aptly applied to describe their profound effect in driving our daily behaviors. However, at any given moment, one drive can prove to be dominant over the other. Evidence of an awareness of psychoanalytic laws can even be found in the bible. The Apostle Paul expressed his awareness that psychic determinism is an inherent powerful part of our being in the following statement.

> Romans 7:19; "For I do not practice the good that I will; but the evil I do not will, that I do."

Although our unconscious mind and various environmental factors play a significant role in shaping our behavior, we do have considerable conscious control over how we behave. Whether we decide to do the things that are constructive and add positive things to our lives: or to do destructive things that worsen or destroy our lives is partially guided by our intent. Each day we must consciously decide whether we will travel on a generally constructive path or on a generally destructive one. By early adulthood we generally know what behaviors of ours are truly 'good' for us or are 'bad' for us. Therefore, a full understanding of our psyche has implications for our overall health.

For instance, we all know that overeating, lack of exercise, smoking cigarettes, using illicit drugs and alcohol, speeding while driving, unprotected sex, etc. are not in our best interest, but millions of people in spite of their awareness of the destructive nature of these behaviors do so every day. However, our knowledge, our will power, and our faith can be used to support our ability to remain on a healthy and constructive path. In reality, we have great influence over the final choices we make though this sometimes may not seem so.

Ego is a term used to describe that part of our mind that experiences the external world (reality) through the senses. It organizes our rational thoughts and through the use of ego defense mechanisms (presented in Chapter 3) governs and directs our behavior. The ego mediates between the impulses of the id, the demands of the environment, and the standards of the superego to keep an individual intact and functioning. Ego defenses would then tend to support and protect our inner wheels. In entities such as institutions and business systems, procedures serve the role of ego.

Superego is a term used to describe that part of our mind that is critical of the self (ego) and enforces moral standards. At a conscious level it uses guilt to punish the ego, and at an unconscious level it generates anxiety and emotional discomfort (angst). In crude terms, it serves as a set of brakes for the ego and the id. Institutions and businesses use rules, regulations, policies, and ethical guidelines implemented through a supervisory structure that is tied to clear penalties. For the institution this serves the role of the superego. Thus, the superego, has an 'I ought or I should', rather than an 'I want' (id), or an 'I can' (ego) quality. The superego is constructed of internalized prohibitions which act to suppress id and ego satisfaction even when there is no possibility of punishment by an external agent. The superego is largely unconscious.

Freud also described a psychic structure that he referred to as the 'sensor' that essentially acts as a filter and gatekeeper for the flow of unconscious material. It acts like an editor of a paper deciding what's fit for print. If the id impulse or unconscious material is too intense for us to handle emotionally, the sensor generates a very uncomfortable emotional state of anxiety that Freud termed 'signal anxiety'. In response to the discomfort felt, the ego attempts to repress (totally hide), to suppress ('sweep under the carpet'), or to transform (disguise) the impulse in an attempt to lessen the anxiety generated.[3]

Why the tripartite model is so important is that it attempts to explain the standard operating procedures for the conscious and unconscious portions of our mind. These operating procedures have a profound impact on the way we think, feel, and behave every moment of our lives. In the field of psychoanalysis: this model and the forces described that govern and regulate our minds are considered to be documented fact and not just theory. It is a model for understanding psychosis versus neurosis.[4]

The term psychic determinism is used by psychoanalysts to describe the tremendous power the unconscious has in shaping and directing our daily actions. Indeed, it tends to dictate the general course of our lives. The gyroscopic method presented in later chapters lays the foundation for a self-directed form of conscious determinism. For the purpose of simplification, I have attempted to diagram the basic parts of Freud's model in Fig. 1 (below).

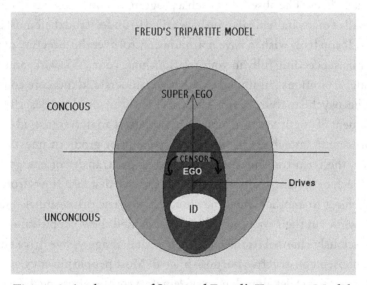

Figure 1: A schematic of Sigmund Freud's Tripartite Model.

Impulses from the id flow through the censor, which operates at an unconscious level. Using the intensity level of signal anxiety as a guide, the censor leads to either the expression of acceptable or the repression unacceptable id impulses. The impulses that are allowed to pass through the censor are fed through the ego, where ego defenses are applied. This then allows for the id impulses to be satisfied through discharge.

The pressure for rapid discharge without regard for the consequences to others (or to the organism itself) is referred to in psychoanalytic theory as the "pleasure principle". The pleasure principle implies that man is basically hedonistic, seeking to maximize his pleasure while attempting to avoid any unpleasantness. The process of learning to delay impulse expression and to take into account the immediate and future consequences of our behavior is referred to as the "reality principle". The tremendous power our basic drives have to direct us towards welcomed greatness or unwanted infamy is surely worth considering.

Our sexual and aggressive drives ultimately supply the power for our actions, and it takes ongoing active mental work to shape and re-shape who we are. An area for improvement in our society is the development of a clear and comprehensive teaching system that helps people to gain a sound understanding of their basic drives and natures and how these affect their daily lives. The absence of such a program of education has led to the downfall of many individuals who have failed to understand their most basic nature. If you truly wish to have optimum control over the direction of your life while succeeding fully in your relationships, your life's work, and your personal aspirations it is imperative that you understand this core concept.

The psychoanalytic term "cathexis" is often used to describe the attachment of our drives to an object. In the purest analytic sense, id energy is "cathected" (attached) to the object, person, or group in question. In science, the term transduction is defined as the transfer of energy from one object, or system, to another. Such as the way that heat flows from one metal object to another when they touch. Our basic drives are also felt to 'flow' while on their way towards being satisfied. Few people know how to consciously channel (transduce) their sexual or aggressive drive energy into a chosen constructive purpose or goal. Most people never even think about this subject, let alone have a systematic way of addressing it. I believe that this lack of knowledge and awareness can lead to unwanted or highly undesirable outcomes, which I discuss later in this book.

3

The Ego Defense Mechanisms

DURING 1894, AS A PRACTICING NEUROLOGIST, STRICT SCIENTIST, AND Secretary of the German Society of Naturalists and Physicians, Sigmund Freud branched out to the field of psychiatry by describing his first set of defense mechanisms. At first this may sound confusing, but I assure you it will become much clearer as you proceed with your reading. Freud had observed that not only could our affect and emotions be "dislocated or transported" from ideas through unconscious mechanisms he would later refer to as repression, dissociation, and isolation, but that they could also be "re-attached" to other ideas which he referred to as displacement. He also noted that subject and object could be cognitively reversed by the process he termed projection.

Before discussing our defense mechanisms, and in order to get a deeper understanding, it is important to discuss the topics of tension and anxiety. Freud noted that a major drive for people is the reduction of tension and that a major cause of tension is anxiety. He identified three different types of anxiety:

Reality Anxiety

This is the most basic form of anxiety and is typically based on fears of real and/or plausible events, such as being bitten by a dog, struck by a car, falling from a ladder, being struck by lightning, etc. The most common way of reducing the tension felt is to avoid or to get away from the feared situation or event (i.e., by avoiding any possible contact with dogs, by avoiding crossing any roads, by refusing to climb a ladder, or by avoiding being outside on cloudy or rainy days).

Neurotic Anxiety

This is a form of anxiety that arises from an **unconscious** fear that the basic primitive impulses of the Id will take control of us, make us misbehave, and eventually lead us to be punished for our 'bad' actions. An example would be a fear of acting inappropriately in response to one's sexual urges while at work and being punished for it. Importantly, with neurotic anxiety the sexual urges are totally unknown to the person; all they experience is the anxiety and don't know why. They may seek help with their anxiety, and not have a clue as to why they are feeling anxious.

Moral Anxiety

This form of anxiety comes from a fear of violating values and moral codes and gets expressed as feelings of guilt or shame. When moral anxiety occurs, the mind first responds by an increase in active thinking and problem solving. The mind often seeks rational ways of escaping the situation. If this doesn't work, a range of "defense mechanisms", covered next, may be triggered. This can then lead to very complex behaviors and interactions.

Freud also described how the Ego uses a wide-range of "defense mechanisms" to handle the interactions between itself, the Id, and the Superego. This while simultaneously meeting our needs and protecting us. This 'protection' is why they are often referred to as ego 'defense' mechanisms. Freud highlighted the role of repression in normal mental functioning. He saw repression as being central to, and a critical component of, his theories of mental function.

Repression is where the mind unconsciously excludes painful, unwanted or conflicted thoughts, feelings, impulses, and/or memories from our conscious awareness. Repression is the primary ego defense mechanism, and all others tend to assist or reinforce it. Thus, restating the aforementioned, a number of phenomena are used to aid in the maintenance of repression, and these are termed the Ego Defense Mechanisms. The terms "Mental Mechanisms" and "Defense Mechanisms" are essentially synonymous.

The primary goals of the ego defense mechanisms are:

1. To minimize anxiety.
2. To protect the self.
3. To maintain repression.
4. To service the needs of the id.

Ego defense mechanisms protect us from being consciously aware of a thought or feeling we would otherwise find difficult to deal with or to tolerate. The defense mechanisms allow for the unconscious thought or feeling to be repressed (shoved and locked away under the surface), or to be expressed indirectly in a disguised form or fashion.

By distorting reality, there is a change in perception that allows for a lessening of anxiety with a corresponding reduction in the tension felt. Repression is useful to the individual since it prevents discomfort, and leads to some economy of time and effort. Wow! That's a mouthful! But all true! J

Thus, All Defense Mechanisms share two common properties:

1. They most often appear unconsciously.
2. They tend to distort, transform, or otherwise falsify reality.

Anna Freud greatly expanded upon the original list of ego defenses described by her father, Thus, leading us to a deeper appreciation of their nature and impact on our lives. At this point, in an attempt to better understand these concepts, it would be good to examine a common life example of how the id, ego, and superego can work in unison to the benefit of an individual.

Let's take the example of a young man who recently met a girl whom he finds to be highly attractive and sexually desirable. His immediate impulse (id) is to be sexually intimate with her. However, they have just met. If he were to approach her with a request that she be sexually intimate with him, the odds are quite great that she would reject him immediately. Aside from that, she might embarrass him by telling others about his highly inappropriate request for sexual intimacy. His superego would then likely punish him with feelings of guilt and embarrassment. If he acted in a forceful manner, he would run the risk of retaliation and possible legal repercussions. The law would serve as a strong enforcer of punishment for his indiscretion in addition to his own superego's form of punishment.

So instead, he develops a plan to win her favor: the ego in action. He decides to ask her out on a date (Sublimation: See definition: Appendix A) with the hope that things will progress well from there. A movie and dinner seem a good idea for a safe first date. As their eagerly awaited date begins, things start-off well, they make a good connection and he begins to realize that she is somewhat taken by his appearance and behavior. They then walk to a local movie theatre, buy their tickets, purchase popcorn and soda and then take their seats.

As they sit in the movie theatre while the movie is running, he debates the idea of placing his arm around her shoulder: id impulse in action. After a moment of sweating out the decision he decides not to do so. This, out of neurotic anxiety (described above), his fear of rejection and his fear of intense feelings of guilt over having violated her trust: super ego in action. His fear is that if he were to make such a mistake that he would surely beat himself up mentally for days and possibly for months afterwards. He would also jeopardize his chance of forming a romantic relationship with the girl in question.

Interestingly, as an aside, if you were to ask him about the content of the movie they were watching, he might not have a clue, or would have a very patchy report to give. He would have been in a highly distracted state of mind during the movie. However, regardless of this, and as a result of his good behavior, they complete their first date and go on several more dates. After a few months of dating, they develop an intimate relationship and their initial id impulses get satisfied (i.e., sexual intimacy). They experience their first kiss. This all occurs in a socially acceptable manner which safeguards both of the individuals involved from any moral or societal negative repercussions. In the meantime, their id impulses get satisfied. I know what you're thinking: some people are on a faster track when dating. But in general, they tend to follow similar rules of behavior.

Everyone has heard of athletes and politicians who have had sexual indiscretions that put them in the hot bright spotlight of infamy. They break the rules of acceptable societal behavior. In many of these cases, I feel that the athletes and politicians involved have failed to understand the true nature of their basic drives. They very often have failed to contain their sexual energy (construdo) and their aggressive energy (destrudo) into appropriate channels (i.e., their work) instead of their sexual indiscretions and/or abusive and assaultive behaviors. Like some people, they assume or were led to believe that their unconscious 'sexual' urges (in reality: construdo) are present only for the purpose of sexual activity. Likewise, they assume or were led to believe that their 'aggressive' urges (in reality: destrudo) are present only for the purpose of hostility and violence. Their ego defenses fail them and their core personality style overshadows the needs of others.

Quite often they have failed to anticipate and understand that the expression of one's sexual and aggressive drives often becomes heightened with success, notoriety, and political power. This is further fueled by their continued accomplishments and increasing sense of power and self-esteem. During the course of their work athletes and politicians can quickly become overwhelmed and corrupted by the many urges they experience. It can become intoxicating to the individual, much like the 'call of the ring' in J.R.R. Tolkien's "The Lord of the Rings". In that book, the ring tempts its potential wearer with ultimate power over all things if only they would simply wear it.

Psychiatrist, Alfred Adler, believed that "character" was the result of a unique interplay between two opposing forces: a need for personal power and aggrandizement and a need for "social feeling" and togetherness. The many urges felt by people of notoriety and power can make them act in seemingly uncharacteristic and self-destructive ways. It is well known that the use of alcohol or drugs can have a profoundly negative impact on one's character. There is a saying in psychiatry that 'the superego is soluble in alcohol'. Some feel that money can change a person's character. However, I am reminded of the quote which states that having money and power doesn't change a person's character, it only reveals it! It is worthwhile to read psychiatrist Carl Jung's description of how "archetypes" can direct our choice of sexual and life partners. In fact, there are many authors who have written about relationships and the driving forces behind them.

As such, it would be ideal if the people involved in scandals entered psychotherapy to better understand and control the urges they experience from a personal perspective. This with the eventual goal of mastering the how and the why of transducing (channeling) their urges toward a more constructive, positive, fulfilling, and productive end for themselves. This could also potentially help them to avoid a great deal of personal loss, embarrassment, public humiliation, and ridicule. It could lead to politicians being better able to govern more effectively. It is often quite painful to see people stumble from great heights due to their lack of knowledge in this area of human experience. It is often a disheartening spectacle to observe people who do not know their own natures. They often appear stunned by and usually somewhat oblivious to the serious nature of their transgressions when their behaviors are spotlighted by others.

It is both interesting and informative to study the various ego defense mechanisms. As you study them, you will soon begin to notice the ones that you, your friends, your family members, your co-workers, your boss, and your politicians use most often. Our unconscious drives, hopes, fears, fantasies, and perceptions fuel our most predominant pattern of ego defenses which then underlie our own individual personality styles. As you study the words and actions of others, remembering to study your own as well, you may find yourself better able to spot the multiple examples of ego defenses that impact upon and shape your daily life and relationships.

The defense mechanisms are by definition unconscious and therefore are not consciously recognized by people during the normal course of their daily activities. Therefore, it would be difficult to directly confront an individual about their use of defense mechanisms, because they would simply be unaware of what you were talking about. Thus, confronting them would be impossible to attempt without precipitating an involved and lengthy discussion. It would truly be a teaching moment!

How you handle these defenses can have a huge impact on your life. For example, let's take the ego defense of identification. If you have a friend or family member who you strongly identify with and who you see as being weak and ineffective. Then likely you will see yourself as weak and ineffective. This would affect the choices you make and thus the limits of your personal power. It will heavily influence the outcomes of your actions and ultimately the direction of your life. But the defenses are unconscious so that you would most likely be unaware of their presence and impact. That is one reason why therapy can be helpful.

What is important to remember is that the ego defenses have a purpose and are there to keep us 'stable' and 'safe'. They help to repress (hide) our unacceptable thoughts and/or impulses from our conscious mind. As such, people are sometimes totally unaware of the true origin and nature of their conscious thoughts, feelings, and/or behaviors. The ego defenses are a vital and integral part of our mental health.[5] See Appendix A for a list of the ego defense mechanisms and their definitions.

It is also important to note that there is a generally accepted hierarchy for the defense mechanisms. There are those that are considered to be the more mature ones such as humor and altruism, and then there are those that are considered to be the less mature ones such as projection, denial, and reaction formation. However, they are all vital and we tend to use them all. The fact that humor is considered a higher "more mature" defense mechanism gives me much joy and pleasure. Just knowing that we're being mature even when we're being silly! ☺

4

Mood, Affect, Emotion, and Temperament

ASIDE FROM OUR UNCONSCIOUS MENTAL ACTIVITY ONE CANNOT overstate the awesome power that our moods and emotions have in both directing and responding to the events of our daily lives. Our mood and our thoughts directly influence and help shape our emotions and behavior in a give-and-take manner. The terms mood and emotion are often used interchangeably. However, for the sake of greater clarity and understanding, the term mood should be distinguished from the term emotion.

According to the Merriam-Webster dictionary, the word "mood" is derived from the Old English word 'Mōd' which referred to military courage. And the word "emotion" dates back to 1579, when it was adapted from the French word *émouvoir*, which means "to stir up". The French word 'émouvoir' is based on the Latin word 'emovere', the 'e' meaning 'out' and 'movere' meaning 'move'. Emotions are aroused in people by situations or objects in their environment. However, the earliest precursors of these words likely date back to the very origins of language.

Let's further examine the term mood. The term mood is often defined as a conscious state of mind with a predominant feeling state. Moods may last for long periods of time whereas emotions tend to last for shorter periods of time. Emotions tend to be more transient in nature. One is said to emote as they express their feelings. Moods tend to be less specific and less intense than emotions and are less likely to be triggered by a specific event or stimulus.

How many moods can you name? The field of psychology recognizes five basic moods. Our five basic moods are Sadness, Happiness, Anger, Anxiety, and Apathy. When considering our various moods, we can plot them out over time as illustrated in figure 2 (below). Take note that with any extreme mood, irritability and agitation may occur. That in the extremes of mood, emotions are more likely to arise.

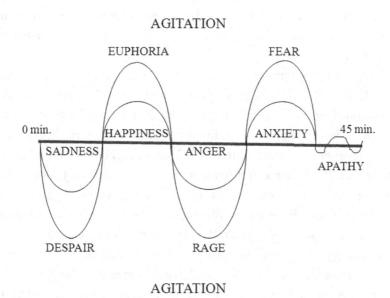

Figure 2: Moods and Emotions Graphed over Time.

In review, emotions are often experienced at the extremes of mood and are states of being that are somewhat transient in nature when compared with moods. Moods tend to be more enduring and are deeply felt by the individual who may not express them openly. The term affect is used in psychiatry to describe what the examiner observes (i.e., sad face, dejected posture, trembling, etc.) as they attempt to ascertain what a person's mood and emotions might be over a span of time such as a 45-minute interview. A person's mood, however, is generally accepted as what the person being evaluated states they feel (i.e., sad, happy, angry, anxious, apathy) when asked by the examiner.

Further defined, emotion is also a conscious mental reaction based on an underlying mood (i.e., sadness, happiness, anger, anxiety, apathy) that is subjectively experienced as a strong feeling usually directed toward a specific object and usually accompanied by physiologic and behavioral changes. Emotions are characterized by psycho-physiological expressions, biological activity, assumed mental states, and quite often by behavioral expressions. Emotional expression is directly related to mood, temperament, personality, disposition, thinking (cognition), and motivation. It is also felt to be directly influenced by biological factors such as hormonal status and neurotransmitter activity (i.e., dopamine, serotonin, noradrenaline, GABA, oxytocin, cortisol, etc.). Emotion is often the driving force behind motivation.

Some examples of emotions are: Affection, Angst, Anguish, Annoyance, Arousal, Awe, Boredom, Contempt, Contentment, Courage, Curiosity, Depression, Desire, Despair, Disappointment, Disgust, Distrust, Dread, Ecstasy, Elation, Embarrassment, Emptiness, Envy, Euphoria, Excitement, Fear, Frustration, Gratitude, Grief, Guilt, Happiness, Hatred, Hope, Horror, Hostility, Hurt, Hysteria, Indifference, Interest, Isolation, Jealousy, Joy, Loathing, Loneliness, Love, Lust, Outrage, Panic, Passion, Pity, Pleasure, Pride, Rage, Regret, Remorse, Satisfaction, Shame, Shock, Shyness, Sorrow, Suffering, Surprise, Terror, Trust, Wonder, Worry, Zeal, Zest, etc.

As already mentioned, emotions tend to be induced by extremes of mood. When sadness becomes profound it can be experienced as the emotion of despair. When happiness becomes extreme it can be experienced as the emotion of euphoria. When anger becomes extreme it can be experienced as the emotion of rage. When anxiety becomes profound it can be experienced as the emotion of fear. Apathy, due to its very nature of not caring and not feeling can be experienced as the emotions of emptiness, isolation, and boredom.

Using these definitions of mood and emotion we can examine situations where emotions are created. When we attach our thoughts and our feeling of 'happy' to a gift (object) we receive for our birthday we may then experience the emotion of 'joy' (strong feeling) and as a result feel 'butterflies" in our stomach (physiological response) and dance and shout uncontrollably (behavioral change).

When we attach our mood of anxiety to a tiger (object) that we think is about to attack us (i.e., our thoughts) we may experience the emotion of fear and, at least for me, utter dread (powerfully strong feelings)! We may begin feel our heart pounding, our breathing increase, and feel 'shaky' inside (physiological response) and attempt to run screaming through the streets (behavioral change), although running from tigers, even paper ones, isn't often recommended by the experts. ☺

Cognition (thinking) greatly influences the state and shape of one's emotions. For example, the cognition of danger (i.e., the thought that one might be attacked while walking alone down a dark street at night and the other possible dangerous outcomes one specifically imagines in response to those thoughts) can cause an activation of one's central nervous system leading to a rapid heart rate, rapid breathing, sweating, muscle tension, trembling, etc. As the person becomes aware of their physiologic response this can induce more fear and start a vicious cycle of feedback. This can then set the stage for abject fear and a state of panic. This may affect the individual's behavior causing them to run and seek help. The classic fight-or-flight response.

However, if they have walked those same seemingly dangerous streets many times in the past and they have a gun with them for safety, the mere sense of familiarity with the area and the *thought* of having the gun may provide a sense of safety, real or imagined, which can shape that individual's eventual emotions. Feeling secure, they may choose to walk more slowly and not to run which would attract unwanted attention. They may change their behavioral response by deciding to stay and fight rather than take flight. Granted that while this is an extreme example, it gets across the point I wished to make.

In addition to our five basic moods and the numerous emotions that were described above, we are all born with a particular temperament. This describes a person's innate "baseline" emotional disposition. Synonyms for temperament include: nature, temper, grain, and disposition. Temperament is present so early in our lives that indeed it is considered to be an innate (inborn) quality that we each possess. Within groups of infants, toddlers, adolescents and adults, we see clear individual differences in their temperaments. This persists throughout people's growth and development and has a huge impact on their perspective of the world.

Temperament plays a significant role in who we are. How we interact with others and how we go about living our lives. Secretly, we may ask ourselves certain questions when we are first getting to know an individual.

23

Is this person usually calm and pleasant or irritable and moody? Are they mostly 'even-tempered', easily irritated or 'hot-headed' or 'cool thinking'? The following scenario demonstrates the strong influence that mood and emotions can have on our behavior:

Picture an old man sitting on a park bench reading a newspaper. It's a beautiful spring day. The sun is shining brightly, the sky is blue, the birds are chirping in the trees, and children are happily playing in a nearby playground. Suddenly a child leaves the playground and tosses a beach ball toward the old man. The ball rolls and lightly touches the old man's leg. He puts down his newspaper and picks up the ball. He then begins tossing the ball back and forth with the child as they both laugh and play with great delight.

Now let's take the same scenario. Except this time someone comes along with a sledge hammer and forcefully strikes the old man's left foot. The old man is now in excruciating pain. His mood becomes angry and he develops the emotion of rage. If at that very moment the child were to toss the beach ball toward the old man's leg, it is very likely that the old man would angrily kick the ball away. He might curse at or scold the child while yelling get away from me! Can't you see that I'm in pain here?! Expletives deleted!

What is quite significant is that the only thing that has changed between the first and the second scenarios is a shift in the old man's mood. It is the same sun, the same birds, and the same child as the first scenario. In the first scenario the old man's mood is happy and content. While in the second his mood is angry and enraged and he is in pain. In the first scenario his perspective is that the world is a happy and beautiful place to be. In the second scenario his perspective is that the world is a horrible, hostile, and painful place to be. We then witness the emotion of rage and a behavioral change. His perception of the world changes abruptly and dramatically.

He suddenly feels that the sun is beating down on him, that the chirping birds are irritating and annoying, and that the playful child is hostile and intrusive. Same world, same sun, same trees, same birds, same child. He just sees them quite differently. He sees the exact opposite of what he did initially! Therefore, our moods and emotions can serve to distort our sense of reality. Our moods color and distort our perceptions and thereby directly impact our conclusions which then shape our subsequent perspectives and behavior. As a result of his mood shift his view of the world becomes distorted and his behavior towards the child and indeed towards the world changes dramatically as well. It can also strongly influence the choices he makes.

What is also very interesting about this situation is the role that timing plays in the formation of our perceptions. If you were to ask the old man about his negative behavior towards the child while his foot was still hurting, he would likely attempt to justify his behavior. He might state my foot is killing me and he threw a ball at me! Couldn't he see I was in pain! Which would be a more immature response. However, if you were to question him several weeks later after his foot no longer hurt, he might express intense guilt and remorse over his behavior towards the child. He might make a strong argument that he loves children and would never do anything to hurt a child. That it is truly neither his character nor his personality to act in such a manner with children. That he would never have behaved the way he did were it not for the intense pain and anguish he had experienced. A more mature and rational response.

Such feelings of intense guilt and remorse are often judged by most to be unnecessary under the aforementioned given set of circumstances. In that it is generally recognized and accepted by society at large that as his mood shifted with his experience of intense pain while being victimized. That the old man's ability to think clearly and to behave rationally changed as well. That the situation had placed him outside the pale of his ability to control his response. It is important to note that his angry behavior at the time of the incident had little to do with the old man's true nature, his character, or his personality. As a result of his horrific experience, he might even further change his behavior. For instance, by starting a neighborhood watch Anti-Foot Whacker society to prevent such atrocities in the future! ☺

It is also important to know that we have an unwritten hierarchy for our five basic moods. Just as there is a hierarchy for our various ego defense mechanisms there is also one for our five basic moods. This often unstated, socially imposed ranking system is usually in constant operation. The following paragraphs describe the nature of our mood hierarchy system.

Most of us will accept a 'happy' person who walks in the room. Usually, they tend to make us feel somewhat happy too. We are most often inclined to like such experiences. If an 'apathetic' person walks in the room, they don't care we don't care. Thus, they are usually dismissed and ignored by all present. If a 'sad' person walks in the room they would be somewhat less welcome. They are often seen as a slight emotional burden by others. This is why many people often hide any feelings of sadness they may have. So as not to be a burden to others. If an 'anxious' person walks in the room everyone wants them to calm down immediately. It's hard for people to tolerate. We ask them to sit down and tell us what is wrong. To not be so anxious! The least accepted is the 'angry' person who walks in the room. Most people want them to leave the room immediately! Get them out of here! If they exhibit any angry behaviors, to call security!! However, although some may be less desirable than others all five basic moods are a natural integral part of our psyche. Being able to tolerate and deal with all of our basic moods and emotions is necessary for our emotional health and wellbeing.

Another important fact to keep in mind concerning moods is that we tend to mirror the emotions we see in others. I had alluded to this in the previous two paragraphs. If someone is happy, we tend to feel happy. If someone is anxious, we tend to feel anxious. When an anxious person enters a room the people in the room will ask them to take a seat, get control over their emotions, and calm down. Anxious people make us feel more anxious! This is generally experienced as an uncomfortable and sometimes painful emotion by most. This is why everyone in the room wants the anxious person to calm down immediately. Likewise, if someone approaches us in an angry manner, we tend to feel and act angry in response.

If we simply mirror the emotions of others in a blind fashion we are doomed to be controlled by our own emotions, the emotions of others, and by the general emotional tones set by the moment. It takes some practice not to respond to the emotional tones set by others, but it can be done with practice. This is a vital step to take if you wish to manage your own moods and emotions and eventually your own destiny. In the epic martial arts film, "Enter the Dragon", Bruce Lee instructs his student to use "focused emotional content" and "not anger" in his fighting techniques. The student is expected to master their moods and emotions, rather than become a reactive puppet and slave to them.

In review: When our mood is attached to a particular object, target, or event, which then causes an emotion with a coordinated set of responses which may include verbal, physical, and neurologic mechanisms this can cause a change in our behavior. People's moods can lead to the formation of emotions that can then uncover moods and provoke emotions in others.

The following is a relevant story from my own personal experience. As a ten-year-old child I had become quite curious about how many of the mechanical devices around my family's home worked. Much to my family members dismay I would occasionally take things apart to take a look inside. I was simply curiously exploring what really made things work. I took apart clocks, toasters, radios, telephones, electric can openers, you name it. If it moved or ticked or made a sound, I took it apart to figure out how it worked. Most of the time I was able to put the things I had dismantled back together. Other times, however, much to my dismay I was quite unsuccessful. This would cause me a great deal of frustration and anger at myself for having taken the darn thing apart in the first place. I also lived with the fear of inevitably being caught and punished or killed!

I remember quite clearly working frantically one day while trying to put my mother's radio alarm clock back together. I figured that she might need it to wake-up the next day. I had returned home from school after 3PM and my mother was soon due home from work after 5PM. Oh my God, what had I done! Panic set in! I had become so frustrated, overwhelmed and anxious that I could not use my hands in an effective manner. My trembling hands felt awkward and clumsy as if I had lost full control over them. At that moment it struck me how powerful and absolutely paralyzing and counter-productive our moods and emotions can be. That they can actually become our worst enemy.

At that very moment I made a conscious decision and pledged to rule my moods and emotions rather than to have them rule me. For if I let my moods and emotions rule me, they would make me incapacitated and ineffective and thereby dictate my future. That experience had a profound effect on my life. It gave me the opportunity to experience a great insight! It let me realize that indeed I could experience moods and emotions, but I did not have to relinquish control and become a slave to them in the process. At that moment I was ready to receive any punishment doled-out because I realized that through that experience, I had gained something priceless. My freedom from being ruled by my emotions!

The opportunity to confront the power of your moods and emotions comes through many venues and activities. Try not to ignore opportunities that arise and allow for you to master your most intense moods and emotions. It will eventually free you to fully direct your own destiny. In dealing with one's moods and emotions every person who wishes to control their own destiny must take this stand!

There are those who routinely succumb to their moods and emotions. Some are overwhelmed by their anxiety to the point of feeling inadequate and may become avoidant of other people. Some make anger the center of their daily lives and act in a destructive manner which offends and alienates people. There are those who make an angry mood and the emotion of hatred the central theme of their entire existence. For them, people and the world at large are the bane of their existence. The path of hatred towards individuals, groups, and/or systems most often leads to devastating effects on society at large. Those people who are drenched in hatred walk on a dark, dangerous, and often tragic path. They are lost and are the enemies of society. They are truly unfortunate! Later chapters will take a closer look at this topic.

In the realm of personality types, one of the standard assessment tools is the Myers-Briggs Type Indicator (MBTI) which from its early form has been around since the 1940's. It is used by many employers today as part of their applicant and employee assessment process. During a Christmas vacation Isabel Briggs brought home her boyfriend Clarence Myers. Isabel's mother Katherine noted that while she liked Isabel's boyfriend, he was quite different from their family members. She subsequently developed an interest in categorizing people by personality types. Katherine discovered the book "Psychological Types" by psychiatrist Carl Jung and it became the basis for her lifelong work on defining personality types. She also became aware of psychiatrist Alfred Adler's work on introversion vs. extroversion. Isabel Briggs eventually married Clarence Myers, Thus, the Briggs-Myers label.

Prior to her death Isabel Briggs Myers wrote with the assistance of her son Peter the book "Gifts Differing: Understanding Personality Type" which is a must read if you are interested in the thinking behind personality typology. The MBTI defines 16 possible personality types expressed as a four-letter code. Examples are ENTP, INTJ, ESFP, ISFP, etc. If you are interested, there is a website where you can take the test for free to determine your personality type. The test is in a yes-no format and takes approximately twelve minutes to complete.

The website is: www.16personalities.com/free-personality-test

Once you discover your personality type, 'google' it and you will get a wealth of information about yourself. It is a very interesting and informative exercise. See if you agree!

5

Mood Gone Wrong and Emotional Laziness

EMOTIONLESS LAZINESS IS A STATE OF BEING THAT IS OFTEN misunderstood or overlooked. It is a feeling of emptiness, indifference, or indifference about anything or anyone. It is a state where one lacks the motivation to act or even care about the outcome of their efforts. It is a feeling of apathy where nothing seems to matter or have any importance.

It is important to understand that emotionless laziness is not a sign of weakness, but rather an expression of suppressed emotion. Emotions can be suppressed for a variety of reasons such as fear, guilt, or shame. For example, a person may feel ashamed of their failures and be unwilling to take risks or face challenges. As a result, they may become emotionally shut down and avoid any challenges or interactions with others.

We are actually prone to laziness and we are inherently lazy for a reason. That reason is at least partially biological and is genetically driven. Since it is usually easier for us to see how things affect us in the physical realm I will start there. Since prehistoric times we have been genetically engineered and programmed to maintain our bodies in a state best suited for our own individual and our collective survival and procreation. This to ensure the 'continuation of our species'. As you continue to read on you will undoubtedly wonder: Where is he going with this? Trust me that it will become clear by the end of this chapter.

Our DNA directs the creation and very composition of every cell in our body. Our bodies want to conserve energy whenever possible to ensure that they can function and thereby survive. Since fat is a better source of energy than is muscle (specifically, fat has 9 kcal/mole vs. protein which has 4 kcal/mole), the body is pre-programmed to prefer a higher amount of body fat than muscle mass to ensure adequate energy stores. The proposed rationale for this is that during times of famine the body is able to feed-off-of its own fat stores for the energy needed to survive. You really don't want to break-down your muscles which you need to move with in order to get energy just to survive. That wouldn't work well. Fat, however, serves as a highly efficient storage system. Animals in the wild make use of this fact constantly as their various available food sources wax-and-wane throughout the seasons. This system helps to prevent starvation when food supplies are not available.

While this may serve some grand and practical biological purpose it tends to serve as a source of great frustration for those wishing to lose weight through dieting. For dieting runs directly counter to the body's natural programmed desire to consume the calories required to maintain high energy fat stores. Again, our bodies find survival security in being fat. People will sometimes starve themselves in short spurts in a futile attempt to attain long-term weight reduction. However, this runs directly counter to nature's long-term goal of ensuring a person's survival. Only a sustained long-term reduction in calories consumed will lead to sustained weight loss. As noted, the body is programmed to want the fat and does not care about one's own individual health goals or even their intense burning desire to obtain a 'model-like' figure.

I believe that just as we are pre-programmed to maintain higher fat stores to ensure adequate energy reserves, we are also programmed to be emotionally lazy to help conserve our psychic energy stores. That is, our bodies are programmed to avoid prolonged highly intense energy exhausting mental activities, moods, and emotions whenever possible. This has to do with our body's attempt, on the physical plane, to conserve energy that is directly related to the biochemical activity rooted in the cells and tissues of our bodies and most importantly the neurons and neurotransmitters of our brains. For instance, sustained high emotions tend to 'burn-up' the major neurotransmitters serotonin, dopamine, and norepinephrine in our brains through increased neuronal activity.

Sustained high emotions can also lead to physiologic states that require large amounts of energy to power and maintain them and thereby significantly deplete our bodies of biological energy. For example, intense moods (anger, anxiety, etc.) can increase the heart rate and raise our blood pressure. The increased pumping action of our heart, increased muscle tension, and increased physical activity burn energy at a very rapid rate. As a result, we can feel 'emotionally drained', 'physically drained', and 'exhausted' all at once. At that point our bodies send us a message (through exhaustion) to slow down and to rest for the sake of conserving of our energy.

Avoidance of intense emotions, overly demanding interactions, and conflict allows us to conserve energy. Thus, we are all biologically programmed to be emotionally passive and lazy whenever possible and by our very natures we are prone to always take the shortest most energy efficient physical and emotional paths to follow. Like how I snuck this in here? ☺ In addition to this, as I had mentioned during the introduction, we are strongly gyroscopic (covered in Chapter 7). We wish to remain 'stable' with our old beliefs, ideas, views of others, and views of the world. This reinforces our tendency to avoid some of the potentially energy draining tasks and activities we are presented with on a daily basis.

There you have it we are all basically lazy and resistant to change for biological as well as psychological reasons. Increased anxiety and stress serve as deterrents to deeper intra (internally) or extra (externally) directed psychic activity. This is a lot to overcome when an easier path is presented to us. Most often it is the path of inaction. The path of inaction can prove to be of no great consequence. However, as we are all aware, inaction can sometimes lead to undesirable outcomes and consequences.

Our drives, desires, moods, fantasies, experiences and perceptions fuel our most predominant pattern of ego defenses and color our own individual personality styles and emotions. As mentioned earlier temperament also plays a big role here. A person's predisposition can profoundly impact their approach to the world. Some of the paths that people may choose to follow can be quite destructive to them as individuals and to the people around them.

Anger and anxiety are frequently the most difficult moods for us to deal with and to master. Their associated emotions of hatred and fear are difficult to master as well. Indeed, they are the most difficult of moods and emotions for the world at large to deal with and to master. We all know what anger is and we've all felt it. Whether it occurs as a fleeting angry feeling or as full-blown rage it captures our immediate attention. When it gets out of control it can become destructive and cause problems at work, at home, with your relationships, with your health, with your safety, and with the overall quality of your life.

Anger can be caused by both external and internal events. You can be angry at a specific individual (i.e., your friend, your spouse, your co-worker, your supervisor, your boss), or an event (i.e., a flat tire, a traffic jam, a long wait on a grocery store line, a canceled airplane flight), or your anger can be caused by you mentally reviewing and brooding about your personal problems and past events. Memories of past traumatic enraging events can easily serve to trigger angry feelings and emotions.

Our instinctive drive compels us to act in an aggressive manner when we express our anger. Anger is a natural adaptive response to threats. It inspires powerful, often aggressive, feelings and behaviors which allow us to fight to defend ourselves when we are attacked. Anger, therefore, is seen as being necessary for our survival. However, we shouldn't lash-out at every person or situation that annoys us. That may have worked during prehistoric times, but not now. Laws, social norms, safety concerns, and just common-sense place limits on how far we can take our anger.

As noted earlier, people use a variety of conscious and unconscious processes to deal with their angry feelings. The four main ways we deal with anger are: repressing it, suppressing it, expressing it, and mentally calming ourselves to take a short break from a provoking event.

Expressing your anger in an assertive manner and not in an aggressive or hostile manner is the healthiest way to express your anger. To do this you have to learn how to make clear what your concerns, feelings and needs are, express how they can be met, and do so without hurting others in the process. Being assertive does not mean being pushy or demanding; it means being respectful of yourself and others as you express your feelings and needs in an honest and non-threatening manner.

Anger can be suppressed, and then through focused rational thought and introspection be converted into more constructive and positive behavior. Potential problems can arise when dealing with suppressed anger. Especially when the anger is turned inward on the self, but is never dealt with. Anger turned inward on the self and not dealt with can lead to depression, high blood pressure, fatigue, a decreased immune response, muscle tension, headaches, just to name a few. Holding on to anger and hatred is like drinking a cup of poison and hoping that the other person gets sick. In reality it only makes the angry person sick. Like actual poison sustained anger and hatred can lead to a person's untimely demise through physiologic mechanisms (i.e., weakened immune system, hypertension, cardiac problems, etc.).

Holding on to anger can also lead to pathological expressions of the suppressed or repressed anger through passive-aggressive behavior (getting back at people indirectly) or a personality style that is perpetually hostile and cynical towards others. People who constantly put others down, criticize everything, and make cynical comments have not learned how to deal with anger in an effective manner. Not surprisingly, they are not likely to have many successful relationships.

Intense anger can become hatred. However, in order for anger to become hatred something must happen. The mood of anger must have an identified target. That is, a person, specific object, group, system, or symbol must be identified to attach the anger to. The same is true of fear where anxiety must be attached to an identified target. The attachment of anger and anxiety to identified targets is a natural process. However, it can lead to horrific outcomes when a specific person, group, or institution becomes the direct target of the generated hatred or fear.

What further compounds this situation is the fact that most people tend to take the easiest path to follow. It's easier to hate an entire group than to spend the time and energy required to get to know people as individuals. Consider all of the energy that must be expended to get to know all the people you may encounter as individuals. And to, only then, decide who to like or dislike and to what extent or degree.

People of reason have commented on our various moods for centuries. Consider the following quotes concerning anger.

> Anger is a wind which blows out the lamp of the mind.
> **Robert G. Ingersoll (1833-1899)**

> When anger rises, think of the consequences.
> **Confucius (B.C. 551-479)**

When angry, count ten before you speak, if very angry, a hundred.

Thomas Jefferson (1743-1826)

The greatest remedy for anger is delay.

Seneca (B.C. 3-65 A.D.)

Anyone can become angry - that is easy, but to be angry with the right person, to the right degree, at the right time, for the right purpose, and in the right way - that is not easy.

Aristotle (B.C. 384-322)

An angry man opens his mouth and shuts his eyes.

Cato the Elder (B.C.234-149)

Usually when people are sad, they don't do anything. They just cry over their condition. But when they get angry, they bring about change.

Malcolm X

Although you may spend your life killing, you will not exhaust all your foes. But, if you quell your own anger: Your real enemy will be slain.

Nagarjuna (100-200 A.D.)

6

Cognitive Dissonance

ANOTHER IMPORTANT CONCEPT TO BE AWARE OF IS THE CONCEPT OF cognitive dissonance. Whenever an individual simultaneously holds two thoughts, ideas, attitudes, beliefs, or opinions (cognitions) that are psychologically inconsistent (i.e., are at odds with each other); cognitive dissonance occurs. Cognitive dissonance is experienced as an unpleasant, sometimes painful state of mind caused by a conflict between what one already knows and believes and conflicting information that is brought to one's awareness. The discomfort felt is often experienced as mental stress, mental pain (angst), or anxiety.

Since cognitive dissonance is presumed to be unpleasant, theory (i.e., the pleasure principle) predicts that people will strive to avoid or reduce it. There is usually a strong emotional urge to resolve, as soon as possible, the stress and anxiety that result from cognitive dissonance.

Typically, this is done by:

1- Adding thoughts that are clearly consistent (consonant cognitions) with one or the other of the dissonant cognitions. Essentially adding new thoughts to strengthen one side of the argument over the other.

2- Reducing dissonance by making it a smaller part of the total. Seeing the global picture and making the dissonant cognitions insignificantly small in your mind's eye.

3- By directly changing one of the dissonant cognitions. This leads to self-persuasion with resultant distortion of objective reality.

This is a key concept that will be covered more fully in subsequent chapters concerning psychotherapy and our ability to change. Now for clarification of what this means and how it works. The following are examples of thoughts that can lead to cognitive dissonance:

Examples:

>Cognition 1: I like smoking cigarettes.
>Cognition 2: Cigarette smoking causes lung cancer.
>Cognition 1: I love to eat.
>Cognition 2: I'm overweight.

The result in both cases equals cognitive dissonance and mental stress. In an attempt to reduce cognitive dissonance, specifically with respect to the example just presented concerning cigarette smoking;

1- One can add consonant cognitions:

>To support cognition 1, I like smoking cigarettes, they taste great; one can think of other pleasurable aspects of smoking and the alertness it brings to help one stay focused on the job.

>To support cognition 2, cigarette smoking causes lung cancer; one can think of all the harm it does to one's health, the impact it has on the lungs, the financial impact it would have, the impact on one's family life, and the fact that they plan to quit smoking soon and begin working out at the gym.

2- One can make it a smaller part of the total:

>For cognition 1: Yes, I like to smoke cigarettes, but that's not the major reason, the major reason is they help to keep me alert and mentally sharp while I'm working and they don't have as much an impact on my health as eating red meat, using salt, and inhaling pollution do.

For cognition 2: Yeah, my long-term health is important, but there are other things that are more important right now, like being productive at work and putting food on the table.

3- One can just change one of the dissonant cognitions:

Change cognition 1:

Change: I like smoking cigarettes. To: I hate smoking cigarettes.

Change cognition 2: Cigarette smoking causes lung cancer. To: Plenty of people smoke and never get cancer, cigarettes don't cause cancer, that's just media hype! Look at George Burns; he smoked cigars until he died at the age of 100.

Unfortunately, cognitive dissonance can interfere when there is a critical need to accommodate or to assimilate new ideas and perspectives. It may cause us to reflexively reject new ideas or perspectives in a careless manner. Even when they might save our life! Thus, dissonance-reducing behavior (a defensive behavior) can be considered irrational or maladaptive in the sense that while it is good for an increased sense of mental stability, it often prevents a person from solving very real problems. It can block our ability to grow and to change. It can prevent us from successfully working-through and addressing a real-life problem or issue we face.

On the other hand, when we are enlightened, cognitive dissonance may alert us to new opportunities for personal growth. It prompts us to consciously keep our own beliefs, biases, and perspectives at bay while allowing for us to become more open to consider new or different ideas and perspectives. Thus, cognitive dissonance may cause us to pause, most often in an uncomfortable way, and directly challenges our propensity toward mental and emotional laziness.

Cognitive dissonance can also lead to an activation of our ego defenses which then rid us of the conflict and its accompanying discomfort altogether, this through the unconscious process of repression. When this occurs, we are totally unaware of what has taken place. Therefore, we remain unknowingly blinded to the issue at hand. We may then be doomed to fully succumb to the dictates of our moods, our unconscious minds, and our environment. Unless we consciously decide to examine our thoughts, feelings, and behaviors to get at the underlying root causes of such, we will remain blinded to some of our important personal issues. We lose true control of our lives in exchange for the false perception of being fully secure, fully informed, and fully in control.

Cognitive dissonance was first investigated by Leon Festinger and his associates. The original work arose from an observational study of a cult who believed that the earth was going to be destroyed by a flood. The research group closely studied what happened to that cult's members as time passed. Some of the cult members had been so committed to the cult as to give up their homes, possessions, and jobs in order to spend their full time working for the cult. Eventually, when the flood didn't happen, some fringe members of the cult recognized that they had made 'fools' of themselves both locally and in the national public eye and needed to just 'put it down to experience'.

However, the very committed members were more likely to re-interpret the evidence (of no flood) to show that they had been right all along, that the earth was not destroyed because of the faithfulness and prayers of the cult members. Therefore, both groups worked to resolve their cognitive dissonance in different ways: by changing their original cognition or through the use of consonant cognitions. The common end being that they both could move on with their lives.

Depending on how we respond to cognitive dissonance, it can either help or hinder our ability to gain new insights and perspectives, and ultimately our ability to be mentally flexible. How we deal with this issue can have a profound impact on our ability to master our lives and our place in this world.

7

The Gyroscopic Model

DURING THE INTRODUCTION I USED THE TERM GYROSCOPIC. THIS IS core to the model which I will be presenting. To provide greater clarification, I will begin with the standard definition of a gyroscope taken from Webster's New World Dictionary:

> **Gylro-scope** (ji'rō skōp', -rə-) **n.** [**GYRO-** + **-SCOPE**] a wheel mounted in a set of rings so that its axis of rotation is free to turn in any direction: when the wheel is spun rapidly, it will keep the original direction of its rotation axis no matter which way the ring is turned: gyroscopes are used in gyrocompasses and to keep moving ships, airplanes, etc. level

Figure 3: Picture of a Gyroscope.

If you were to take a gyroscope and wind a string around its central axis and then rapidly pulled the string; the central wheel would begin to spin at a very high speed. If you then placed the gyroscope on a tabletop the gyroscope would stand upright much like a spinning top. If you then attempted to push the gyroscope over onto its side the gyroscope would resist your actions and attempt to return to its previous position. Gyroscopes resist any attempts that are made to change their axis of rotation (position in space).

The physical forces involved are readily observable and can be quite powerful. The forces involved can actually be felt while manipulating the gyroscope in mid-air. If you have never seen or handled a gyroscope it would be worthwhile to gain access to one just to witness, firsthand, the powerful physical forces generated by gyroscopes. Quite importantly, this would allow for you to directly experience their great resistance to any attempts that are made to change their axis of rotation. This physical resistance to being manipulated can be extrapolated to the experience of mental resistance to manipulation.

By observing and analyzing this phenomenon of gyrotropism it occurred to me that it could be used to serve as the core of a theoretical construct that would support a universal model to explain people and systems. It is known that the faster the wheel of a gyroscope spins, the more difficult it becomes to change its axis of rotation. All people and systems behave in this way as well. The power exerted by gyroscopic forces transcends all areas of our existence. I noted during the introduction that I refer to this innate quality of people and systems as gyrotropism. That I believe it exists as a natural ubiquitous law of the universe, much like inertia, gravity, and the conservation of energy. Thus, it has a transcendent quality.

Now imagine a person to be a gyroscope. As our inner gyroscopic wheels spin, they keep us locked-in and resistant to change. We inherently resist any attempts that are made to change our perspectives or behavior. Every person and every system has an inner wheel. What would then power a person's inner wheel to spin are all their thoughts, ideas, memories, moods, emotions, hopes, fears, desires, needs, conscious and unconscious beliefs, biases, perceptions, learned information, and life experiences. The gyroscopic state is truly an indelible part of every person and of every system. The gyroscopic force lies at the core of our being. It transcends the source of our inner power and weakness. It greatly influences our ability to change and to grow. It also resides at the core of the persuasive power that information, people, systems, and perspectives can exert on us.

The information one uses to populate their inner wheel comes from multiple sources. Among them are the things taught by one's family members, peers, friends, members of the community, teachers, coaches, co-workers, casual acquaintances, religious affiliations (churches, synagogues, mosques, temples, etc.), books, movies, the media, their government, etc. From infancy we instinctively seek-out new information to add to our own inner wheels and we do so at an ever-accelerated pace. We often add information that is mentally transformed by us based on our own experience, perception, or interpretation of our environment. Sometimes we add filler information that we simply imagine to be true or valid.

As time passes, more information is added to our inner wheel, and as this occurs the wheel gets further energized. It begins to spin faster. Eventually, our inner wheel spins so fast that we begin to become more rigid in our thinking and perspective of the world. We see the world from our own point of view and thus become more resistant to change. We develop rigid perspectives (platforms) based on our own individual experiences and interpretations and our rigidity tends to increase as we age.

This increased rigidity results from having a longer time to selectively seek out corroborating information consistent with our previously held beliefs and experiences. We seek out that information which will support and reinforce our own beliefs and perspectives. We want to prove that our perspective is correct to anyone who wishes to challenge our beliefs. This sense of being right gives us a sense of stability. Thus, as we age, we tend to become more rigid in our thinking. The awareness of this phenomena very likely led to the saying "You can't teach an old dog new tricks". That old dogs will reject any new tricks presented. Asserting that old people are too far gone to learn or accept anything new. Fortunately, this is not always true.

The term momentum is used in physics to describe the nature and behavior of objects and their impelling physical forces. Having been trained in a scientific educational framework, I tend to use scientific terminology to describe things. So please bear with me. Hopefully this will make sense. Momentum is defined as the product of an object's mass times its velocity. The term vector is used in physics to describe the magnitude and direction of natural forces. Mental gyroscopic forces are also powerful forces that have focused direction. Thus, I feel the term vector can be aptly applied to mental forces. People and systems are vector-like in that they have magnitude, force, and direction. They directly impact each other and their respective environments with a given resultant. Figure 4 (below) shows an illustration of an individual's 'gyroscope.

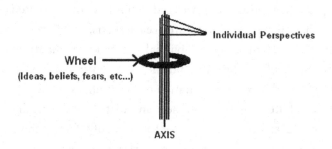

Figure 4: Schematic of an Individual's
Gyroscope Components.

When I teach students about the art of doing psychotherapy I use the gyroscopic model as a core theoretical construct. For just as a gyroscope seeks a central axis of stability, people also seek a central axis of stability (i.e., a stable state of mind or being). With no framework to refer to therapists can easily become lost and confused when attempting to understand what drives and motivates the thinking, mood, emotions, and behaviors of the individual seated before them. For the sake of brevity, I will frequently refer to people's thoughts, beliefs, ideas, biases, myths, memories, perspectives, hopes, fears, etc., simply as elements.

Therapy is often recommended if a particular pathologic platform (unhealthy fixed perspective) is causing problems for an individual or the people they encounter. This is particularly true in the case of personality disorders, psychotic disorders, and delusional disorders. It is generally accepted that such a pathologic platform (perspective) should be directly confronted for the distorted perception of reality that it is. That it should somehow either be transformed or discarded. But keep in mind, for the previously mentioned gyroscopic reasons, that any attempts made to change that person's distorted perspective will very likely be met with great resistance. It is also important to keep in mind that even a pathologic platform may be a source of security and stability for the person afflicted.

I noted earlier that people have a central axis (state-of-being). By combining the words state and axis, I refer to a person's axis state as their staxis. Pronounced as 'stack-sis'. Actually, people have multiple axes (axis states). The multiple form of the word being 'staxes'. Pronounced as 'stack-sees'. The reason for use of the terms staxis and staxes is to avoid the misconception that the axes are in a fixed state. I have incorporated the word state to emphasize the dynamic nature of each staxis. They are each in a state of constant flux with their own individual and shared elements. Each staxis has its own state of equilibrium and they are continuously transforming or morphing based on new information or experiences. As such, staxes are fully malleable (alterable) through the manipulation of their individual and collective mental elements. This lies at the heart of effective therapy.

A person's Major Staxis, or dominant staxis, is the way in which they usually present themselves. It takes center stage. The Minor Staxes are subordinate and are by definition less prominent than the major staxis. They tend to hide in the shadows of the unconscious mind. They often come into play in response to specific major life stressors. However, independent of specific major events or stressors, we have some degree of conscious control over calling subordinate staxes forward to take center stage. We can play the role of parent, or friend, or lover, or executive, or coach, or son, or daughter, or brother, or sister, or teacher, or neighbor, or caretaker, or patient, etc. All of these roles are distinctly different selves.

All of one's staxes combined comprise one's core personality with all its various nuances. In this way, the subordinate staxes form the major structural 'skeleton' of our conscious and unconscious minds. Although we have a specific identity, we think and behave differently as we take on our various roles in life. Subordinate staxes are state dependent, in that they usually come into operation when called upon during specific stressful life events or when we consciously call upon their service in the context of specific daily tasks, routines, needs or environments. This is often accomplished through the sheer use of our mental focus and will power.

As an aside, with specific reference to psychoanalytic theory, I believe that a major purpose for suppression and repression is to lock-away one's subordinate staxes into one's subconscious mind. Thereby keeping the subordinate staxes both hidden and inactive until needed. This serves the purpose of attempting to keep some portions of our unconscious life from directly interfering with our center-stage active major staxis presentation. It allows for us to more easily choose how we present ourselves to others. Thereby directly aiding the major ego function of preservation of the self by utilizing the most advantageous defense mechanisms along with the choices we make. Incidentally, I believe this process lies at the core of acting where actors create a subordinate staxis or "character" to portray and then bring it to life.

Chapter 3 discussed our ego defense mechanisms. The ego defense of dissociation plays a major role in keeping subordinate staxes separate. Dissociation involves the 'splitting-off' of a group of thoughts or activities from the main portion of one's consciousness (compartmentalization). This complex system allows for one's dominant major staxis to maintain center-stage in a stable manner. An example would be a military soldier who is trained to kill the enemy, and is still able to sit at a pretend tea party with his young daughter and acting as a prince (actually a devoted parent) while ignoring his military self. Once again, this complex system allows for one's major staxis to maintain center-stage in a stable manner. Otherwise, an individual would appear quite unstable as they randomly and repetitively shifted from subordinate staxis to subordinate staxis before your very eyes. I feel this abnormal shifting between staxes underlies some of the mental instability witnessed in some mental disorders.

Though locked away, the subordinate staxes are held in a 'neutral' state and are ready to take center stage when called upon to do so. Very much like an engine can be kept in a neutral or idling state but stands ready to be shifted into drive or reverse when needed. Normally there is a continuous intense unconscious conversation that occurs between our various subordinate staxes. This intense conversation also occurs between them and our dominant staxis. This conversation accounts for the sometimes intrusive 'loud thoughts' that can arise from our preconscious or unconscious minds. It also accounts for the sometimes-impulsive behaviors we exhibit, as impulses from our unconsciously held subordinate staxes break-through and attempt to take charge and center stage.

One can experience these spontaneous thoughts or impulses under conditions of increased stress or even under conditions of calm and quiet. I believe that this intense conversation is at least in part the source of the stimuli that produces the auditory hallucinations occurring with frank psychosis. This occurs when the auditory center which is normally suppressed to keep this 'conversation' silent is in some manner provoked to become active. It then serves as a physiologic conduit for the release of unconscious material (elements) either directly or via the framework of a previously inactive subordinate staxis.

The fact that individuals have multiple staxes also accounts for the seemingly different or contradictory stances or perspectives that they may take from moment to moment and from day to day. When a person switches from one staxis to another it may take others by surprise causing them to question that person's true identity, beliefs, or motives. I also feel that this is why people sometimes get cast as being phony, inconsistent, or unreliable. It can also be why people sometimes feel lost or misunderstood. The person themself may be unaware that they have switched staxes. They can be blind to how they are perceived. This can be further compounded by the presence of substance use or mental illness.

As we search among our various conflicting staxes, we can get 'lost' while trying to understand who we really are. Our multiple subordinate staxes also account for why we can have several identities: our business self, our parent self, our fun-loving self, our compassionate self, our dispassionate self, our pacifist self, our warrior self, our savior self, our punishing or murderous self, our sensuous self, our prudish self, our liberal self, our conservative self, our religious self, our agnostic or atheistic self, our radical self, our 'intellectual' self, our 'stupid' self, etc. Subordinate staxes are sometimes created in response to persistent environmental challenges. Thus, they can be adaptive and protective, or they can be maladaptive.

Figure 5: Gyroscopic Diagram: Showing Multiple Staxes.

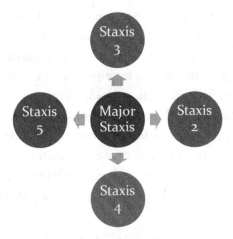

Figure 6: 2-Dimensional Diagram:
Representation of Multiple Staxes.

People often present with different staxes from one therapy session to the next. Each subordinate staxis has its own core identity. This may cause the therapist to question: Who am I really dealing with today? When an individual reports to your office for continued psychotherapy it is important to know which staxis they are presenting with. Today: Is it the businessperson who feels the pressures of their taxing job? Is it the concerned parent who is concerned about their child's school performance? Is it the troubled partner in a relationship who fears they are about to lose their partner? Is it the ultra-religious person, the emotionally defeated person, the conservative thinker, the liberal thinker, the caring (we must feed the poor) person, or the uncaring (the poor need to feed themselves) person?

It is important for you know *who* you are dealing with in each session. Is it the concerned parent, the anxious 'business' person, or the depressed 'I need to be free to find myself' person? You must listen carefully to their lead. When you determine which one it is you can then proceed to address that particular staxis. You will be able to hold their attention and focus much better this way. Your ability to form rapport with a given person will be greatly enhanced as well. If you fail to do so, you may find yourself talking to someone with deaf-ears. Someone who thinks, privately, that you are way off topic and not on the same page or wavelength as them.

For example, it would be quite difficult to talk to the I want to be free to be me staxis about being a responsible parent or businessperson. They just won't want to hear it without a fight. Again, if you don't keep aware of the person's staxes you could find yourself speaking to deaf ears in one session and cause your frustrated client to prematurely drop out of therapy in the next. This phenomenon of multiple staxes can lead a therapist to erroneously believe that their client has a 'multiple personalities'. If the therapist is thinking along those lines, it would be good to keep in mind that we all present ourselves differently most of the time. We also harbor secret subordinate staxes as well, that we consciously or unconsciously keep hidden from others. It can surprise all present when they show-up in the therapeutic setting. These hidden staxes can be revealed and explored, even provoked, in effective therapy.

Eventually your patient will develop a subordinate staxis of being your patient/client. It is important to ask them at the beginning of each session what concerns them today. If they begin to talk about the problems of being a parent, before they attempt to make that conversation dominate the session, it is important to remind them of their role of being a person in therapy. The bottom line being that for optimal therapy to be realized, it is important to be cognizant of the client's staxes. There is an old psychotherapy dictum that continues to hold true. You must meet the person where they are. Effective therapy depends greatly on the "fit" of the therapist with their patient/client. They must both be on the same page or wavelength. For this to happen you must be where they are or alternatively get them to come to where you are. To do so you must know 'who' they are.

When doing psychotherapy, I picture the person as being a gyroscope and myself this way as well. Each of us with our own complex basic structure as previously described. During therapy we make a connection and share ideas. Transference and counter transference are two powerful events that can be used in psychotherapy. Transference occurs when a patient transfers their unconscious feelings and emotions onto the therapist. For example, a patient may transfer their feelings of anger towards their father onto the therapist. In this case, the therapist needs to be aware of the transference and must work with the patient to explore and identify the underlying triggers for the anger. The therapist can then gain insight into the patient's unconscious thoughts, feelings, emotions, and behaviors.

Counter transference occurs when the therapist develops feelings and emotions of their own towards the patient. Both transference and counter transference can have a powerful impact on the patient-therapist relationship and can be either beneficial or detrimental depending on how they are managed. Through this connection something helpful is imparted to the individual through the process of transference and countertransference. New insights are discovered, and thoughts and feelings are processed which leads to greater clarity. An internal change then occurs and there is a conscious re-shaping of the person's major staxis and of that their subsequent behavior. A full discussion of this complex subject, which can be controversial, is beyond the scope of this book.

Below, figure 7, is a sample staxis tacking sheet that beginners can use. If no sheet is used to track the individual's staxes, a brief notation in one's therapy notes can suffice.

STAXIS I	STAXIS II	STAXIS III	STAXIS IV
General Qualities:	General Qualities:	General Qualities:	General Qualities:
Session DATES:			

Figure 7: Staxis Tracking – Reference Sheet

It is important to be aware that your client may use their subordinate staxes in an evasive (defensive) manner by flipping back-and-forth from one staxis to another to avoid being confronted in a particular area of focus during therapy. For example, while you are confronting a businessperson about their self-defeating behaviors at work, they suddenly want to discuss their children (i.e., their role as a parent) or their desire to be a free spirit and recent purchase of a sports car. The switch may be related to their problems at work and deserve exploration, however it can also serve as a smoke screen for their core problems at work. This shifting back-and-forth by the client can leave the therapist frustrated and annoyed as they attempt to determine the true focus of the therapy. Frequently clients 'hang-out' in therapy to get the closeness and company of the therapist while harboring the feelings of having no intention of challenging their previously held perspectives. Thereby causing the therapeutic process to quickly reach an impasse.

It is my belief that the gyroscopic model can be used as a core theoretical construct (framework) upon which all forms of psychotherapy can be superimposed. To serve as a familiar structure upon which to place the various tools of therapy to be employed while delivering psychotherapy. It is intended to tie together many great contributions to the area of psychology by authors such as: Alfred Adler, Aaron T. Beck, Gavin de Becker, Eric Berne, Alfred Binet, Robert Bolton, Edward de Bono, Nathaniel Branden, Isabel Briggs Myers, Louann Brizendine, David D. Burns, Robert Cialdini, Mihaly Csikszentmihalyi, Albert Ellis, Milton Erickson, Erik Erikson, Hans Eysenck, Susan Forward, Viktor Frankl, Anna Freud, Sigmund Freud, Eric Fromm, Howard Gardner, Daniel Gilbert, Malcolm Gladwell, Daniel Goleman, John M. Gottman, Robert D. Hare, Harry Harlow, Robert Harper, Thomas A. Harris, Sheila Heen, Eric Hoffer, Karen Horney, William James, David Jessel, Carl Jung, Alfred Kinsey, Melanie Klein, R. D. Laing, Karl Lashley, Harriet Lerner, Konrad Lorenz, Abraham Maslow, Stanley Milgram, Anne Moir, Ivan Pavlov, Bruce Patton, Fritz Perls, Jean Piaget, Steven Pinker, V. S. Ramachandran, Otto Rank, Wilhelm Reich, Carl Rogers, Oliver Sacks, Barry Schwartz, Martin Seligman, Gail Sheehy, B. F. Skinner, Douglas Stone, William Styron, Harry Stack Sullivan, Robert E. Thayer, John Watson, Max Wertheimer, Carl Whitaker; Wilhelm Wundt just to name a few. It is a very worthwhile pursuit to read their many significant observations, theories and perspectives concerning the nature of our mental functioning to expand your insight and knowledge base.

Aside from doing psychotherapy, the gyroscopic model also allows us to view how the previously presented principles can also be directly applied to understanding other real-life situations. An example which lends itself to such an application involves the area of military training. While undergoing military training, recruits are presented with a large volume of information. They are given new sets of rules, regulations, routines, experiences, ideas, priorities, perspectives, values and ideals that they are asked to absorb and incorporate into their very being. That information which is absorbed provides for the mental elements that are used to populate the inner wheel of a new subordinate staxis. That new subordinate staxis is one of being a soldier which with time can transform into being their major staxis. Their new identity.

It is well known that the incorporation of the new information can be greatly accelerated when tied to high intensity emotions. This tends to overwhelm the person's ego defenses, thus weakening or knocking down potential barriers on the road to inserting new information into an individual's unconscious mind. This tactic is routinely employed by military trainers to hasten the "induction" process. An example would be an unscheduled 3:00 AM waking by the drill sergeant who while banging loudly on a garbage pail with a stick gives orders for the highly disoriented and emotionally overwhelmed recruits to get dressed, gear-up, and go for a three-mile run.

As the recruits absorb the new material presented under duress, it serves to power their inner wheels to create a new subordinate staxis and a new perspective. When the recruit is placed in a war situation that subordinate staxis takes center stage and becomes dominant. Their identity is that of being a soldier. The daily events of war then add further material (elements) and experiences to the new subordinate staxis, thereby strengthening and reinforcing it. During wartime service, the soldier is faced with multiple periods of inner turmoil due to the often-conflicted interface between their 'soldier self' and their 'former self'. I believe that a full understanding of the military indoctrination process is essential and lies at the heart of effective psychotherapy for those involved in the military. Particularly, when treating those suffering from Post-Traumatic Stress Disorder (P.T.S.D.). A case that explores this specific issue and provides for further clarification and for a deeper understanding will be presented in a later chapter.

The role of subordinate staxes goes far beyond the provision of a structure around which the unconscious mind can organize itself. For example, I believe that the system of staxes accounts for the popularity and power that music and songs have in our lives. Musical tones, beats, patterns, tunes and lyrics, by containing common and familiar elements that are periodic and repetitive in nature profoundly affect our subordinate staxes by resonating with them. Songs can momentarily convert us mentally from our current dominant staxis to one of our subordinate staxes.

Music can induce the emergence of a subordinate staxis and thereby put us in touch with an element of our true selves. This resonance occurs within the physical neuronal networks of our brains (such as the limbic system) which serve as the actual physical structures of our staxes. Music can create a sensation of pleasure or pain and can provoke many other powerful feelings and emotions. Music can make us "feel" a certain "way". That "way" is often directly in line with one or more of our subordinate staxes. Music has meaning and calls to mind different pictures, feelings, emotions, ideas, memories and perspectives often contained in our subordinate staxes. This is the reason that music tends to be a personal experience that is open to wide interpretation. Music can serve the useful purpose as a distraction, thereby relieving us from the current tensions of our dominant staxis.

Certain types of music are more powerful in creating reactions and effects. One can use music to intentionally induce the emergence of hitherto subordinate staxes. For example, music is often used by the military ("revelry" for example) to 'rally the troops' to induce 'the fighting spirit'. It gets the troops in touch with, and activates, their military subordinate staxes. The national anthem is used at football games and other sporting events to incite patriotism and loyalty with the crowds of fans. It is ever present at the Olympics in the theme song "The Bugler's Dream". Music is frequently used to induce a romantic atmosphere or response in a partner. When people go to discos, clubs, parties, or celebrations, and music is played it encourages their 'party animal' subordinate staxes to emerge. If you were to attend one of those events you might witness the transformation of a conservative business executive to the singing and dancing life of the party! This would be particularly more likely if that executive became highly disinhibited through their consumption of alcohol. Remember, the superego is soluble in alcohol.

What's interesting is that what you actually might be witnessing is the re-emergence of the previously suppressed 'party animal' subordinate staxis that the executive had created during their college days. It could take many by surprise who were unaware of the executive's past history. It might also represent the emergence of a fantasy driven minor subordinate staxis that the executive created while day dreaming prior to the party. It would likely serve as a source of great embarrassment for the executive if they were highly intoxicated and 'made a fool of themselves' with the people they supervise, only to 'come-around' the next day and realize what had transpired. That their 'secret self' was 'let out of the bag'! Great remorse might follow with multiple apologies, or they might simply just blame it on the alcohol, choose to 'forget' it ever happened, or simply deny that it ever happened.

By combining all of the previous models discussed we get the following diagram which, for the purpose of this book, serves to represent the basic structure of our mind.

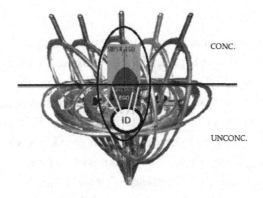

Figure 8: Combined Models of the Psyche.

8

The Weakness Within

NOW THAT I HAVE DISCUSSED THE POWER WITHIN, WHAT IS THE weakness within? When I speak of inner weakness, I am not referring to mental, emotional, physical, or spiritual weakness. I am also not referring to one's inability to tolerate stress. This is a common mistake that many people make when attempting to define the term 'weakness' for themselves. It has prevented many people from examining their own inner weaknesses out of fear of appearing to be "weak". The weakness that I am referring to is the weakness that is inherent in the choices that we make.

Making choices is an intrinsic part of the human experience. It is our choices that make us strong or weak and that leads to desirable vs. undesirable outcomes. Thus, our power and our weakness arise from the very same thing. The indelible link arises in our choices. Life can be viewed as a series of choices that cumulatively shape our identities and experiences. If you wish to master your power or to overcome your weaknesses, you must master your choices.

Each decision, no matter how small, contributes to our personal narrative. Recognizing this interconnectedness can encourage individuals to approach choices with a sense of purpose and intentionality, fostering a deeper understanding of how their decisions shape not only their own lives but also those of others around them. Again, our weakness comes from the choices we make. What lies at the heart of weakness is not our lack of tenacity, willpower, or emotional fortitude, but rather it is a failure to make the right choices.

From the mundane decisions of daily life to the significant crossroads that shape our futures, the choices we make define who we are and influence our paths. At the heart of making the right choices is self-awareness. The ability to make the right choices is not merely about selecting options but involves understanding oneself, weighing various consequences, and considering the long-term impact of those decisions. Understanding one's values, beliefs, and desires is crucial.

When individuals are clear about what matters most to them, they can align their choices with their personal goals and ethics. For instance, a student deciding on a career path must consider not only their interests but also their values regarding work-life balance, financial stability, and societal impact. Self-awareness empowers individuals to make choices that resonate with their true selves, leading to greater satisfaction and fulfillment.

Another essential aspect of making sound choices is the ability to weigh pros and cons. This analytical approach involves gathering information, considering potential outcomes, and evaluating the risks involved. For example, when deciding whether to accept a job offer, one might consider factors such as salary, company culture, growth opportunities, and location. By systematically evaluating these elements, individuals can make informed decisions that are more likely to lead to positive outcomes.

Moreover, making the right choices often requires foresight. This means not only thinking about immediate consequences but also considering how decisions will affect the future. A classic example is the choice to pursue higher education. While it may require significant time and financial investment upfront, the long-term benefits of increased earning potential and career opportunities often outweigh the initial costs. Foresight allows individuals to navigate life with a broader perspective, leading to decisions that foster long-term happiness and success.

However, it is essential to acknowledge that no one is immune to making mistakes. Poor choices can stem from various factors, including unconscious motivations, peer pressure, financial pressures, emotional responses, misunderstandings, lack of information, etc. Whether we choose to use crutches such as alcohol, illicit substances, social withdrawal, avoidance of our problems, laziness, etc. to deal with our life stressors and problems. The key to growth lies in how one responds to these missteps.

Reflecting on past decisions provides valuable lessons that can inform future choices. Embracing a mindset of learning rather than judgment fosters resilience and personal development. Seeking advice from trusted mentors, friends, or family members can provide new insights and perspectives. Collaborating with others can illuminate aspects of a decision that one might overlook. Involving others in the decision-making process can lead to more comprehensive and balanced choices, ultimately enriching the outcome.

Making the right choices for yourself is a lifelong journey. As individuals grow and their circumstances change, so too will their values and priorities. What may have been the right choice at one point in life may evolve to something else as experiences shape one's perspective. Thus, it is essential to remain adaptable and open to re-evaluating decisions as needed. The process of making the right choices extends beyond the individual and has broader implications for relationships, communities, and society at large. Here are some additional aspects to consider:

1. Learning from Mistakes:

Reflecting on past decisions allows individuals to identify mistakes and understand what went wrong. By analyzing these experiences, one can gain insights into the factors that led to a poor outcome, thereby avoiding similar pitfalls in the future. This process fosters personal growth and improves future decision-making skills.

2. Recognizing Patterns:

Reviewing past experiences can help individuals recognize recurring patterns in their decision-making. By identifying these patterns, one can better understand how specific emotions, thoughts, or external influences impact choices. This awareness can lead to more conscious and informed decisions in the future.

3. The Importance of Reflection:

Reflection provides an opportunity to step back and evaluate decisions from a broader perspective. It encourages individuals to consider the context, motivations, and consequences of their choices, leading to a deeper understanding of how those decisions align with their values and goals.

4. Building Confidence:

By reflecting on successful past decisions, individuals can reinforce their confidence in their ability to make sound choices. Recognizing moments of success can serve as motivation and a reminder of one's capabilities, bolstering their self-assurance in future decision-making.

5. Enhancing Problem-Solving Skills:

Analyzing past experiences can improve problem-solving skills. By examining how challenges were approached and resolved, individuals can develop strategies and techniques that can be applied to new situations. This practice fosters adaptability and resourcefulness.

6. Understanding Emotional Responses:

Reflection is a powerful tool in the decision-making process. Reflective practices encourage individuals to learn from their experiences and grow, fostering a continuous cycle of improvement. Taking time to consider past choices, what worked, what didn't, and why, can enhance future decision-making skills. Reflection helps individuals explore their emotional responses to past decisions. Understanding how feelings influenced choices can lead to greater emotional intelligence, allowing individuals to manage their emotions better and make more balanced decisions in the future. Journaling, meditation, or simply setting aside quiet time to think can help individuals gain clarity and insight.

7. Fostering Resilience:

Reflecting on both successes and failures builds resilience. Understanding that mistakes are part of the learning process can help individuals develop a growth mindset, where they view challenges as opportunities for growth rather than as setbacks.

8. Improving Future Planning:

Reflection allows individuals to create better action plans for future decisions. By considering what worked and what didn't, they can develop strategies that take past experiences into account, leading to more thoughtful and effective decision-making.

9. The Role of Values:

Values play a crucial role in decision-making. They serve as a guiding compass that helps individuals determine what is important to them. For example, someone who values integrity may prioritize honesty in their relationships and work, leading them to make choices that reflect this commitment. Understanding personal values can help clarify priorities and lead to more authentic decisions. Reflecting on past experiences can help clarify personal values and long-term goals. By evaluating how past decisions aligned with these values, individuals can make more intentional choices that resonate with their true nature, leading to greater satisfaction and fulfillment.

10. Emotional Intelligence:

Emotional intelligence (EQ) is another vital component in making choices. It involves the ability to recognize and manage one's emotions and the emotions of others. High EQ allows individuals to navigate social dynamics more effectively, which can influence decision-making. For instance, being aware of how stress or anxiety might cloud judgment can lead someone to take a step back and reassess their options before making a significant choice.

11. The Impact of Environment:

The environment in which individuals find themselves can significantly affect their choices. Social circles, cultural norms, and socioeconomic factors can all influence the decision-making processes. For example, a supportive community can encourage positive choices, while a toxic environment may lead to detrimental decisions. Being mindful of these external influences can help individuals make choices aligned with their true intentions rather than succumbing to external pressures.

12. Accountability and Responsibility:

Taking ownership of one's choices is essential for personal growth. Taking the time to reflect promotes accountability. It involves a person recognizing that every decision has consequences, both positive and negative. Individuals are more likely to take ownership of their decisions and understand the impact of their choices on themselves and others if they examine them. This sense of responsibility can lead to more ethical and considerate decision-making. When individuals hold themselves accountable, they are more likely to learn and adapt from their experiences. This sense of responsibility can also enhance trust and respect in relationships, as others see a commitment to integrity and self-improvement.

13. Coping with Fear and Uncertainty:

Fear of making the wrong choice can paralyze decision-making. Embracing uncertainty and understanding that no decision is without risk can empower individuals to take action. Learning to cope with fear, whether through positive affirmations, seeking support, or developing problem-solving skills, can lead to more decisive and confident choices.

14. The Collective Aspect of Decision-Making:

In many situations, decisions are not made in isolation. In professional settings, for example, collaboration and teamwork are often necessary. Understanding group dynamics, valuing diverse perspectives, and practicing active listening can lead to more robust and well-rounded decisions. Engaging others in the decision-making process can also enhance buy-in and commitment to the outcomes.

15. Dealing with unconscious motivations can be a complex process, as these motivations often influence behavior without our conscious awareness. Here are some strategies to help you address them:

    a.   **Self-reflection:** Take time to reflect on your thoughts and behaviors. Journaling can be particularly effective in uncovering patterns and motivations that may not be immediately obvious.

b. **Mindfulness:** Practicing mindfulness and meditation helps individuals tune into their thoughts and feelings without judgment. By quieting the mind and focusing on the present moment, people can develop a heightened awareness of their internal cues and instincts, making it easier to recognize intuitive insights. Practicing mindfulness can help you become more aware of your thoughts and feelings in the present moment, allowing you to identify unconscious motivations as they arise.

c. **Listening to Gut Feelings:** Training oneself to pay attention to gut feelings or bodily sensations can enhance intuitive decision-making. When faced with choices, individuals can pause to notice their physical reactions, which may provide valuable insights into their true feelings about a situation.

d. **Therapy or Counseling:** Working with a mental health professional can provide insights into your unconscious motivations. Therapists can help you explore deeper emotional issues and provide tools to address them.

e. **Journaling:** Keeping a journal can help individuals reflect on their thoughts and feelings regarding past decisions. By writing down experiences, emotions, and outcomes, individuals can identify patterns and intuitive nudges that influenced their choices. This practice can strengthen the connection to one's intuition over time.

f. **Dream Analysis:** Sometimes, our dreams can reveal unconscious desires or fears. Keeping a dream journal and analyzing recurring themes may provide clues about your motivations.

g. **Feedback from Others:** Ask trusted friends or family for their perspectives on your behaviors. They may notice patterns that you are unaware of.

h. **Behavioral Experiments:** Try changing a behavior intentionally to see how it feels. This can help reveal underlying motivations and beliefs that drive your actions and decisions.

i. **Reading and Education:** Learning more about psychology and human behavior can help you understand the dynamics of unconscious motivations better.

j. **Visualizations:** Visualization techniques involve imagining different scenarios or outcomes related to a decision. By mentally exploring various possibilities, individuals can tap into their intuition and observe how they feel about each potential outcome. This process can clarify instincts and preferences.

k. **Engaging in Creative Activities:** Creative pursuits, such as painting, writing, or playing music, can foster intuition. These activities encourage free expression and can help individuals connect with their inner selves. Engaging in creativity can open pathways for intuitive insights to emerge.

l. **Seeking Solitude:** Taking time for solitude can provide the space needed to listen to one's inner voice. Whether through nature walks, quiet reflection, or simply stepping away from distractions, solitude can help individuals reconnect with their intuition and gain clarity on decision-making.

m. **Learning from Past Experiences:** Reflecting on past decisions, both successful and unsuccessful, can enhance intuition. By analyzing what felt right or wrong in previous situations, individuals can better understand their intuitive signals and how to apply them to future choices.

n. **Connecting with Nature:** Spending time in nature can help individuals clear their minds and tap into their intuitive senses. The natural environment often fosters a sense of calm and clarity, allowing for deeper introspection and connection to one's instincts.

o. **Practicing Decision-Making:** Engaging in small decisions regularly can build confidence in using intuition. By intentionally making choices, whether it's selecting a meal, choosing an outfit, or planning a weekend activity, individuals can practice listening to their instincts and observing the outcomes.

p. **Trusting the Process:** Building intuition is a gradual process, and learning to trust one's instincts can take time. Embracing the uncertainty that comes with intuitive decision-making and allowing oneself to experiment with choices can enhance confidence in this ability.

By combining these strategies, you can gain a clearer understanding of your unconscious motivations and work toward aligning them with your conscious goals and values.

Here we see that our power and our weakness both come from the same source. The choices we make. Making the right choices is a complex and dynamic process influenced by a myriad of factors, including personal values, emotional intelligence, environmental contexts, and reflective practices. By cultivating awareness and understanding in these areas, individuals can navigate the often-challenging landscape of decision-making with greater confidence and insight. Ultimately, the choices we make serve as steppingstones towards achieving our goals, nurturing meaningful relationships, and contributing positively to the world around us. Embracing this journey with openness and resilience can lead to a more fulfilling and enriched life. Through this reflective practice, individuals can navigate future choices with greater insight and intention, leading to more fulfilling and meaningful outcomes. Embracing the lessons of the past ultimately empowers individuals to make better decisions in the present and future.

9

Our Ability to Change

PSYCHIATRIST ALFRED ADLER WAS RESPONSIBLE FOR SEVERAL CONCEPTS and terms such as "inferiority complex" (a.k.a. the Napoleon complex or syndrome), "birth order" (the implications of where one comes in the family line), the role of narcissism in forming the "enemies of society", and many others. Adler wrote "The hardest thing for human beings to do is to know themselves and to change themselves." He saw us all as social beings moving through life creating a style of life in response to the environment and to what we inherently feel we lack (our feelings of inferiority). He was quite interested in how children seek to increase their power in the world. He felt that being born as poorly coordinated, illiterate beings, entirely dependent on fully developed adults for survival that children must rise from a position of inferiority.

Adler felt that a fork in the developmental path is reached where we must choose between imitating adults to become more assertive and powerful ourselves or to display weakness to get the help and attention of adults. He noted that this early decision has a very powerful lifelong impact. Adler stated that "a thousand talents and capabilities arise from our feelings of inadequacy", and each child develops in ways to best address their weaknesses. This critical decision leads to either a self-sufficient adult or to a weak and dependent adult. What choice did you make? If you mistakenly made the latter choice to become dependent this can be remedied. However, it will take some work.

Figure 9: A Field at Midnight

With regards to our ability to change, a story might help. Imagine if you will a person walking through a dark field at midnight. There they stand in a pitch-black environment. They have no flashlight and are unable to see anything around them. At that very moment there is a thunderstorm brewing in the distance. Occasionally there is a flash of lightning and for a split second they can see the ground, trees, bushes, water, rocks, and boulders that surround them in their immediate environment. For a split second they see reality. They see the environment as it truly is; and not just as they had imagined it to be.

However, as the flash of lightning quickly disappears, they are again left in total darkness. They are again totally blind to the world around them. The picture they saw begins to fade in their mind's eye. They begin to question what they actually saw and perhaps begin to distort or 'morph' their mental image. They may begin to develop an erroneous perspective of their environment. They may trip and stumble as they attempt to negotiate their immediate environment. Nevertheless, with each successive flash of lightning they can see several more accurate pictures of their immediate environment.

As they accumulate those supplementary pictures, they are then able to fuse the additional pictures together to form a more stable mental image of their environment. That refined mental image can then prove to be quite valuable and useful. They can begin to use that mental image as a roadmap to negotiate their environment. It can prove to be protective by preventing them from stumbling over boulders, walking into trees, falling into holes or deep water, etc. Thus, the map can prevent them from making very bad choices or unsafe decisions. The process of psychotherapy, self-therapy, self-discovery, and inner change involves such a journey.

With this concept firmly in mind, you can begin your journey. It has been stated that the only thing that welcomes a change is a wet baby. From infancy we begin exploring the world of things around us. We instinctively search our immediate environment for new information, experiences, and meanings. We do so in an inquisitive and mostly uninhibited fashion. As infants we are inherently driven to have our own immediate needs met. As we attempt to have our own needs and interests met, we are forced to interact with caretakers who have their own individual needs, agendas, approaches, interpretations, perspectives, and powers. Indeed, we live in a world where there are many powerful forces that incessantly aid or challenge us as we seek to have our own basic needs fulfilled.

As infants and children, we are most often quite flexible and malleable. Ideally, as we age, we hope to retain some of that innate flexibility to learn from our environment. However, as some people age, they choose to live a life defined by their own gyroscopically driven rigid perspectives. Sometimes their beliefs and perspectives are accompanied by blatant non-truths which can distort their sense of reality. Sometimes they live in absolute fantasy. They would rather hold on to beliefs that are consistent with their own perspectives than to see or deal with the truths and realities of our world. This is truly a sad situation for those people from the perspective that they live in total darkness. They are blinded to and mostly isolated from the real world. They stand in the field at midnight and refuse to see the light. They tend to reflexively reject the pictures that they do see. Their sense of community and connection is often stilted, and their spiritual growth is often thwarted.

It is also quite tragic when people are either directly or indirectly indoctrinated with their expected "place" or "station" in life and then blindly accept it. By accepting their 'place' they unwittingly and simultaneously forfeit any possibility for their further personal growth. Now for the question of questions. Are you who you want to be? Or are you who others want you to be? Are you true to who you are? And behave that way? When you attempt to answer these questions are you being truthful with yourself? As you proceed with reading this book you will become better able to answer these questions in a more informed and focused manner.

When attempting to change your life, if you wish to see both your greatest ally and your worst enemy towards change, look in any mirror. It always comes down to you! The bottom line is that every person must make a choice as to whether they will serve as the master of their own destiny, or alternatively, surrender their fate to the will of others or to their life circumstances. If you wish to grow emotionally, to excel in your chosen career, to quit smoking, to lose weight, to get physically fit, to excel in academics or sports, or perfect your ability to play an instrument, whatever it may be, you must first be flexible enough to create a true internal mental commitment to change your thinking and behavior!

Then you must tie that new mental commitment for change to your willpower and your actions. This with the purpose of either creating a new or enhancing an existing subordinate staxis. The next step is to operationalize your new subordinate staxis through your actions which are tied to clearly defined goals. It involves making the right choices. This realization lies at the core of change, growth, and self-perfection. Now for another question: Which usually comes first, motivation or decisive action? If you answered motivation, you are incorrect. Decisive action must come first for anything to happen. Only by acting can we truly begin to build true motivation. Action leads to motivation which leads to more action. Mental motivation without any action is useless and often serves as a major barrier to personal change. Motivation is dependent on action. It ends with a self-defeated attitude and self-criticism when no action is accomplished. People often then procrastinate and deal in the top sixty excuses for not getting started, listed in Chapter 16 on Self-Therapy. Take a quick look.

Carl Jung was a Swiss psychiatrist and psychoanalyst who founded the field of analytical psychology. He wrote extensively on topics such as the unconscious mind, archetypes, and the collective unconscious. He is also known for his insights into the idea of personal change and transformation. He believed that personal change and transformation are essential to living a full and meaningful life. He believed that to grow and develop, people must be willing to challenge their existing beliefs and behaviors and be open to change. He also believed that personal change can lead to greater self-awareness and personal growth. For example, he argued that by challenging ourselves and examining our own beliefs and behaviors we can gain a better understanding of our strengths and weaknesses and this in turn can lead to improved self-confidence and greater self-awareness.

He identified a process of personal growth that he called individuation. Which is essentially the conscious realization of one's true self. It is achieved by integrating one's conscious mind with their unconscious mind and thereby becoming fully aware of who they truly are. Jung felt that only then could we achieve our full potential. This realization of one's true self is felt to be achievable through the active workings of one's own conscious mind, with an emphasis on the exploration of one's unconscious mind. Thus, to get in touch with one's true self requires some mental work. You must enter a mental state or "zone" where you take an honest look at yourself. At the same time, you ideally should be able to evaluate new information that you discover about yourself and possibly assimilate information that you receive from others to move towards greater personal enlightenment and growth.

While our ability to change should never be underestimated, there are some real obstacles to change. One such obstacle is our inherent state of mind with respect to our general outlook on life and our sense of optimism. If one chooses to harbor and nurture a pessimistic state of mind then personal growth and change becomes extremely hard to actualize. Often such people lead a life of depression and bitterness. They secretly harbor feelings of inadequacy and ineffectiveness. They tend to be bored with life and are generally miserable. There is a saying that states: If you are bored, you are boring to be with. Pessimism is a negative perspective that must be corrected for. Only then can a person grow in a healthy, uninhibited, and unencumbered fashion.

In fact, multiple studies have been performed where researchers have attempted to determine the most significant factors that are associated with depression in later life. Among all the factors, which included poor economic status, poor health, environmental stress, losses, lack of education, etc., they found that the most predictive factor associated with depression in later life was whether an individual was raised in a predominantly optimistic versus a predominantly pessimistic environment. The studies revealed that those raised in a pessimistic environment were found to be at a significantly higher risk for depression during their later years. The implications of this study go far beyond the subject of depression. Whether you *choose* to be in an optimistic state of mind versus a pessimistic one profoundly affects your ability to enjoy a fulfilling life. Given a choice, most people would prefer to strive for a positive future, and if asked, would generally prefer to be in a more optimistic than pessimistic state of mind and environment.

However, this ideal state of mind, this optimistic perspective, is often challenged shaken and sometimes broken by our daily experiences and stressors. In addition to these significant barriers to change is our often-inconsistent approach to gaining the new knowledge and perspectives needed to achieve true personal growth. This is often further confounded by our failure to develop and utilize effective coping skills and strategies. The following example will help to illustrate a very important concept regarding personal change.

We are all inherently resistant to change our perspectives. It's as if they are "hard-wired" in our brains. And in fact, neurobiological research says to some degree they probably are. The following example will serve to illustrate my point. Below is a figure which was created by Dr. Edward H. Adelson, Professor of Vision Science at MIT.

Figure 10: Optical illusion published by Edward H. Adelson, Professor of Vision Science at MIT in 1995.

The squares labeled A and B on the illusion appear to be different colors. However, the squares A and B are actually the same color (or shade), although they seem to be different.

Figure 11: Optical illusion published by Edward H. Adelson, Professor of Vision Science at MIT in 1995.

By adding a bridge between the two squares A and B, the fact that they are the same color can be revealed. Squares A and B now appear to be the same color (hue). Convinced? What's important about this in terms of the gyroscopic theory is that the mind rigidly holds on to its' pre-conceived ideas and biases (perspective) until a flash of lightning (i.e., the bridge) occurs.

Figure 12: Optical illusion published by Edward H. Adelson, Professor of Vision Science at MIT in 1995.

Now look at the original figure again (above). The squares labeled A and B appear to be of different colors (hues). Right? This appears to be so although intellectually *you now know* that they are actually the same color. Your mind refuses to let go of its preconceived perspective that they must be of different colors due to the presence of the shadow. Our minds can be quite rigid and resistant to change!

Flipping back-and-forth between the two images reveals how our mind resists the idea of accepting change. Although we know, intellectually, that the two squares are actually the same color (i.e., when the bridge is present) experientially we cannot help but see them as different colors when the bridge is absent.

Please allow me to repeat this point. Even though we know intellectually that the two squares in question, labeled A and B, are the same color, we are unable to overcome our fixed perspective that has been hardwired into our brains that the squares must be different colors because of the presence of the shadow. So too, can our other beliefs and life perspectives be just as resistant to being changed! This is our inherent nature which often stands far beyond our awareness and can close the door to our personal growth.

Only through repeated exposures to new information, coupled with reality, can we begin to see things clearly and progress towards emotional growth and change. That is, we see the new insight or perspective for a glimpse, for a brief moment, as if it is illuminated by a flash of lightning. But then as quickly as it appears it tends to fade away and disappear from our sight. We are left with only an after-image, a shadow of what we briefly saw. Most often we inherently either reject or morph the new information we received. Leaving us, once again, to stand in total darkness.

This leaves us to selectively question what we experienced. This is further complicated by the fact that we are often blinded by our own pre-existing beliefs and perspectives. We reflexively reject anything that is new or that counters our previously held beliefs. We may quickly color, corrupt, and distort what we experienced with our own pre-conceived ideas and beliefs. By doing so we are thrust further back into darkness. It is often this same type of fundamental process that occurs when we attempt to gain insight into a new perspective or a new way of seeing ourselves and others.

When we are momentarily open to new ideas or perspectives, as if it was fully illuminated by a flash of lightning, we get a clearer view of the other person's perspective. If we can examine and then incorporate the new perspective into our existing set of perspectives this leads the way to true personal change and growth. Through repeated exposures to new ideas or perspectives, both in psychotherapy and in life, in the presence of an 'open mind' a clearer and longer-lasting picture of the new insight or perspective can be achieved and employed.

The lessons learned in therapy can then be used as a 'road map' to help guide individuals as they negotiate the events of their lives. That they make an internal change which then changes the nature of their behavior. This method lies at the core of the psychotherapeutic process and lies at the heart of true inner and eventually outer life change. It also lies at the heart of the healing process.

Again, regarding possible obstacles to inner change, our very own nature can serve as an impediment. The axis of our gyroscope is composed of our many singular perspectives bundled together. The elements frequently get activated by both internal and external events. Depending on one's predominant staxis at any given moment the elements that are either activated or received can be either "ego-syntonic" (acceptable) or "ego-dystonic" (unacceptable). Thus, the elements can 'sync' with "who" we are or run 'counter' to "who" we are at any given moment. For instance, our fun-loving subordinate staxis might accept bungie jumping as an acceptable activity while our responsible parent subordinate staxis may not! Our responsible parent subordinate staxis would have a closed mind to such an activity.

If any of these elements or perspectives happen to be at odds with each other; then internal conflict and cognitive dissonance arises. Cognitive dissonance is a psychological phenomenon where individuals experience psychological discomfort when their beliefs, values, and behaviors do not align. It is a state of mental conflict that occurs when an individual holds two or more contradictory beliefs, ideas, or values. The level of mental stress and pain experienced by the individual is directly proportional to how strongly the discordant elements oppose each other. Also at play are the individual's defensive style and the pressure generated by the contextual framework of the environment in which the individual exists. The feelings and related emotions generated by such inner conflict can be quite intense.

I had noted previously that we usually reflexively reject any new information or perspectives presented to us. We often do this in order to

71

avoid the resultant cognitive dissonance with its unwanted internal conflict and mental distress (angst). People tend to stay on their own chosen path to feel safe, secure, protected, and anguish free. This aligns with Sigmund Freud's pleasure principle. Their bundled perspectives may become so strong and rigid that they become that individual's core identity. At that point the individual can become highly inflexible. They may become unable to hear the words and ideas of others. They truly can become deaf and blind to the world around them. Unfortunately, tied to solely self-serving agendas this phenomenon is what makes know-it-alls; know-it-alls, bigots; bigots, and criminals; criminals.

Figure 13: A light bulb.

There is an old joke in psychiatry which goes: How many psychiatrists does it take to change a light bulb? The answer is only one. <u>But</u> the light bulb has to <u>want</u> to change! If you wish to quit smoking, lose weight, get physically fit, excel in academics or sports, grow emotionally there must first be an internal desire for change. Many people start with the idea that they want to make a change in some aspect or area of their life. They might wish to achieve a specific life goal. Unfortunately, many of them don't know how to go about it. They often give little time and serious thought to the often, difficult internal mental change that is required. They also often fail to act. Which I previously discussed as to the pre-requisite need for action prior to the development of motivation.

In summary, the process of personal change often involves acquiring the new knowledge needed to succeed. It requires the reshaping of one's desire, will power, mental attitude, and focus. It leads to the creation of the new perspectives that are required to achieve one's desired goals. True change always begins as an internal process and requires your will and commitment for its fruition. If you need to make a change, or wish to grow, you must take it seriously. You must also act. As I have mentioned, our previous fixed perspectives stand in the way. The longer our platforms (perspectives, staxes) exist the more resistant we become to change.

ONE'S PLATFORM MUST BE CONFRONTED!

I tell many of my patients: If you wish to see your very best friend and your very worst enemy at any time. Look in any mirror! Look in your mirror every morning and ask yourself the following question: Am I going to be my very best friend today or my very worst enemy?

Now for some fun! ☺ Can we truly change our perspectives?

What is: 45 X 11?

Seems like a difficult problem for the average person, right?

You're asking is this fun?!

Actually, if you know the trick: You can make the seemingly difficult: easy.

The trick: 4 + 5 = 9

Place the 9 in the middle.

The answer is: 495

What is: 53 X 11?

Again: 5 + 3 = 8

Place the 8 in the middle.

Answer: 583

Now you can astound your family and friends as you ask them to give you any number, and you give them the answer before they can find the answer while using a calculator!

I have given this example to show how if you put aside your preconceived ideas of what seems impossible or too difficult and open your mind to receive new information (namely, the math trick) you can quite easily change your perspective about what is difficult. You must allow for that 'flash of lightning' to occur. You must be flexible enough to open a window for new information to enter which then allows for a change of perspective to occur.

What is: 95 X 11?

Don't panic! It's the same process.

9 + 5 = 14

Add 14 to the middle.

9 - 5

<u>1 4</u>

Answer: 1045

Practice makes perfect!

Now look at the picture presented next, in figure 14. It is a picture of the St. Louis Arch. Question. Is the arch taller than it is wide, or is it wider than it is tall?

Figure 14: St. Louis Arch

With guidelines added the arch miraculously appears taller than it is wide as portrayed in figure 15.

Figure 15: St. Louis Arch with guide lines drawn.

However, in figure 16, when we add equal sized smiley faces we can see that the arch is as wide as it is tall! ☺

Figure 16: The St. Louis Arch is as tall as it is wide! ☺

Although they <u>know</u> intellectually that it is as wide as it is tall, most people's naked eyes still tell them that it's taller than it is wide!

Figure 17: St. Louis Arch

The following is a personal story about will power, adaptation, and the acceptance of change. While serving as a patrol leader in the Boy Scouts, I had an experience that tested my will power. We had arrived at a campsite after sunset. It had grown quite dark. However, with there being a full moon that night we could see the outlines of the trees and large objects that surrounded us. After unloading our gear, we set out to find wood for our campfires. As we walked through the woods, we came upon a few fallen trees that seemed to have the type of wood we were seeking. We paused by a log and I had placed my foot on the log for support while viewing our surroundings.

As I scanned the area, I noticed that one of the scouts had been carrying an axe without its sheath. That could prove to be quite dangerous in the dark. He noted that he had no sheath with him. As the patrol leader, I instructed him to bury his axe until we were ready to chop the wood. Not seeing my right foot on the log, he struck my foot with the axe's blade as he attempted to bury it in the log beneath us. I first heard a thud as I felt a tremendous force strike my foot. I reached down and touched my hiking boot and realized that it had been cut open!

I then rubbed the opening in my boot to lessen the pain I was beginning to experience. As I brought my hand back towards my face I could see blood on my hand. It then hit me that my foot had been cut. My heart began pounding and I knew that I had to make it back to the campsite to assess the extent of the damage to my foot. As I walked as quickly as I could back to camp, I had to summon my will power not to panic and run, which I knew would only increase my risk of suffering significant blood loss. We were approximately half-a-mile from our campsite.

On the way back I was met by our Assistant Scout Master and I explained to him what had happened. He then carried me on his back the rest of the way to the campsite. After we arrived at the campsite our Scout Master went to the campground headquarters and got a jeep to bring me to a local hospital emergency room. While riding in the jeep on the trail out of the campgrounds a highly intoxicated young camper ran into the side of the jeep while brandishing a handgun. This surely added more stress to my experience though it seemed quite surreal to me at that moment. Surreal enough to make it easier to disregard what had happened and focus on getting to the hospital.

Fortunately, that situation was quickly handled by another scoutmaster who had joined us for the trip. Luckily the overall ride to the hospital was of a relatively short duration. During the ride I imagined what it must be like to be a wounded soldier, especially in a foreign land far away from home and family. The feelings I experienced during the ride left a lasting impression that I can relate to even today.

After examining my foot, the doctor left the room to speak with my Scout Master. When he re-entered the exam room, he asked me if I wanted him to attempt to "save" two of my toes that had been cut very badly (almost completely severed from my foot). To a 12-year-old boy, this question was quite frightening, but I answered "yes" immediately without hesitation. He cautioned me as he began to suture them that there was no guarantee that the toes would "heal properly" and that they might have to be removed later if gangrene set in. Once I was done and my foot had been wrapped, I was returned to the campsite.

The Scout Master stated that he would bring me home in the morning if I wanted to do so. After some thought, I decided not to be defeated by what had happened. I informed my scout master that I had decided to stay for the remainder of the camping trip. A drastic change in my situation had been thrust upon me and served as a direct challenge to my will. I decided to adapt to my situation. I met with the scout who had cut my foot. He was feeling quite guilty about what had transpired the previous night. Having had already decided to forgive him, I then joked with him to reduce his guilt and forgave him.

The next morning the Assistant Scout Master, was playfully taunting a scout by calling him while holding a belt in his hand, as if he planned to hit the scout with the belt. I crept up behind the Assistant Scout Master, as the Scout Master watched with great amusement. I was quietly hoping on my left foot, while supporting myself with a crutch on the right. I was quite pleased and honored that our Scout Master didn't give me away! He just smiled at me. The Assistant Scout Master didn't seem to hear or notice what I was doing. At least not until I grabbed the belt out of his hand from behind and then ran from him. He then burst into laughter when he realized what I had done. In spite of the events which had occurred the previous day, I was having fun.

I knowingly took a chance to stay at the campsite with my toes in jeopardy. Perhaps one might think that my judgment was off and maybe they are right, but I did gain something in the process. Those events were critical to my early growth, as they allowed for me to further learn about the nature and power of my own will power. It taught me to take risks and to fight on in the face of fear, despite possible future losses. It taught me that we must adapt to change to move forward. By the way, my toes are just fine all these years later.

We all experience such pivotal events in our lives, and we should take them seriously. They are opportunities to grow emotionally and to sharpen our will power. They are opportunities to expand our 'emotional IQ' and rally towards change and personal growth. I tell this story because it relates directly to the therapeutic process which can involve fear of the unknown and the mental stress it can invoke. As a result, therapy often requires courage, will power, and tenacity. However, given one's perspective it can also involve fun as well! It requires some sense of optimism as you go along.

True insight and growth can be attained by individuals who actively and repeatedly work on their emotional and mental flexibility. In order to change and grow you must deal with the ideas, beliefs, perceptions, emotions, defenses, etc. that power your inner wheel. You must actively add new elements and make changes to those existing items that need to be changed or deleted. Focused repetition of new ideas and perspectives is essential when you are attempting to change a deeply held erroneous or unwanted perspective. It is critical that you link your thoughts to your emotions as you attempt to 'work-through' the central issues at hand.

Quite often when a person in therapy gains a new insight, they treat it as if it occurred during a flash of lightning. They find it interesting at first but quickly drop the insight and move on. This is like a person walking aimlessly through a desert in search of a well, and when they find one, they take only a sip of water and then continue walking aimlessly through the desert in search of another well. Most would agree that such a person is not being efficient and seems truly lost. By walking away from insights gained with their opportunities for growth we curtail the advantage that the therapeutic process has to offer.

The unconscious mind listens more seriously to conscious ideas that are firmly attached to feelings and emotions. As new perspectives replace older ones they may eventually become fully established. They can strengthen your inner wheel by adding greater momentum. This process can lead to a lasting change in your perspectives and in your axis of stability. What can also be gained is further mental flexibility and personal growth. This happens on a long-term basis only by repeated glimpses of new information and the active focused consideration and incorporation of different perspectives over time. When such a process is attached to a purpose it can be quite powerful.

As people age, they become more rigid in their thinking and perspectives. Thus, they tend to become more resistant to change. As noted previously, this general observation probably led to the adage: 'You can't teach an old dog new tricks.' This general observation has also been historically supported by clinical experience. I believe that as a person absorbs more information and life experiences over time it causes their inner wheel to spin faster which then gains greater momentum. As a result, the individual then becomes more powerfully driven to remain rigid in their beliefs and perspectives. We all seek information to confirm our own perspectives which in turn makes us feel more secure.

The following quote by Pearl S. Buck underscores this matter: "You can judge your age by the amount of pain you feel when you come in contact with a new idea."

However, age need not be a barrier to personal growth and change. As previously stated, a general assumption I make is that as a person ages, the more rapidly their inner wheel spins. This as a direct result of the passage of time that provides for the selective incorporation of more beliefs, life experiences, perceptions, ideas, information, etc. that serves to reinforce one's major and subordinate staxes. This then further powers one's inner wheel to spin more rapidly. Succinctly, the greater one's life experiences, the greater the amount of fuel available to power the spinning wheel, the greater one's resistance to change. Though somewhat basic in its design the model of a functioning gyroscope provides a concise picture of the general processes described.

I mentioned earlier that the faster that the wheel of a gyroscope spins the more difficult it becomes to shift its axis. However, the mind responds to the focused repetition of new ideas and perspectives at all ages, which is a skill that becomes better with practice. In this way it truly becomes possible with practice to direct a change of one's core axes at any age. Fortunately, we are not rocks that are confined to the physical parameters which limit the malleability of inanimate objects. Remember this: We are what we practice.

Keep in mind that all people are gyroscopic and have their own issues and dynamics. People will put forward the premise for one or more of their perspectives to influence your thinking, emotions, and behavior. Sometimes they will 'sync' with your own perspectives and dynamics. Sometimes they will not. Sometimes their input will be good and constructive for you. Other times their input will be bad and destructive for you. Sometimes people's actions will 'bounce-off' of you causing you to experience feelings of inner-conflict and a temporary sense of instability as you stand there wobbling!

Occasionally people will 'push your buttons' while attempting to deal with their own issues. This may cause you to become reactive. Try not to mirror their behaviors. Doing so will ultimately cause you to lose focus and control over your own life. Sometimes their behavior and interactive styles will open your eyes to a personal area of yours that you need to examine or change. Other times their behavior and interactive styles will further blind you to a personal area of yours that needs to be changed. They may reinforce bad habits or behaviors. Addressing this can prove to be quite challenging. Indeed, it can be quite tricky trying to both comprehend and manage multiple inputs amid multiple daily interactions.

Hopefully the model and method presented here will provide some tools you can use to sort things out in a clear and objective manner. So that any personal changes you may need or decide to make will prove to be positive ones for you. Some people approach this task with trepidation. Try to think of it as a creative process. In fact, you can become quite creative in the way you visualize the process of self-therapy. One way of visualizing it will now be presented.

Think of your unconscious mind as an open kettle lying below a sand sifter. Think of your many experiences, exposures to others thoughts and perspectives, as well as your own thoughts, perspectives and secret fantasies as grains of various colored sands. Blues, reds, yellows, greens, purples, etc. The more of blue you put in the sifter, the more of blue that gets sifted into the kettle below to become a part of your unconscious which then colors your subsequent view of the world. Thus, you must choose wisely which thoughts and perspectives will enter to serve as your central focus and thereby color your life.

Consider the following quote from Buddhism which was cited by Mahatma Gandhi:

"Keep your thoughts positive, because your thoughts become your words.

Keep your words positive, because your words become your behaviors.

Keep your behaviors positive, because your behaviors become your habits.

Keep your habits positive, because your habits become your values.

Keep your values positive, because your values become your destiny."

- Buddha

When attempting to achieve personal change and growth it is important to consider the power and influence of one's own self-esteem. I believe that no one is ever born with self-esteem. That it is not a natural or innate part of our psyche. Self-esteem is something that we create. We create it by setting and by achieving goals. We set a goal, act, and when we make the goal, we say to ourselves good job! We feel good about ourselves. Then we set another goal and when we make that goal, we feel even better about ourselves. We feel great! Then, we set another and when we achieve that goal, we feel fantastic about ourselves!

However, just as we can build our self-esteem by setting and making goals, we can also lose our self-esteem by missing goals. For example, if you were to take a highly successful and self-confident businessperson and gave him or her three years of bad business returns with huge losses, even that person would begin to lose several points on the self-esteem scale. When a person's self-esteem is low it weakens their own faith in their ability to tolerate change and to achieve personal growth. They can become highly discouraged and emotionally stuck! They can become 'gun-shy' in the face of life's challenges.

Thus, our self-esteem is directly tied to our faith that we can change and to our ability to adapt and grow. It is essential for adolescents and young adults to work on and to be nurtured in this area of development.

There is certainly nothing novel in this statement. It is also important to keep in mind that self-esteem is multifaceted. It is divided into specific areas of ability such as physical prowess vs. intellectual ability vs. parenting ability, etc. This is because each area is comprised of its own set of specific goals that must be accomplished. This is why a person can feel great about their intellectual ability while being quite unhappy with their athletic abilities. So that an individual can have high intellectual self-esteem, but have low athletic self-esteem, and vice versa. Unfortunately, sometimes individuals consciously choose to develop just one specific area of ability to the exclusion of others and thus become unbalanced and unhappy with themselves. It often leaves them feeling great in one aspect of their life and totally inadequate in another.

Due to the sense of stability, it provides, the gyroscopic effect might seem as if it would lead to the most desirable state of being. In earlier passages of this book, I alluded to the fact that a person's major staxis can support a fixed and pervasive dysfunctional state of being. In psychiatric clinical jargon we refer to this type of dysfunctional state as being a 'personality disorder'. Such people are sometimes referred to as being 'stably unstable' by clinicians. If one exists in a fixed dysfunctional state, it can sometimes lead to devastating consequences. Those dysfunctional states can range from an inadequate ineffective personality type to that of the utter sociopath. Unfortunately, psychotherapy does not always help such people. Very often due to the individual's mental rigidity and rejection of help.

However, there are more subtle types of disfunction that affect us all. Let's take the common example of a man who has high blood pressure but refuses to acknowledge it or to seek treatment. Already his doctor has informed him that he needs to have his blood pressure monitored and treated, lest he have a stroke. He then goes about working every day forgetting about (suppressing/repressing) his doctor's concerns and advice. He 'forgets' to take his medications. He may even resort to sporadic compliance with his medications or the use of ineffective home remedies or alternative treatments. By doing so he can reduce his own level of anxiety and cognitive dissonance over his problem with high blood pressure. This allows him, for the most part, to maintain his original perspective that all is well and that there's really nothing to worry about. He chooses not to change his behavior and to let the ego defense of denial dominate.

At some point however, he might have a stroke, a heart attack, or over time might develop severe kidney failure. Let's say he suddenly has a stroke. A new perspective (reality) is thrust upon him. Now he is not only physically ill, but also becomes mentally distraught. Fear rushes in to chase his new reality now unmasked. He has left-sided paralysis, impaired speech, and is unable to take care of himself. He is then forced into the unfortunate position of having to accept a new undesirable perspective of being ill. Also, of having now missed the window of opportunity to avoid his now highly undesirable situation. Cognitive dissonance and remorse set in with their accompanying mental anguish.

He likely will feel anger at himself for not having been more serious about the need for him to comply with his treatment. He likely will feel guilt over the severe negative impact that having a stroke has on his family and the 'burden' he has placed on them regarding his new physical care needs. Also, his inability to work to earn a living. Thus, the seemingly protective defensive gyroscopic forces that initially allowed him to keep the perspective that all was well, blinded him to the dangers of his chronically elevated blood pressure that eventually led to a disastrous outcome.

In general, most people either directly or indirectly reject any new negative information provided concerning their health. Most people are in a mental fog after getting bad news concerning their health. As patients are treated for their medical illnesses, part of what a doctor must do is to shift that patient's perspective concerning their state of health so that the gravity of their illness is understood and incorporated by the patient. The patient must develop a new perspective of having an illness. During that process, they also develop a new "identity" as a person with hypertension, or diabetes, or cancer, etc.

This process can allow for a positive and desired major shift in their perspective regarding their own active role in their treatment. In this way, they can access the necessary education concerning their illness, the available resources and supports, and the professional medical guidance required for their treatment. This is a very powerful thing. It lies at the very core of the healing process. It serves as an opportunity for an open window that connects the patient with their healer.

I had mentioned earlier our very common and natural reflexive rejection of any new information or perspectives that counter the elements and perspectives of our inner wheels. As a result, when new bits and pieces of information are presented to us, it is as if we were walking through a thunderstorm with brief flashes of lightning. Likewise, in a medical setting we are only able to see brief flashes of information. We tend to hear only small portions of the information presented to us. This is especially true when we receive bad news about our health or during the stress of our initial visits for a medical concern or condition. It is very common to hear a patient state, 'the doctor told me I have cancer, but I can't remember anything the doctor said after that'.

Such information can be too overwhelming to an individual's ego defenses and threatening to their axis of stability. The time interval is just too short for a complete realignment of that individual's perspectives during one visit. That person's mind just shuts down and defends against a major blow to, and shift in, its axis of stability. It is assumed that if a person doesn't fully accept the gravity of their illness and their need for care, that they are more unlikely to follow-up with treatment. Those people tend to have a poorer prognosis and therefore poorer outcomes. Unfortunately, all too often such scenarios lead to tragic outcomes.

10

Quotes Concerning Change

SINCE A MAJOR PORTION OF THIS BOOK DEALS WITH THE SUBJECT OF change, I have decided to dedicate this chapter solely to quotes on change. I have included numerous quotes which embody centuries of though and wisdom concerning the subject of change. They can be used to better understand the nature of change. They can be used for reference by the reader when the opportunity for change presents itself. They can also be used to raise the hope and spirits of a person who has just been confronted with a difficult life change. They can simply be used for solace. They are concise, yet full of wisdom. They are truly invaluable for all the enlightenment and words of wisdom they provide concerning the subject of change.

Consider the following Quotes about change:

> "They always say time changes things, but you actually have to change them yourself."
>
> **- Andy Warhol**

> "Education is the most powerful weapon which you can use to change the world."
>
> **- Nelson Mandela**

"We have a powerful potential in our youth, and we must have the courage to change old ideas and practices so that we may direct their power toward good ends."

- Mary McLeod Bethune

"Things do not change; we change."

- Henry David Thoreau

"I felt that it was not until one wanted the world to be different, that one could look at the world with will and emotion."

- Richard Wright

"He that will not apply new remedies must expect new evils; for time is the greatest innovator."

- Sir Francis Bacon

"Change your thoughts and you change your world."

- Norman Vincent Peale

"The real voyage of discovery consists not in seeking new landscapes, but in having new eyes."

- Marcel Proust

"When you are through changing, you are through."

- Bruce Barton

"They must often change, who would be constant in happiness or wisdom."

- Confucius

"You must be the change you wish to see in the world."

- Gandhi

"You can judge your age by the amount of pain you feel when you come in contact with a new idea."

- Pearl S. Buck

"No person is your friend who demands your silence, or denies your right to grow."

- Alice Walker

"If you have always done it that way, it is probably wrong."

- Charles Kettering

"It is not the strongest of the species that survives: nor the most intelligent, but the one most responsive to change."

- Charles Darwin

"The important thing is this: To be able at any moment to sacrifice what we are for what we could become."

- Charles Du Bois

"In times of change, learners inherit the Earth, while the learned find themselves beautifully equipped to deal with a world that no longer exists."

- Eric Hoffer

"If you want to make enemies, try to change something."

- Woodrow Wilson

"To exist is to change, to change is to mature, to mature is to go on creating oneself endlessly."

- Henri Bergson

"When we blindly adopt a religion, a political system, a literary dogma, we become automatons. We cease to grow."

- Anais Nin

"Everyone thinks of changing the world, but no one thinks of changing himself."

- Leo Tolstoy

"The whole course of human history may depend on a change of heart in one solitary and even humble individual - for it is in the solitary mind and soul of the individual that the battle between good and evil is waged and ultimately won or lost."

- M. Scott Peck

"The universe is transformation; our life is what our thoughts make it."

- Marcus Aurelius

"A person needs at intervals to separate from family and companions and go to new places. One must go without familiars in order to be open to influences, to change."

- Katharine Butler Hathaway

"Be not angry that you cannot make others as you wish them to be, since you cannot make yourself as you wish to be."

- Thomas a Kempis

"The heresy of one age becomes the orthodoxy of the next."

- Helen Keller

"Change is the law of life. And those who look only to the past or present are certain to miss the future."

- John F. Kennedy

"A man may fulfill the object of his existence by asking a question he cannot answer and attempting a task he cannot achieve."

- Oliver Wendell Holmes

"The first problem for all of us, men and women, is not to learn, but to unlearn."

- Gloria Steinem

"I am always doing that which I cannot do, in order that I may learn how to do it."

- Pablo Picasso

"I cannot say whether things will get better if we change; what I can say is they must change if they are to get better."

- Georg C. Lichtenberg

"Life is a process of becoming, a combination of states we have to go through. Where people fail is that they wish to elect a state and remain in it. This is a kind of death."

- Anais Nin

"Most of the change we think we see in life; is due to truths being in and out of favor."

- Robert Frost

"All conservatism is based upon the idea that if you leave things alone you leave them as they are. But you do not. If you leave a thing alone you leave it to a torrent of change."

- G. K. Chesterton

"How wonderful it is that nobody need wait a single moment before starting to improve the world."

- Anne Frank

"Never doubt that a small, group of thoughtful, committed citizens can change the world. Indeed, it is the only thing that ever has."

- Margaret Mead

"What man actually needs is not a tensionless state but rather the striving and struggling for some goal worthy of him. What he needs is not the discharge of tension at any cost, but the call of a potential meaning waiting to be fulfilled by him."

- Victor Frankl

"We change, whether we like it or not."

- Ralph Waldo Emerson

"If you're in a bad situation, don't worry it'll change. If you're in a good situation, don't worry it'll change."

- John A. Simone, Sr.

"There is nothing wrong with change, if it is in the right direction."

- Winston Churchill

"When you're finished changing, you're finished."

- Benjamin Franklin

"Change your thoughts and you change your world."

- Norman Vincent Peale

"To learn is to change. Education is a process that changes the learner."

- Anonymous

"Change the changeable, accept the unchangeable, and remove yourself from the unacceptable."

- Denis Waitley

"Life is change. Growth is optional. Choose wisely."

- Anonymous

"If you do not change direction, you may end up where you are heading."

- Lao Tzu

"You must welcome change as the rule but not as your ruler."

- Denis Waitley

"People underestimate their capacity for change. There is never a right time to do a difficult thing. A leader's job is to help people have vision of their potential."

- John Porter

"If the facts don't fit the theory, change the facts."

- Albert Einstein

"Growth means change, and change involves risk, stepping from the known to the unknown."

- Anonymous

"He who rejects change is the architect of decay. The only human institution which rejects progress is the cemetery."

- Harold Wilson

"One does not discover new lands without consenting to lose sight of the shore for a very long time."

- Andre Gide

"Maintaining a complicated life is a great way to avoid changing it."

- Elaine St. James

"Politicians are like baby diapers. They need to be changed frequently and for the same reason!"

- Larry L. Taylor

"In all things that involve social pressures if we want to see change we have to force the envelope outwards."

- Gary Lee Phillips

"To change your language, you must change your life."

- Derek Walcott

"If you ain't the lead dog the scenery never changes."

- Edmund Wilson

"The mind has exactly the same power as the hands: not merely to grasp the world but to change it."

- Colin Wilson

"Only fools and dead men don't change their minds. Fools won't. Dead men can't."

- John H. Patterson

"Change and growth take place when a person has risked himself or herself: and dares to become involved with experimenting with his or her own life."

- Herbert Otto

"Some people change their ways when they see the light; others when they feel the heat."

- Caroline Schroeder

"The only person who is educated is the one who has learned how to learn ... and change."

- Carl Ransom Rogers

"He who rejects change is the architect of decay."

- James Harold Wilson

"A foolish consistency is the hobgoblin of little minds."

- Ralph Waldo Emerson

"To exist is to change, to change is to mature, to mature is to go on creating oneself endlessly."

- Henri Louis Bergson

"Simply pushing harder within the old boundaries will not do."

- Karl Weick

"Money does not change men it only unmasks them."

- Mme. Riccoboni

"If you don't create change, change will create you."

- Anonymous

"Change is inevitable, except from vending machines."

- Unknown

It is only the minority of people who seek self-improvement or personal growth. This is because whatever one's self-criticisms, one secretly really believes that one's way of being is okay and probably the only correct one. They are alright as they are, and all problems are caused by other people's selfishness, unfairness, and by the external world.

- David R. Hawkins

Further quotes on change made by the Rev. Martin Luther King, Jr.:

"Put yourself in a state of mind where you say to yourself, 'here is an opportunity for me to celebrate like never before, my own power; my own ability to get myself to do whatever is necessary."

"The ultimate measure of a man is not where he stands in moments of comfort and convenience, but where he stands at times of challenge and controversy."

"If you succumb to the temptation of using violence in the struggle, unborn generations will be the recipients of a long and desolate night of bitterness, and your chief legacy to the future will be an endless reign of meaningless chaos."

"Change does not roll in on wheels of inevitability but comes through continuous struggle. And so, we must straighten our backs and work for our freedom. A man can't ride you unless your back is bent."

"I refuse to accept the view that mankind is so tragically bound to the starless midnight of racism and war that the bright daybreak of peace and brotherhood can never become reality."

"Rarely do we find men who willingly engage in hard, solid thinking. There is an almost universal quest for easy answers and half-baked solutions. Nothing pains some people more than having to think."

"Every man must decide whether to walk in the light of creative altruism or in the darkness of destructive selfishness."

"Darkness cannot drive out darkness; only light can do that. Hate cannot drive out hate; only love can do that."

- Rev. Martin Luther King, Jr.

11

Dealing with Stress and Assertiveness

STRESS IS DEFINED AS A NON-SPECIFIC RESPONSE OF THE BODY TO ANY demand placed upon it. The term non-specific means the body needs to readjust in multiple non-specific ways (both mental and physical) to deal with the demand. Stressors are the events or conditions that produce the stress response. Any chronic intense response that is unpleasant or harmful is called distress. That which motivates us and increases our productivity and satisfaction is called eustress.

When we think of stress, we usually think of it in negative terms: waking up late for work or a planned event, discovering the gas gauge is on empty while on the highway, it's raining and you need to get to work on time for an important meeting and you're running late, you drop the juice container and it spills all over the kitchen floor, etc. Stress, however, is not always unpleasant (i.e., marriages, having a baby, the holiday seasons, buying a new car or house, etc.). What really counts here is that a demand is placed on you to readjust. The evaluation of whether the stress is either positive or negative is determined by our own thoughts, interpretations, and perspectives.

Key Points about Stress:

- It is a misconception that we should eliminate stress altogether.
- Stress is a necessary and vital part of life.

- Without stress there are no challenges and often there is no personal growth.
- Complete avoidance of stress is to do nothing: and thereby to become emotionally dead.
- What is stressful for one person may not be stressful for another person.
- Any condition or life event can be stress-producing, depending on the individual's perception of the event.

Sometimes it may seem that there's nothing you can do about your stress. Your bills keep coming. There are never enough hours in the day to feel free to do as you wish. Your career and family responsibilities seem like they will always be overwhelming and demanding. However, you have more control than you might think. In fact, the simple realization that you're in control of your life is one of the foundations of stress management. Managing stress is all about taking charge of your thoughts, your emotions, your schedule, and the way you deal with your problems.

Stress management begins with identifying the sources of stress in your life. This is not as easy as it may sound. The true sources of your stress aren't always obvious, and it's all too easy to overlook your own stress-inducing thoughts, feelings, and behaviors. Sure, you may know that you're constantly worried and stressed about your work deadlines. But maybe it's your procrastination rather than the actual job demands and deadlines that leads to your stress.

To identify the true sources of your stress, look closely at your habits, attitudes, and excuses (the chapter on self-therapy discusses the topic of excuses):

- Do you justify stress as just being temporary, so that you don't have to deal with it? (i.e., 'I just have multiple things going on right now, so I can't stop to take a break and work on this stress thing.' Even though you really can't remember the last time you took a break?)
- Do you justify stress by defining it as an integral part of your work or home life? (i.e., 'Things are always crazy around here.' or define it as a part of your personality: 'I just have a lot of nervous energy, it's the way I tend to deal with things, that's all'.)

Do you tend to blame your stress on other people or outside events? Do you consider excessive stress to be normal? Until you accept responsibility for the role you play in creating or maintaining it, your stress level will remain outside of your control. Think about the ways in which you currently manage and cope with stress in your life. If your way of coping with stress isn't contributing to your greater emotional and physical health, then it's time to find healthier methods. There are a lot of healthy ways to manage and cope with stress, but they all require change. You can either change the situation or change your reactions to the stressors as they present themselves. Stress is carried both mentally and physically. Where do you mostly carry your stress?

Since everyone has a unique response to stress, there is no 'one size fits all' solution for managing stress. Thus, no single method or action works for everyone in every situation. So, it becomes important to experiment with different techniques and strategies. It is a good idea to focus on what makes you feel both calm and in control. The following is the general format used by those doing stress management therapy and education. When deciding which option to use it's helpful to think of the traditional four A's of stress management: avoid, alter, adapt, or accept.

Stress management strategy #1: Avoid unnecessary stress

Not all stress can or should be avoided. Most often it's not healthy or wise to avoid a situation that you need to address. If you address them directly you might be surprised by the large number of stressors in your life that you can actually eliminate.

- **Learn how to say "no"** – Know your abilities and limits and stick to them. Whether in your personal or professional life, refuse to accept added responsibilities when you're already near to or at your limit. Taking on more than you can handle is a certain recipe for stress and for failure.
- **Take control of your environment** – If driving in heavy traffic has you stressed-out, change the times you travel or take a longer but

less-traveled route. If the evening news makes you anxious, turn the TV off. If you hate grocery shopping and find it an unpleasant chore, do your grocery shopping online.

- **Avoid people who stress you out** – If someone consistently causes stress in your life and you can't turn the nature of your relationship around, limit the amount of time you spend with that person or end the relationship entirely.

- **Avoid 'hot-button' topics** – If you tend to get upset over certain topics like religion or politics, cross them off your conversation list. If you have repeatedly argued about the same subjects with the same people, stop bringing them up or excuse yourself when the topics arise in discussion.

- **Trim down your to-do list** – Analyze your schedule, responsibilities, daily tasks, and your short-term and long-term projects. If you've got too much on your plate, distinguish between the "I should do's" and the "must do's." Either drop tasks that aren't truly necessary to the bottom of the list or just eliminate them entirely.

- **Manage your time better.** Poor time management can cause a lot of unnecessary stress. When you're stretched too thin with multiple tasks and are running behind, it's hard to stay calm and focused. But if you plan ahead and arrange your schedule to make sure you don't overextend yourself, you can greatly reduce the amount of stress you're under.

Stress management strategy #2: After the situation occurs

If you can't avoid a stressful situation, try to change it. Figure out what you can do to modify things so that the problem doesn't present itself in the future.

- **Express your feelings instead of holding them in.** If something or someone is bothering or irritating you, communicate your concerns to those involved in an open and respectful way. If you don't voice your feelings, you may find yourself feeling resentment, and the situation will likely remain the same.

- **Be willing to compromise.** If you ask someone to change their behavior, you should be willing to do the same. If you both are willing to bend just a little, there's a good possibility you'll find a happy middle ground.
- **Be more assertive.** Don't be passive. You are ultimately responsible for directing your own life. Deal with problems head on. Do your best to anticipate and prevent problems. If you have a project to complete for work and your chatty fellow employee just entered your work space, state up front that you only have ten minutes to talk with them and stick to just ten minutes.

Stress management strategy #3: Adapt to the stressor

If you can't change or avoid the stressor, then you must change yourself. You can adapt to stressful situations and regain your sense of control by changing your expectations and attitudes regarding your stressors.

- **Reframe your problems.** Try to view unavoidable stressful situations from a more positive perspective. Rather than simmering emotionally while stuck in a traffic jam, look at it as an opportunity to pause and relax, listen to your favorite music, or enjoy singing your favorite songs, or remembering jokes that you found to be very funny, etc.
- **Focus on the positive.** When stress gets you down, take a moment to reflect on all of the positive things you can appreciate in your life. Look also at your own attributes and blessings. This simple strategy can go a long way in helping you keep things in perspective.
- **Look at the big picture.** Take a global perspective of the stressful situation. Ask yourself how important it will be in the long run. Will it really matter in a week? A month? A year? Ten years? Is the stressor really worth getting upset over? If the answer is no, focus your time and energy on more important issues.
- **Adjust your standards.** Perfectionism, which is often based in non-reality and is most often unobtainable, is a major source of avoidable

stress. Stop setting yourself up for failure by always demanding self-perfection. Set reasonable goals and standards for yourself and others, and learn to be okay with the term "good enough" which is most often fully sufficient.

- **Adjusting Your Attitude.** How you think about your problems and stress can have a profound effect on your emotional and physical well-being. If you habitually think negative thoughts about yourself, you can create an unhealthy inner tension that in the long term may cause ill health effects.

Stress management strategy #4: Accept the things you can't change

Some sources of stress are unavoidable and unchangeable. You can't prevent or change stressors such as a serious illness, loss of your job when your company goes out of business, the death of a loved one, a flood, a national recession, etc. Acceptance may be difficult to accomplish, but in the long run, it's easier than fighting against a situation you can't change.

- **Don't try to control, uncontrollable things.** Many things in life are beyond our control, particularly the thoughts and behaviors of other people. Rather focusing on the things that you can't control; focus on the things that you can control, such as the way you choose to react to problems as they occur. One example would be not responding in a reflexive, knee-jerk fashion to the emotional tones set by others, as discussed in the earlier chapters on mood and emotions.
- **Look for the advantage.** As the observation by Friedrich Nietzsche goes, "What doesn't kill us makes us stronger." When facing difficult, stressful challenges, try to look at them as opportunities for personal growth and change.
- **Share your feelings.** Talk to a trusted friend or make an appointment to speak with a therapist. Talking about what you're stressed about can be very cathartic, even if there's really nothing you can do to change the stressful situation.

- **Learn to forgive others.** Accept the fact that we live in an imperfect world where people are fallible and make mistakes. Let go of your anger and resentments, and free yourself from negative energy by forgiving others and by moving on.

Stress management strategy #5:
Make time for relaxation and for fun activities

You can reduce your overall level of stress, simply by nurturing yourself. If you take time for relaxation and fun on a regular basis, you'll be in a better place to handle life's stressors when they arrive. Don't get so caught up in life's demands that you forget to take care of your own need for nurturing. Nurturing yourself is an actual necessity, not a luxury. Go for a nice walk, take a warm bath, get a massage, listen to music, watch a good movie, make a cup of tea, light scented candles, etc.

- **Set aside relaxation time.** Schedule rest and relaxation into your daily schedule. Don't allow other obligations to encroach on your personal time. This is your time to take a break from all your responsibilities in order to recharge your batteries.
- **Connect with others.** Spend time with supportive positive people who enhance your life. A strong support system will buffer you from the negative effects of stress.
- **Do something you enjoy every day.** Schedule time for leisure activities that bring you joy and fulfillment, whether it is dancing, exercising, playing an instrument, playing chess, painting, whatever makes you feel good.
- **Exercise your sense of humor.** Develop the ability to laugh at life and to even laugh at your own silly predicaments. The actual act of laughing has been shown to help our bodies fight stress in a number of ways.

Stress management strategy #6:
Adopt a healthy lifestyle

You can increase your ability to counter stress by strengthening your physical health.

- **Exercise regularly.** Physical activity and regular exercise play a key role in reducing and preventing the ill-effects of stress. Schedule time for at least 30 minutes of exercise, three times per week.
- **Eat a healthy balanced diet.** Well-nourished bodies are better prepared to cope with stress.
- **Reduce caffeine and sugar.** The temporary "highs" that caffeine and sugar provide often end in with a crash in mood and energy as the caffeine leaves your system and the glucose gets locked into storage by insulin. Try reducing the amount of coffee, soft drinks, chocolate, and sugar snacks in your diet, or even eliminate some or all of them, very likely you'll feel more relaxed, and you'll sleep better too.
- **Avoid use of alcohol, cigarettes, and drugs.** Self-medicating with alcohol or drugs may provide a quick and easy escape from stress, but the relief is only temporary, and as many substance users will tell you, the problems are still there when they 'come down' and are usually much worse. Deal with your problems head on and with a clear mind, this tends to produce much better results.
- **Get enough sleep.** Adequate sleep allows your mind a restful break from daily stress. It also allows your body to get its rest. Feeling tired and exhausted will increase your stress level and will often tax your ability to think clearly.

In addition to handling your stress level it is also important to be aware of the more global need to restructure those things in your life that are directly associated with and produce your stress. One needs to be assertive in that pursuit. The following paragraphs attempt to clarify the distinction between the terms assertiveness, passiveness, and aggressiveness.

Assertiveness involves standing up for one's own personal rights by expressing one's thoughts, feelings, and beliefs in direct and appropriate ways that do not violate another person's rights. The act of assertiveness involves a focus of respect rather than one of dominance. The respect has two aspects: respect for oneself (by expressing one's own thoughts, feelings, beliefs and needs while defending one's own rights) and respect for the other person (the other person's needs and rights). The non-verbal cues of assertiveness are: a clear and well-modulated voice, good eye contact, and relaxed, confident, and polite gestures.

Passiveness involves violating one's own rights by failing to express one's honest feelings, thoughts and beliefs; thereby permitting others to violate oneself. The goal of passivity is to appease others and to avoid conflict at any cost. The underlying message is 'I don't count, my thoughts, feelings, beliefs, and needs aren't important, so you can disrespect and take advantage of me'. The non-verbal cues of passivity are a soft voice, poor eye contact, and weak body gestures and posture.

Aggressiveness involves standing up for one's own personal rights and expressing one's thoughts, feelings and beliefs in ways that are inappropriate and violate the rights of others. The usual goal of being aggressive is domination and winning one's own way. The underlying message being: 'I want, what I want, and what you want isn't important'. The non-verbal cues of aggressive behavior are a loud voice, a stare-down, and threatening gestures and body postures.

Of the three defined approaches: assertiveness, passiveness, and aggression, the assertive approach tends to have the best outcomes and tends to establish a much better foundation for relationships with others.

Assertiveness done correctly is a win-win proposition, where both parties involved get some or most of their needs met through a supportive and collaborative process. How can one further increase their mental flexibility and their ability to change the parts of themselves they wish to? The next chapter begins the journey towards a real answer to that question.

12

Confront Your Fear

TRADITIONAL THERAPY OR EVEN SELF-THERAPY CAN BE A SCARY THING at first for those who have never done so. Therapy is often filled with many unknowns as one begins the process. Some people let their imaginations run wild about what therapy involves. Many people don't know where to start and fear their own thoughts, emotions, potential behaviors, and potential embarrassment. We are given many negative images of therapy by the media, by our community, by religious groups, etc.

When starting therapy, that first 'flash of lightning' which reveals the true nature of one's life situation can be truly uncomfortable or frightening to some. However, one must overcome the fear of their thoughts and emotions. This is essential. To free yourself to think in an unrestricted manner about your problems and emotional concerns, you must first overcome your own fear that your thoughts and emotions can somehow harm you. That your thoughts or feelings will somehow destroy you or make you 'go crazy'. Many people secretly hold this fear.

I mentioned earlier that as unconscious material passes through one's sensor (as described in the Freudian model), the sensor can cause repression of the unconscious material, or it can produce 'signal anxiety' as it allows the unconscious material to pass through. The signal anxiety is experienced by the individual as tension or anxiety. Combining this with the information previously covered concerning our moods and emotions it becomes much clearer how intense unconscious material can generate feelings of intense anxiety and even fear, intense anger and even rage.

However, I want to focus on anxiety and fear here. Intense anxiety and fear can serve as major barriers to the work of effective therapy. However, when therapy is approached in a gradual, rational, and consistent fashion, there is nothing to fear. You will encounter difficult feelings to work through, but the emotional growth and freedom you will experience as a result will be well worth your hard work.

The following is a list of common fears:

1. Fear of emotional pain – This type of fear is rooted in wanting to avoid the potential negative emotional consequences of your actions.

2. Fear of failure – This type of fear has its roots in the irrational misconception that everything you do has to be 100% successful.

3. Fear of success – This type of fear is based on the idea that success is likely to mean more responsibility and attention, coupled with pressure to continue to perform and succeed at a very high level.

4. Fear of being judged – This type of fear comes from an often-exaggerated fear of criticism and the need for approval that most people develop in childhood. It is tied to one's self-esteem.

5. Fear of embarrassment – This is a fear of appearing foolish, weird, or inappropriate. This type of fear is often a result of empowering others to judge you when you demonstrate that you're only human by making mistakes and having obvious lapses of judgment.

6. Fear of being abandoned or being alone – This type of fear is related to fear of rejection and may be tied to low self-esteem.

7. Fear of rejection – This type of fear comes from personalizing what others do and say and the thinking that it will lead to your being rejected.

8. Fear of expressing your true feelings – This type of fear holds you back from engaging in open, honest dialogue with the people in your life.

9. Fear of intimacy – This type of fear manifests itself by an unwillingness to let others get too close, less they discover the 'real you.'

10. Fear of the unknown – This type of fear manifests itself as needless worry about all of the bad things that could happen if you decide to make a change in your life. This is sometimes tied to the baseless fear of 'going crazy' or finding out that you're 'crazy'.

11. Fear of loss – This type of fear is related to the potential pain associated with no longer having something or someone of emotional significance to you.

12. Fear of death – The ultimate fear of the unknown. What will happen once our spirits leave our bodies?

Do any of these fears stop you from moving forward?

What are you doing about them?

A very good book to read on the subject of fear is the book entitled "The gift of fear" written by Gavin de Becker. The following chapter provides numerous quotes regarding fear.

13

Quotes Concerning Fear

Just as courage imperils life, fear protects it.

Leonardo Da Vinci (1452-1519)

A good scare is worth more to a man than good advice.

Edgar W. Howe (1853-1937)

There is no passion so contagious, as that of fear.

Montaigne (1533-1592)

Fear is the mother of foresight.

Henry Taylor (1800-1886)

Where fear is present, wisdom cannot be.

Lactantius (260-340 A.D.)

The only thing we have to fear is fear itself.

Franklin D. Roosevelt (1882-1945)

We fear things in proportion to our ignorance of them.

Livy (B.C. 59-17 A.D.)

Just as courage imperils life, fear protects it.

Leonardo Da Vinci (1452-1519)

A good scare is worth more to a man than good advice.
Edgar W. Howe (1853-1937)

There is no passion so contagious: as that of fear.
Montaigne (1533-1592)

Fear is the mother of foresight.
Henry Taylor (1800-1886)

Where fear is present, wisdom cannot be.
Lactantius (260-340 A.D.)

The only thing we have to fear is fear itself.
Franklin D. Roosevelt (1882-1945)

We fear things in proportion to our ignorance of them.
Livy (B.C. 59-17 A.D.)

14

The Gyroscopic
Method of Therapy

THERE ARE MANY SCHOOLS OF PSYCHOTHERAPY. AND THERE ARE MANY more opinions and perspectives than schools on how psychotherapy should be done. The list includes but is not limited to: psychoanalysis, psychodynamic psychotherapy, insight-oriented psychotherapy, cognitive therapy, cognitive behavioral therapy, dialectical behavior therapy, family therapy, couples therapy, marital therapy, brief intensive psychodynamic psychotherapy, positive psychotherapy, gestalt therapy, hypnotherapy, meta-psychiatry, narrative therapy, integrative psychotherapy, role-play therapy, expressive therapy, interpersonal psychotherapy, body-centered therapy, and group psychotherapy; just to name a few.

I will now present an approach to psychotherapy based on the gyroscopic model. What I am attempting to do with the gyroscopic model is to provide a solitary unified method that transcends all methods of therapy. A unifying theory that ties all forms of therapy together through a central universal construct. It is not so much the method as the structure which is of first concern. The essential question is how can we get someone to change, to get better, and to heal?

As noted, people develop platforms (rigid perspectives) based on their own life experience. If those platforms are causing no specific problems for the individual, then they very often can be left alone while doing psychotherapy. Here one can take the highly apropos 'don't fix what's not broken' approach. Some things are better left untouched. However, if an individual's particular platform is pathological and thereby causes them problems, it can be directly confronted in therapy for the dysfunctional distortion of reality that it is.

Psychiatrist Pierre Morrell's Maxim states: "The best predictor of future behavior is past behavior". This certainly is in line with the gyroscopic forces and model previously outlined. The goal of psychotherapy is to directly challenge and defeat an individual's basic dysfunctional platform and thereby win the battle for change and personal growth! Superior healers know how to avoid the pitfalls of their own personal needs, biases, prejudices, and desire for personal gain as they decide if and when to intervene. Remember, however, that not everyone can or wants to be helped! There are times when ending therapy is the correct answer.

A direct parallel to the art of providing psychotherapy can be made with respect to the earlier analogy concerning a person walking through a darkened field at midnight during a thunderstorm. As a person begins therapy there is a generally awkward exploration of their present and past experience which can be full of apprehension. Once individuals are fully engaged in therapy and they have shared a significant amount of information about themselves, a point is usually reached where the therapist shares their own thoughts and observations with their client.

Those thoughts and observations are partly based on the client's own expressed thoughts, feelings, experiences, and/or behaviors, and partly on the therapist's own experiences. This sharing of the therapist's thoughts and observations is often done with the hope that the individual will gain greater insight into both the internal (intra-psychic) and the external (environmental) sources of their difficulties and problems. That the individual will begin to examine the choices they have made and the impact that those choices have made on their life.

The hope then becomes that with their newfound insights the person in therapy will be better equipped and able to understand and handle their problems and to make any necessary changes in their lives and/or behavior that are called for. If the client does 'get it' (i.e., the therapist's perspective or point) very often the client will report that they are surprised by and delighted with their newfound insight. However all-to-frequently in clinical practice the client's newfound insight tends to be short-lived and seems to fade from their mind as quickly as it had entered. Analogous to the situation where the afterimage created by a flash of lightning fades from our mind. As a result, no clearly apparent significant lasting change is seen in that individual's thoughts, emotional state, and/or their behavior.

As time passes, they may even adamantly deny ever having been exposed to or having gained the new insight at all! This often proves frustrating to both the individual who is then challenged to remember what they 'forgot' and to their therapist who is left to wonder what has happened. This is often covered under the topic of repression as described by Freud. I also believe that this sequence of events is an expected reflexive rejection of new information and perspectives and is directed by the gyroscopic forces of our minds. I believe that this common event in therapy can be explained by an individual's inner wheel's drive to maintain its state of stability by reflexively rejecting any new information that might possibly destabilize the self (staxis) and give rise to cognitive dissonance.

A person's rejection of new insights can occur no matter how undesirable and dysfunctional their previous state of being may have been. This is because, quite often, that previous state of being is what the individual finds to be most familiar, safe, and stable for them. Thus, they can remain 'stably unstable' as they continue in accepted blindness. There they sometimes find false stability and comfort by living in the shadows of the past in a matrix void of the need for change or truth. This choice often puzzles and frustrates their loved ones and their therapists.

The window of open communication (analogous to the flash of lightning) is a two-way street shared by the individual and the therapist. It is important to note that from the individual's perspective, the physical entrance of the therapist can be perceived as being just as provocative as an actual flash of lightning. This can provoke the individual to respond with a flight-or-fight response. Thus, the individual may retreat from engagement with the therapist (flight), or exhibit aggression directed at the therapist (fight), or just freeze (like a deer caught in headlights). This is partially due to activation of the individual's limbic system via the amygdala. This activation leads the initiation of an involuntary physiologic response.

One result of this physiologic response is that brain (cortical) function gets dampened or shut down. Thus, the individual can become quite unable to process information and even to use adequate reason. Therefore, time should be allowed to pass for this response to fully settle before effective therapy can proceed. This we often do intuitively when we allow an individual to 'get comfortable' before beginning a session or stop briefly when an individual seems to be feeling truly overwhelmed. We often enhance this by engaging in 'small talk' before the session or by showing concern or empathy during a session. We want the individual to proceed with clarity of thought and the ability to gain new emotional and behavioral insights.

Once the individual is receptive to the therapist's comments this allows for what Freud referred to as transference to occur. Transference is a phenomenon characterized by unconscious redirection of feelings from one person to another. One definition of transference is "the inappropriate repetition in the present of a relationship that was important in a person's childhood." At that point the therapist must remain flexible enough to keep the established window open to truly listen to the individual's perspective. This then allows for a personal change in the therapist which will then allow for the generation of a counter-transference reaction to occur.

During therapy, when confronting an individual about a particular problem area that they have resisted examining, you may eventually get them to "break-through" their own defenses. Thereby, allowing them to see their problem area more clearly and from a different perspective. As you help them to break-through their defenses (particularly denial) they may also begin to see their own role in their dysfunctional state. If they don't, you should gradually try to make sure that they do. They should eventually take responsibility for their own actions and/or inactions. As in my field at midnight example it takes multiple 'flashes of lightning' (multiple 'pictures' or 'insights') before the individual in therapy can form a more stable mental image of what is being presented and only then begin to incorporate those various absorbed elements to form a new corrected image or personal perspective.

Frequently, as individuals go through the psychotherapeutic process, they will go through stages like those of death and dying as described by Elisabeth Kübler-Ross. As you break through their defenses, the person may become aware of the role they have played in creating and perpetuating their own dysfunctional state. At this point, they may express great remorse over the role they have played in creating their own dysfunctional state of being. During the latter stages of therapy, they may witness the transformation or death of one of their dysfunctional staxes, and grieve the loss (i.e., the death of the 'party animal' in them, or the death of the 'alcoholic personality' in them, etc.).

The Kübler-Ross model, commonly known as The Five Stages of Grief, includes denial, anger, bargaining, depression, and acceptance. Kübler-Ross originally applied these stages to people suffering from terminal illness. She later expanded this theoretical model to apply to any form of catastrophic personal loss (job, income, freedom, etc.).

The five stages of dying:

Denial — 'No, really...I'm okay...I feel fine...' "This isn't happening...not to me." Denial is a defense mechanism, and some people can become stuck in this stage. Denial is usually only a temporary defense for the individual. This feeling is generally replaced with a heightened awareness of possessions and individuals that will be left behind after death. Denial can be a conscious or an unconscious refusal to accept facts, information, or the reality of the situation.

Anger — It's not fair!"; "How could this happen to me?"; '"Who caused this?" "Why: me? Once in the second stage, the individual recognizes that denial cannot continue. They break-through their defenses and come directly into contact with reality. Because of their anger the person can become very difficult to care for. This is often due to their misplaced feelings of envy and rage. Anger can manifest itself in different ways. People can be angry with themselves or with others; especially with those who are close to them. It is important to remain detached and non-judgmental when dealing with a person experiencing anger from grief.

Bargaining — "I'll do anything for a few more years...I will give my life savings to charity...I'll change the way I behave...I'll pray more often...anything!" The third stage involves the person's hope that they can somehow postpone or delay death. Usually, the negotiation for an extended life is made with a higher power in exchange for a reformed lifestyle. Psychologically, the individual is saying, "I understand I will die, but if I could just do something to buy more time."

Depression — "I'm so depressed...why bother with anything?"; "I'm going to die soon, so what's the point?"; "I miss my loved one, why go on?" During the fourth stage, the dying person begins to understand the certainty of death. Because of this, the individual may become silent, refuse visitors and spend much of the time crying and grieving. This process allows the dying person to disconnect from things of love and affection. It is not recommended to attempt to cheer up an individual who is in this stage.

It is an important time for grieving that must be processed. Depression has been referred to as the 'dress rehearsal for the aftermath'. It is a kind of acceptance with a strong emotional attachment. It's natural to feel sadness, regret, fear, and uncertainty when going through this stage. These emotions can reveal that the person has begun to accept their situation.

Acceptance — "I can't fight it", I may as well prepare for it." "It's going to be difficult, but I'll be okay." In this last stage, individuals begin to come to terms with their mortality, or that of a loved one, or some other tragic event. This stage varies according to the person's situation. People who are dying can enter this stage a long time before the people they leave behind do. Those people they leave behind must pass through their own individual stages of dealing with the grief.

As mentioned, these five stages can be applied to circumstances other than the dying process. The following passages are some examples of how the five stages can be applied to other life situations.

116

Grieving the end of a relationship:

Denial – The person getting 'broken-up' with is unable to admit that the relationship is over. They may try to continue to call the person when that person wants to be left alone.

Anger – When the reality sets in that the relationship is over, it is common for the person to feel anger or even rage. They may demand to know why they are being broken-up with. This phase can make them feel like they are being treated unfairly and it may cause them to become angry at people close to them who want to help aid the situation.

Bargaining – After the anger stage, one will try to plead with their former partner by promising that whatever caused the breakup will never happen again. Example: "I can change. Please give me a chance".

Depression – Next the person might feel discouraged that their bargaining plea did not convince their former partner to change their mind. This will send the person into the depression stage and can cause a lack of sleep, eating and even disrupt daily life tasks such as bowel movements.

Acceptance – Moving on from the situation and person is the last stage. The person accepts that the relationship is over and begins to move forward with their life. The person might not be completely over the situation, but they are done going back and forth to the point where they can accept the reality of the situation

Grieving in substance abuse recovery:

Denial – People feel that they do not have a problem concerning alcohol or substances. Even if they do feel as if they might have a small problem, they believe that they have complete control over the situation and can stop drinking or doing drugs whenever they want. Example: "I don't have to drink all of the time. I can stop whenever I want"

Bargaining – This is the stage that drug and alcohol abusers go through when they are trying to convince themselves or someone else that they are going to stop abusing. This is usually done to get out of trouble. Example: "God, I promise I'll never use again if you just get me out of jail." "Mom, I promise I'll stop drinking, if only you'll let me stay with you."

Anger – The anger stage of abusers relates to the anger they experience at having the disease of addiction. They may be angry that they can no longer use drugs. Some of these examples include "Why am I an addict!" "Everyone uses drugs, why is a problem when I do!" "Why can other people use, and I can't!"

Depression – Sadness and hopelessness are important parts of the depression stage when dealing with a drug abuser. Most abusers experience this when they are going through the withdrawal stage quitting their addiction. It is important to communicate these feelings as a process of the healing. Often, they can begin experiencing emotions and concerns that they have suppressed with alcohol and drugs for years.

Acceptance – With substance abusers admitting you have a problem is different than accepting you have a problem. When you admit you have a problem this is more likely to occur in the bargaining stage. Accepting that you have a problem is when you begin to own the problem and start the process of resolving the problem.

It is important to note that Kübler-Ross felt that these stages do not necessarily come in a fixed order, nor are all stages experienced by all patients. She stated however, that a person will always experience at least two of the stages. Often, people will experience several stages in a "roller coaster" effect: switching between two or more stages, returning to one or more several times before working through it.

While it is important to keep the focus of therapy on the individual, it is also important to acknowledge that an individual and their community are indelibly tied together. The members of one's community have a huge impact on an individual's course in psychotherapy. Members of the community can exert their impact by either reinforcing or by countering the elements of that individual's staxes. They may consciously or unconsciously attempt to reinforce or to completely undo what the individual has learned in therapy. They may also either directly counter or reinforce some of the behavioral changes that an individual is attempting to make as the individual attempts to grow.

The therapist has great odds to overcome here. If a therapist sees a client one hour per week for a year that is at most 52 hours out of the 8,760 hours of that client's life that year. This amounts to just 0.59% of that client's life that year. Their family friends and co-workers will see them very likely a combined 16 hours per day, or a total of 5,840 hours each year. This amounts to 66.6% of the client's life that year. The therapist can be at a distinct disadvantage when battling the forces of influence in their client's lives. So, therapy must be highly focused and pertinent to be effective. The therapeutic process can be greatly enhanced by using a highly structured approach and by properly managing the various transference and countertransference interactions that arise between the therapist and their client.

With the previous therapeutic concerns having been stated, the following is a general approach to the provision of psychotherapy using the concepts, principles, and methods contained in this book. Subsequent chapters of this book present a series of condensed case studies that are intended to reinforce those same concepts, principles, and methods. When starting therapy with a client:

First: Ask yourself the following questions:

Who is this individual?

What are they asking for?

What is my mental image of this individual?

What positive images do I hold?

What negative images do I hold?

Did they seek help on their own, or are they here to please someone else?

Are they here under the threat of negative repercussions from loved ones, their employer, or the law?

How receptive and flexible do they seem?

There are more questions you will need to ask as you go along.

Therapy must be individually tailored to each client based on their presenting problems, their needs, and their intellectual and emotional quotients (i.e., IQ and EQ). When you begin working with a person on their issues and problems it is important to honestly assess how you feel about the person before you. If you have a low regard for your client or have too high a regard you will run the risk of doing them more harm than good by harboring an unbalanced view of your client. You must work on developing a balanced perspective of your client before you can truly help them in therapy!

The belief of a potential for positive change must exist in your mind, before you begin the therapeutic process with your client. Without this belief, what would motivate you to work with your client? What would be the point of doing therapy if there is no hope? If you are doing it for other reasons (i.e., financial gain, the need to feel competent, physical attraction to the client, etc.) you are quite simply walking down the wrong path. It might pay well, but eventually that can lead to an unfulfilling career. Inherently, we tend to want the people we help to 'like' us and to live 'a better life'. But being 'liked' in this regard would be more about the therapist's needs than those of the client. Our own definition and concept of what constitutes 'a better life', however, tends to fit within our own paradigm. Quite simply, your dreams of what a perfect outcome might look like may not be congruent with those of our clients.

Given the expansive nature of our world, it is important to understand that we as individuals have a relatively narrow and relatively inflexible view of our world and its possibilities. It is important to understand that we are shaped and very often bound by who we are in terms of our age, gender, race, ethnicity, education, religious affiliation, nationality, upbringing and life experiences, etc. We are all inherently strongly biased in our views of others and of the world: which we generally can't escape. We all have strong pre-conceptions of what a person's age, gender, race, and station in life mean about a person. This: even without knowing anything else about that person.

The term implicit bias refers to the attitudes or stereotypes that affect our understandings, actions, and decisions at an unconscious level. It is a form of bias that is subtle, automatic and operates below the surface without conscious awareness. This type of bias is often difficult to detect, as it is unintentional and deeply rooted in our minds. Despite this, there are certain signs that can be used to identify implicit bias.

One sign of implicit bias is the use of language. The words we use can reveal our underlying biases, even if we are not aware of them. For example, if someone refers to a group of people as "those people" or "those minorities" instead of using more inclusive language, it could indicate an underlying bias. Similarly, using language that is derogatory or demeaning towards certain groups of people can be a sign of implicit bias.

Another sign of implicit bias is behavior. If someone reacts more harshly to a situation involving a certain group of people than they would to a similar situation involving a different group of people, this could indicate an underlying bias. Thus, implicit bias can manifest itself in a variety of ways, from our behavior and the language we use to our automatic reactions to certain situations. By being aware of these signs, we can identify and address implicit bias in our daily lives. This can help to create a more inclusive and tolerant society and reduce the effects of bias on our decisions.

What images and thoughts come to mind for you when viewing the following, albeit incomplete list of person types?

young black man	young white woman	young Latino man
old black woman	young white man	young Chinese man
old white woman	young Latina girl	old Indian woman
old Arab man	old Russian man	old white man
Catholic man	Jewish man	Muslim man
Lawyer	Doctor	Banker
Priest	Teacher	Etc...

Figure 18: List of Person types.

Questions: Do you hold positive or negative images and emotions for each person-type listed? Where do they come from? Are they strong images and emotions? Why so? What is your automatic image and conception of who they are? Are your thoughts biased or stereotypic? Do they stand in the way of you expanding your life experience and perspective of Do your views separate you from other people? the world? Are there any mental images you need to change?

Only you can answer these questions for yourself. Your answers are core to your own 'gyroscope' and are directly tied to your flexibility and effectiveness as a therapist.

The Implicit Association Test (I.A.T.) is an interesting test of biases that was developed by Anthony G. Greenwald, Mahzarin Banaji, and Brian Nosek.[6] It is a test that was designed to reveal our unconscious associations and racial biases. More than 80% of all those who have taken the Race I.A.T. Thus, far ended up having "pro-white" associations. Of 50,000 African Americans who have taken the test, 50% had "pro-white" associations. That is, they proved to unconsciously have stronger positive associations (thoughts, ideas, and perceptions) of white people than of other black people!

Do you think this might cause some problems for them? If you would like to try the race I.A.T. you can find it at https://implicit.harvard.edu/implicit/demo/.[7] You can also complete a self-test of your unconscious levels of bias about age, gender, self-esteem, and mathematics vs. art at this site. The results may reveal things about you that will surprise you. How do you think these things affect the way you interact and deal with other people and how they interact and deal with you in return? Malcolm Gladwell mentions this site in his book "Blink" which is an excellent read.

Try to keep aware of and avoid the following pitfalls that can occur during the provision of psychotherapy:

The narcissistic view that 'I can treat anyone' is just as much in error as 'anyone can be treated'. An individual therapist cannot treat all clients. It is well documented that the effectiveness of therapy is directly related to the 'fit' of the therapist with the client. No individual therapist can be an excellent 'fit' with every client that walks through their office door. Also, not every person can be treated! There are some individuals who are too rigid and too closed minded to hear any perspectives that are different from their own.

They at heart are not interested in change or further growth. Remember, the light bulb must want to change! Other potential pitfalls in therapy include but are not limited to rescue fantasies; power issues; transference and countertransference impasses; issues of narcissism; the tendency we have to want to complete a task once started; sadistic / masochistic / erotic dynamics; issues of abandonment; in the client and/or the therapist.

Again, transference in psychotherapy is the client's unconscious tendency to assign to their analyst or therapist emotions and attitudes that had significance in the client's early life. Especially the patient's transference to the analyst or therapist of their feelings and attitudes associated with a parent. The client may begin to act and react as if their analyst or therapist is their parent.

Counter-transference, on the other hand, is the transference reaction by a psychoanalyst or psychotherapist to their client. The surfacing of an analyst's or psychotherapist's own repressed feelings through identification with the emotions, experiences, or problems of a client undergoing treatment may be transferred to the client at an unconscious level by the analyst or therapist. For instance, the analyst or therapist may see their client as being like their irritating and controlling mother, or their emotionally cold unfeeling father, and treat their client accordingly.

A common precipitant to transference / counter-transference problems is a personal crisis in the life of the therapist (serious illness, financial pressures, marital problems, divorce, family problems, work-related problems, death of a loved one, miscarriage, etc.). Such stressors can easily weaken the therapist's objectivity and ability to set limits (boundaries) early in therapy. It is important for the therapist to monitor the impact of their response to their own life events on the course of therapy with their individual clients.

Next: Clearly identify what the client's presenting problem is, and why they are seeking help. Try using their words to describe the problem or issue.

Identify if they are there solely for advice, administrative assistance (i.e., to fill out disability paperwork, etc.,), emotional support, clarification (to get a better understanding of their current problems/concerns), confession (feeling intense guilt), reality contact (want to be reassured that they are not 'going crazy'), or just to ventilate ('let it all out'), etc. A great deal of time can be wasted when the client does not see a need for therapy. When they are not there to examine or change a particular perspective or aspect of their life through the process of personal growth.

Next: Determine if the client truly wants to change. If you agree on starting therapy, get from them their verbal commitment to change (in writing if you must).

Change is an internal process that requires the client's will and commitment to emerge. You cannot do it for them. That is unless you plan to run some form of boot camp with an involuntary participant. Even then, true inner change and growth will not occur under such conditions. Warning! If you do plan to run a boot camp, your methods will eventually demand strict forms of punishment for the non-adherent who would dare to resist your suggestions. You can't beat or threaten true emotional growth into your client. I'm sure you get the point. Fascism uses such techniques, and we all know how that tends to go. A fully willing and truly motivated person is always the best scenario.

Next: Identify the individual's various staxes.

But first: An important term to be aware of is the word affectation.

Af·fec·ta·tion from the Merriam-Webster Dictionary is defined as:

1 a: the act of taking on or displaying an attitude or mode of behavior not natural to oneself or not genuinely felt

b: speech or conduct not natural to oneself: artificiality

2 obsolete: a striving after

Synonyms: pretense, affectedness, grandiosity, inflation, pretension, pretentiousness, fake behavior, put on to impress others, and as younger people say; 'he's just fronting'

Many people entering therapy, especially if it's for the first time, are preoccupied with how they will appear to you. They will often present themselves in such a way that is not their true self. They will often present themselves in a way that fits what they think you want to see, to seek acceptance, to not look 'crazy', to appear better than they are truly doing, to appear worse than they are truly doing, to be a 'good patient', to challenge your authority, etc. The bottom line is that clients often don't walk into your office presenting their true selves.

Staxes share common elements and so can be difficult to decipher, but what we are looking for are the general broad characteristics that define a staxis. Often you can use general terms to help guide you to define the staxes (i.e., the parent, husband, wife, friend, brother, sister, volunteer, church member, boss, employee, etc.) The interactions of the various staxes of an individual can be quite complex. See Figure 19 (below).

Figure 19: Staxes are inter-connected
and share common elements.

1- Identify the Major and a few Minor Staxes (various 'personas' if you will). This is how the client generally presents themself, and is in line with what they see as their 'true identity'.

2- Collect and record the elements that support the client's major and minor staxes. Their specific thoughts, ides, beliefs, experiences, etc.

3- Identify problem areas that are causing the client anxiety or concern.

4- Identify what truly needs to change. Identify challenges and roadblocks that have prevented effective change.

5- To lay the foundation for change it is necessary to challenge the person's perspectives. Gently question the person's beliefs to clearly define their significance. For example: Is that what you really believe to be true? Do you think there's another explanation or way to look at it? Did you really think that what you did would you make your situation better?

The cognitive model holds that a given situation can provoke "automatic (negative) thoughts" which then leads to an emotional response, a physiologic response, and finally to a behavioral response. The process of cognitive therapy confronts the person's thoughts and beliefs which are felt to be exaggerated or unfounded and counterproductive. The following is an example of how cognitive therapy can be delivered:

A person enters therapy stating that they think they are a "bad" person. The therapist asks the following questions:

1. What makes you think you're a bad person?
2. How strongly do you believe this?
3. What type of things have you done, that make you bad?
4. On a scale from 0-100% with 100% being the worst person you could imagine, where would you fall?
5. Where would other people, put you on this scale?
6. How often would you say you act as a 100% bad person?

7. Who would you consider to be a "good" person?

8. Would you say that person has never done anything bad?

9. In terms of becoming a better person, how helpful is it for you to criticize yourself when you do something wrong?

10. If you truly don't want to do bad things in the future, what are some things you can work on in therapy?

11. What do you think would happen if you worked on ways of reducing your self-critical thoughts and feelings, and the way you behave around others?

6- Gradually introduce new information and perspectives that reinforce the more positive elements: as you attempt to negate and erase the more negative elements of the chosen staxis. Ego-syntonic material is information that is easily accepted by the individual and fits with their perspective at that moment. Ego-dystonic material is information that is poorly received by the individual and doesn't fit with their perspective at that moment. It is easier to introduce ego-syntonic material than ego-dystonic material. People tend to automatically reject negative information that is presented to them. However, it is always necessary to present both positive and negative information if change and personal growth are to occur.

7- As you help them to break-through their defenses (particularly denial) they may also begin to see their own role in their dysfunctional state. If they don't you should make sure that they do. They should eventually take responsibility for their own actions and/or inactions.

8- In some cases, you may need to identify a subordinate staxis that would do better being dominant. In that case you would search for a desirable subordinate staxis and re-enforce it with new information to make it stronger and eventually dominant. An example would be replacing a client's major staxis (core identity) that they are a lowly addict with a healthier subordinate staxis that they are a sober and responsible member of society. Such a clinical case scenario will be presented in a subsequent chapter.

9- I previously had mentioned that a theoretical construct should serve as a reference point (oft times as a beacon) to help one if they were to stray off-course while providing psychotherapy or while attempting self-therapy. Staying on course should eventually become the shared responsibility of the client and the therapist; for true insight lies at its core.

10- The client should set aside an hour each evening between therapy sessions and mentally review what was covered in their therapy session. The sooner the better because that "flash of lightning" will quickly disappear and close the window of inner vision. They should ask the following questions of themselves:

What was covered?

What did I learn?

What did I actually incorporate?

Did it change my behavior and interactions with others?

What happened as a result of those changes?

15

Relaxation and Meditation Techniques

MEDITATION IS A GOOD STARTING POINT TO GET IN TOUCH WITH ONE'S ideas, beliefs, feelings and perspectives. At the core of meditation lies the ability to create a state of inner peace and serenity that can allow for deep introspection and reflection. The actual long-term practice of meditation involves repeatedly re-achieving that peaceful state of mind. For those familiar with Taoism or Zen, it involves achieving a state fully consistent with and reflective of the Tao. With practice, one can create a subordinate staxis state consistent with deep meditation. Meditation is a tool that can be used to maintain one's sense of focus and inner balance: Thus, it can be aptly applied to serve as a foundation for the therapeutic process.

A simple method that can be used as a gateway to reach the peaceful state required for meditation involves the technique of progressive muscle relaxation. This is where one sequentially tenses and relaxes the various muscle groups of their body, while practicing proper controlled deep breathing. This method has also been applied to the practice of self-hypnosis for induction of the hypnotic state. Hypnosis is a state of heightened awareness contrary to the common belief that it is a state of mental passivity. The following passage provides the steps to follow for progressive muscle relaxation and meditation.

Step 1: Find a quiet and comfortable place to sit. A comfortable chair or couch is fine. A comfortable floor mat is fine too.

Step 2: Clear your mind. Use your imagination to visualize yourself alone on a quiet beach, an island, a meadow, a cloud, a mountain top, or any other peaceful place of your liking. You can even picture yourself leaving the earth and floating off into space if that works better. If thoughts occur, let them happen without paying much attention to them. Don't fight them. Just let them be, without attaching any emotions or significance to them. No need to focus on them. Let them leave your mind as quickly and quietly as they entered. Just let them enter and leave freely without having any significant attachment to them. They are only thoughts and have no real significance at this moment. Just let them float through. This gets easier to do with time and practice.

Step 3: Breathe very slowly and deeply: in through your nose, to a count of eight, and out through your mouth, to a count of eight. Don't overfill your lungs to the point of causing pain or discomfort. With continued practice one can feel the immediate relaxing effect afforded by the technique of controlled breathing. It can be of benefit to imagine that you are inhaling 'purity' and 'calmness' and then exhaling 'toxins' and 'stress' from your body. You are doing so from a biological perspective. (i.e., inhaling life sustaining oxygen: and exhaling toxic carbon dioxide).

To practice deep breathing you can also perform the following exercise:

a. Lie on your back with a pillow underneath your head for comfort.
b. Bend your knees to allow your stomach to relax.
c. Put one hand on your stomach, midline, just below your ribcage.
d. Slowly breathe in through your nose, as you feel your stomach rise.
e. Exhale slowly through your mouth while emptying your lungs completely, as your stomach falls.
f. Repeat this exercise several times until you feel calm and relaxed.

Step 4: Begin with your toes. Curl your toes tightly and hold that position for a few seconds, then extend them back towards your knees, then relax them. Repeat this several times until your toes feel relaxed. Wiggle your toes.

Step 5: Slowly, flex, extend, and rotate your feet and ankles and then relax them. Repeat this several times until your feet and ankles feel more relaxed.

Step 6: Tighten your calf muscles and hold the tension for several seconds, and then relax them. Repeat this several times until relaxed.

Step 7: Tighten the muscles of your thighs and hold the tension, then relax them. Repeat this several times until relaxed.

Step 8: Tighten your buttocks and hold the tension, and then relax. Repeat this a few times until relaxed.

Step 9: Next, slowly rock your pelvis a few times to loosen and relax the muscles surrounding your hips. Do this several times until relaxed.

Step 10: Next, gently tighten (arch) and relax the muscles of your lower back several times and relax.

Step 11: Focus on your breathing for a minute or so, and feel your diaphragm push against your upper abdomen as you inhale. Feel yourself relax.

Step 12: Next, tighten your shoulders and chest, and then relax them. Repeat this several times and relax.

Step 13: Next, simultaneously tighten your biceps and triceps muscles and hold the tension; then relax. Repeat this a few times. Then relax.

Step 14: Next, tighten your fists and forearms and then relax them. Repeat this several times until they feel relaxed.

Step 15: Tighten and relax your shoulders again. Repeat this several times.

Step 16: Next, move your head backward and forward with mild tension several times. Avoid moving your head from side to side, as this can injure your neck (cervical spine). Then sit still as you continue with your controlled breathing technique.

Step 17: Next, tighten your facial muscles several times and then relax them.

Step 18: Continue to feel yourself relax. With each breath you can feel yourself fall deeper into calmness. Continue to clear your mind. Let thoughts enter and leave freely. You are in complete control of whether thoughts are allowed to remain, or instead disappear into thin air. Practice this often. The greater the practice, the more effective it becomes.

Good luck with your practice of meditation. ☺

16

Self-Therapy

WORDS OF WISDOM AND ADVICE THROUGH THE AGES HAVE ECHOED THE phrases: 'Know thyself' 'Know who you are.' 'To thine own self be true.' The following quote by Lao Tzu, author of "The Art of War", affirms our innate sense of who we are.

> 'At the core of your being, you know who you are, and you know what you want'.
>
> Lao Tzu

If you have identified an area of yours that you feel you need to work on, work on it now. If it's worth doing, it's worth doing now! Procrastination, coupled with excuse making is the #1 reason why people fail to achieve their lifetime goals! Why people fail to make necessary changes! The following is a list of some of the excuses that people use to avoid acting on issues that require their attention. They all lead to inaction and ultimately to failure. They are often 'automatic thoughts' that we have. Avoid them like the plague!

Learn to Avoid the Top 60 Excuses for not getting started:

- It's too difficult to do.
- I don't feel like doing it right now.
- I have a headache.
- Delaying this won't make much of a difference in the long run.
- It may be important, but it's not really an urgent issue right now.

- It might be too painful to complete.
- It will be too painful to complete.
- I really mean to do it, but I keep forgetting; I'll make a note to myself.
- Somebody else might take care of this, if I wait.
- Maybe it will take care of itself, if I don't do anything.
- It might be really embarrassing if someone sees me trying to do this.
- I have no idea of where to begin.
- I need a good stiff drink first.
- I should have something to eat first.
- I'm too busy right now.
- I'm too tired right now.
- It will drain me.
- It's boring.
- It might not work.
- I've got to shower and get dressed first.
- I need to sleep on it.
- We can get by with things the way they are.
- I don't really know how to do it.
- I'll wait until I find someone to help me.
- There's a good program / game on TV.
- As soon as I start, somebody will probably interrupt me.
- I need to study this further.
- My horoscope indicates this is the wrong time to do this.
- Nobody is complaining about this yet.
- If I do this now, I'll just end up with something more to do.
- The weather's too bad today.
- The weather's too good to spend on doing that stuff.
- Before I start, I think I'll take a short break.
- I'll do it as soon as I finish some of my other tasks.
- My biorhythms are out of sync with this task right now.
- If I rest now, I'll have more energy to get caught up.
- I'll wait and make this a New Year's resolution.
- It's way too late to start now, anyway.
- I don't have a comfortable space to do my work.
- It's not really vital to do this.

- I work better when I'm under pressure.
- It's too early in the day to start on this.
- It's too late in the day to start on this.
- I don't have any of my notes, books, or references with me.
- I'm too young.
- I'm too old.
- I don't have the money or materials to do it right now.
- I don't have enough time.
- I'll probably fail.
- I've failed too many times before.
- There are many other things I can do with my time.
- They'll laugh at me if I fail again.
- If I don't try, no one will have to know about it.
- It won't work anyway; without all the things I'll need.
- No one will understand what I'm doing.
- There's no market for this.
- They'll think I'm crazy for proposing this.
- It's not worth the time.
- No one will ever be able to fully appreciate my hard work.

I could go on and on and on, but I think you get the point! The poem entitled "Excuses" puts the topic of excuses clearly in focus.

"Excuses are the building blocks of nothing. They serve as monuments to inadequacy, and those who excel in them, seldom do so in anything else."

- Author Unknown

The point is that many of the excuses that people may choose to use can hold them back from accomplishing their goals. Often what it takes to reach your goal is to acknowledge some of the possible reasons it might not work, but to do it anyway! Initial action must be taken! It sets the stage for further action that can lead to the eventual accomplishment of one's goals. Remember, we are just as responsible for the things that we do, as we are for the things that we don't.

But please also remember not to be too critical of yourself. You are your own best friend. True there may be hard work to be done, and some failure may be inevitable, but even superman needed to use some track to stop a speeding train! Remember that failure at some level is always a part of the equation. For those who are wise, failure is accepted and often leads to personal growth and enlightenment.

If you truly want change and personal growth: Do it now! No excuses!

The following is an outline of the Gyroscopic Method that can be used for self-guided therapy. The ultimate goal of self-therapy is personal growth and change. This method is intended for frequent and consistent practice to continuously assess and modify one's own ideas, beliefs and perspectives. It is also intended that this method be actively and frequently applied to one's daily activities to reach one's chosen daily and long-term goals.

It's a good idea to schedule specific times to practice your self-therapy. You can use your scheduler, or the pictures of clock faces to block out those times (as pictured below). It's a good idea to fill-out the clock faces for the 24 hours of all 7 weekdays to see where your time goes. Few people do this. Many people are surprised by what little time they have left for self-reflection and "me-time" at the end of their busy day/week. Few people ever take the time to really think about the structure of their life and the power they have to change it.

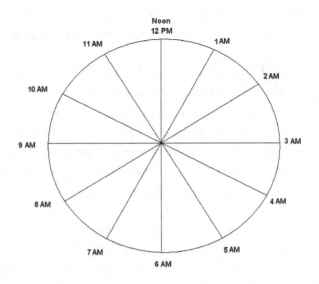

Figure 20: Clock Face: Morning Hours –
Monday through Sunday.

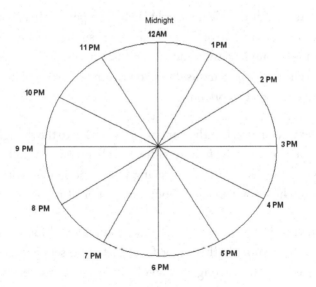

Figure 21: Clock Face: Evening Hours –
Monday through Sunday.

1- Practice in a quiet place where you can get in touch with your thoughts and feelings without being interrupted. Begin with meditation. You must establish a peaceful platform to work from.

2- You should then attempt to establish a clear picture of where you are emotionally and what areas of concern you have. Pick an idea, thought, belief, or perspective that you want to work on, challenge, or change. There are countless topics one can choose from. Write it on a piece of paper; preferably use a diary that you can refer to between sessions. The use of a diary is not an absolute requirement but can serve as a useful reference for some.

Possible areas of focus include relationship problem(s), work problems or stressors, low self-esteem, health issue(s), sexual issues/problems, religious beliefs, racism/bigotry, identity issues, issues of aging, etc. Feel free to make up some areas of focus of your own. Keep in mind the structure of the gyroscopic model and how it represents the structure of your psyche.

3- Underneath the idea, thought, belief, or perspective, write down some of your positive thoughts about the subject. Then, write down some of your negative thoughts and associations that come to mind. Then place the diary aside as you begin to contemplate what you have chosen to work on.

4- Next, get in touch with your true gut reaction to the thoughts, ideas, or perspectives. Be honest with yourself, no one is watching. It can be quite therapeutic and freeing just to be honest with yourself about how you truly feel about a subject or situation.

5- Next, explore the origin of those thoughts and ideas. Were they taught to you? Do they come from past or present experiences you have had? How strong are they? Do they dominate certain areas of your life?

6- Next, determine what fuels them and how they fit within your core axis of perspectives.

7- Next, determine how they fit with, and are reinforced by, your other related perspectives.

8- Now, determine the true validity of your perspective and how it benefits you or weakens you as a person.

9- Do you accept it because it truly benefits you, or is it easier just to accept it?

10- Does the perspective tend to blind you from differing points of view?

11- Determine if you truly wish to change the idea, thought, belief, or perspective. Examine how it fits with or counters your previous perspectives and your daily life.

12- Write down the new idea, thought, belief, or perspective for review.

13- Actively repeat the new desired idea or perspective multiple times in your mind to begin the process of making it stick. Repetition is critical. Attach your emotions, sexual energy, and aggressive energy to your idea. Review the new perspective daily and look for examples of when the new perspective is called into play or is challenged.

14- Keep a regular diary or log for later reflection.

15- Practice this method regularly and you will begin to see that you are able to change your perspectives in an organized self-guided manner. You will then begin to greatly increase your mental flexibility and self-mastery as described earlier. As a suggestion, you can program your PDA with a daily reminder to do these exercises at a convenient time.

16- It is important to set personal goals for yourself. While setting a goal, you should examine how the goal is going to affect you in the four areas of life: body, mind, heart, and spirit. You should set meaningful, realistic and professional 'development goals' to make progress towards your ideal life. Setting long-term goals is as essential as setting weekly or daily goals. From the business world approach: you need to set SMART goals, no matter where you work or what type of work you do, because SMART goals are based on the principle that goals could be easily achieved if they are Specific, Measurable, Attainable, Relevant, and Time-Bound.

Some additional thoughts and suggestions to consider:

1- Never underestimate the power of **your own** ideas or beliefs.

Beware of the images you keep (harbor) in your mind. Have you ever tried to change the way you react to a situation by rejecting your previously held ideas or beliefs? This in the hope of changing the way you would typically respond to such a situation; only to find yourself acting exactly as you have before. At that point, you are confronted by the power of your own ideas, beliefs, and habits, as well as, by your own level of conviction for change.

Therefore, to make a lasting change in your behavior you must first know yourself (i.e., your own ideas, beliefs, habits, motivations, and perspectives) before you can entertain the notion of making a change. Not knowing yourself will leave you feeling unstable at times, especially when you are bombarded with other's ideas, beliefs and perspectives that may knowingly or unknowingly reinforce or directly counter your own.

Quote: If you don't understand yourself, you don't understand anybody else.

Nikki Giovanni

2- Never underestimate the power and influence that other's ideas and beliefs have on you.

Never let anyone tell you who or what you are! This pertains to areas such as your core identity, your racial identity, your cultural identity, your professional identity, your body type, your sexual orientation, your religion, etc. Other people will always attempt to get you to see things from their perspective. Sometimes they will be right. Sometimes they will be wrong. Sometimes there will be no clear right or wrong answer.

3- Do you love yourself?

Unless you are an unrepentant axe murderer: Never let negative self-images survive. Kill them all! They are vexations to your spirit! The next time you look in a mirror, look deeply into your eyes. Then notice how your body feels and responds when you say to yourself "I love you". Does your body's reaction tell you that the statement true, or do you feel that you are lying to yourself?

Self-loving people tend to see themselves as a whole person when they look into a mirror. Other people tend to see either their positive characteristics or their negative characteristics (as if their 'ugly' nose, or their 'beautiful' hair, or that hideous pimple on their forehead somehow represents their whole person). Self-loving people like what they see, despite their flaws. They don't see themselves as parts. The next time you walk down a street and catch your reflection in a store window, notice what your gut reaction is to your own reflection. Is it positive or negative?

If these examples make you realize that you do not love yourself very much today, then use them to remind yourself of times when you actually did feel self-loving. Explore why you could feel that way then, and what you can do today, to get back to feeling that way. This serves as a major part of the foundation of one's self-esteem, which is critical to find happiness in life. If you feel you have never loved yourself, get into therapy to discover why, and then work towards loving yourself. It feels much better! Believe me.

Search for and destroy any negative self-images or ideas that have been planted in your mind either by you or by others. They are counterproductive to you as an individual. Create a mental picture of a high-speed coffee grinder sitting in the middle of your mind. As you identify negative thoughts and perceptions about yourself, your children, your culture, whatever it is: mentally drop them into that running grinder for their rapid destruction. As the grinder grinds them into sand, let the sand fall deep down into an abyss and disappear forever.

Begin replacing them with positive thoughts and perceptions and strengthen them through mental repetition until they become permanent. Thereby mentally freeing you from negativity in the process! This is an extremely important mental exercise to cleanse your mind of the damaging items that are destructive to you as an individual.

As I have stated previously, and will cover in subsequent chapters, many negative images have been placed there by others. See Appendix A: Manipulative Thought Insertion definition. More concerning this important subject will be presented in a later chapter concerning application of the gyroscopic theory and model to the community.

Self-loving people realize that they can make mistakes. Since they live their lives seeking joy and happiness, they tend to take risks by trying many new things. Since they aren't dumb or self-destructive, these experiments work out well most of the time. However, sometimes they do go wrong. When this happens, self-loving people are not devastated! Quite simply, they apologize, if necessary, fix anything that can be fixed, and then move on with their lives. The underlying message here is that self-loving people are responsible: Not guilty. Self-loving people don't make many excuses: Especially to themselves. They realize that the road of life has many bumps!

4- If you settle with your core axis, you will find your center of stability.

To find your core axis it is required that you take an open and honest view of the central ideas, beliefs, and perspectives you hold. By using the gyroscopic method, you can achieve this in an orderly and comprehensive manner. By finding the center of your axis, this allows you to get in touch with your core perspectives and to view the ideas and beliefs that support them. If you are able to feel at peace with these, then you can feel at peace with yourself.

However, this does not mean that your state of mind is ideal. Many horrible people feel at peace with themselves, it is best to make sure that you are not one of them. Ask yourself: Do I want to bring good or bad to this world and to others? The answer is your property. When there is much inner mental conflict, significant uncertainty and unrest can arise. One can find that their mind is in utter chaos, and the source of great pain and unrest. One should work towards inner change and inner peace. Free yourself!

5- Keep an open mind. Be flexible. Be adaptive.

There is a story about a very old and very wise martial arts expert. He was highly sought after by many young martial artists who wanted to learn what he knew about the arts. One day a young man entered the expert's house, seeking his teachings. But before the expert could speak, the young man went on and on about how many different styles of the martial arts he had already studied and mastered.

He told the expert several well-known names of the instructors he had already studied under. It became quite apparent that the young man was quite impressed with and full-of himself. The expert smiled at him and stated, 'You have travelled a long distance to find me. Before we begin, let us have some tea'. The young man agreed and sat at the expert's table.

The expert placed a cup in front of his young visitor. As he began pouring the hot tea into the young man's cup, the young man watched the cup intently. Suddenly, the cup began to overflow onto the table and began pouring of the tables' edge onto the young man's lap. He leapt up stating: 'Can't you see that the cup is overflowing old man!'

The expert then smiled and placed the teapot on the table. He stated 'You are like this cup. If you are so full of yourself, there is no room for anything else. If there is no room for new ideas and concepts, then there is nothing that I can teach you. First empty your cup (mind) and then you will find space for what I have to teach you.'

Quote: I'm a rootless man, but I'm neither psychologically distraught nor in any wise particularly perturbed because of it. Personally, I do not hanker after, and seem not to need, as many emotional attachments, sustaining roots, or idealistic allegiances as most people. I declare unabashedly that I like and even cherish the state of abandonment, of aloneness; it does not bother me; indeed, to me it seems the natural, inevitable condition of man, and I welcome it. I can make myself at home almost anywhere on this earth and can, if I've a mind to and when I'm attracted to a landscape or a mood of life, easily sink myself into the most alien and widely differing environments.

Richard Wright

6- Never underestimate the effect that time, fate, and luck have on you.

The passage of time can either strengthen or weaken our capacity for change. If we choose to remain mentally passive, time reinforces our old beliefs, patterns, and behaviors: simply by allowing for their constant repetition. As such, we then choose to live in a state of mental stagnation. As a result of making such a choice, we then become quite rigid in our thinking. However, by choosing to actively seek personal change, we can make time work in our favor. For the longer we can sustain our focus on new ideas, beliefs and perspectives, and actively practice them, the greater the likelihood that they will lead to greater mental flexibility and to a lasting change in us.

The following passage is taken from the novel "The Hobbit", by: J.R.R. Tolkien. In the passage Bilbo Baggins (a hobbit) is lost in a cave with Gollum (a hideous tortured creature). Gollum possesses a ring that gives its wearer endless power, but for Bilbo to gain possession of the ring he must risk his life and solve a riddle that Gollum poses. Bilbo rightfully fears that his very life is at stake.

Gollum:

This thing all things devours
Birds, beasts, trees, flowers,
Gnaws iron, bites steel
Grinds hard stones to meal,
Slays king, ruins town
And beats high mountain down!

Bilbo sat in the dark thinking of all the giants and ogres he had ever heard of, but not one of them had done all these things. He had a feeling that the answer was quite different and that he ought to know; but he could not think of it. He began to get frightened, and that is bad for thinking! Gollum began to get out of his boat. He flapped into the water and paddled to the bank. Bilbo could see the eyes coming towards him. His tongue seemed to stick in his mouth. He wanted to shout, "Give me more time! Give me time!" But all that came out was Time! Time!

Gollum: *Sssss…*Arrghh! (Gollum hissed out of anger and frustration with an agonized groan)

Bilbo was saved by pure luck, for "time" was the answer! The answer to the riddle was time. More specifically, the power that time holds. Don't underestimate the power of time is the message! It waits for no one. It allows for great things to be built, but eventually will lay ruin to all things great and small. Although time has the ultimate say, don't let it cause you to live in a state of hopelessness and despair. Make good use of time. Never waste it!

7-   Try not to overdo it.

There is another story about a martial arts student who wanted to learn karate and earn his black belt. He went to an instructor and asked how long it would take for him to earn his black belt if he worked on his techniques as directed. The instructor then answered that if he were to work on his techniques six hours a day, it would take him approximately five years. The ambitious student then stated, 'What if I worked on my techniques fourteen hours a day, how long would it take then?' The instructor smiled and stated, 'Then it would take you twelve years.' The moral of the story being that over doing it can set you back. Over-sharpening the blade can make it dull. When doing self-therapy, it should not be all absorbing of your time and attention. It is necessary to continue to live to your fullest to make the changes you are striving for. Growth requires living.

8- If you decide to enter a long-term relationship with your partner, make sure that your axes are similar and aligned with each other.

When doing couples therapy, I first bring the man into a room by himself and ask him to describe their relationship to me. Then I ask where he envisions where the relationship will be in five years, ten years, and finally thirty years. I next bring the woman into a room by herself and ask her to describe their relationship. I also ask her where she envisions it will be in five years, ten years, and finally thirty years.

What I have found over the years is that, most often, when couples are having problems with their relationship, they each have an entirely different picture of their relationship than does their partner. That when I attempt to superimpose their individual pictures of their relationship, they don't fit together. Those areas of non-fit can lead to a great deal of conflict and pain for the couple as they grapple with those differences. I attempt to ascertain if the couple truly hold positive images of each other and show signs of positive regard and support: or do they hold negative images of each other and take frequent shots at each other. This is a major determinant of whether a couple can have a healthy, loving, and fulfilling relationship.

Often when people enter a relationship, they immediately begin forming their own fantasy of what the relationship will be, and often fail to share that fantasy with their partner. The initial focus tends to be more on the lustful and romantic side, rather than on the practical side. Questions such as who is this person and what do they want from a relationship often gets no true in-depth assessment. Unfortunately, people often do more research, questioning, and analysis when buying a new car, a computer, or a washer and dryer for that matter; than they do in examining their new relationships.

Therefore, be aware of the difference between you and your partner with regard to your individual flexibility and desire for growth and change. That difference is what causes people to either grow together or to grow apart over time. If your partner has a very different staxis than your own, you may come to find yourself in constant conflict with your partner. If one partner in a relationship has a more stable axis than the other, then congratulate the less stable one and pity the one who is more stable. Actually, you may need to pity them both because both of them will suffer.

You may be familiar with the old saying: Fool me once, shame on you. Fool me twice, then shame on me. But fool me three times, shame on us! Too many relationships involve a foolish dance of continuous conflict couched in misery. When you are involved in a relationship, never turn control of your inner wheel over to your partner, even if you rightfully decide to absorb some of their more positive attributes. This can lead to a co-dependent relationship and to eventual feelings of resentment.

We are taught to judge our relationships from a legal perspective. With law we judge things with the 'scales of justice'. When this type of thinking is used to judge our relationships, we can easily get caught-up in what is termed 'relationship ambivalence'. There are these good things about my partner...but then there are these bad things...but then there are these good things...but then there are these bad things... but then there are these good things...but then there are these bad things and on and on. Snore! To prevent such a state, if there is something that is happening in your relationship that is totally unacceptable to you, and your partner is unwilling or unable to change, get out of that relationship! Life is too short!

9- Never blindly trust that another person, institution, or system will do what is in your best interest.

Take full responsibility for your thoughts and actions. You must actively control your own destiny. People who turn control of their lives over to others often end up blaming others when things don't go right. By blaming others for your condition, you throw away your innate power to make needed changes in your life. Don't blame others if you don't take charge.

10- Don't focus solely on your strengths and positive attributes, to the neglect of your areas of weakness that need improvement. For instance, if you completed the Myers-Briggs test, what are your areas of weakness, and do you plan to address them? Do you plan to actively work on your areas of weakness so you can grow?

It is easy to become self-absorbed when we acknowledge our most positive attributes. Because focusing on these makes us feel emotionally better, more secure and intact. It is extremely important that we do so, because it allows for us to bolster our self-esteem. However, being overly absorbed with our strengths can blind us to our weaknesses. Over time our weaknesses can leave us more vulnerable to life's mishaps and may cause us to fall short of our full potential. So, it is important to take stock of them, and to address them in an appropriate manner.

17

Linda's Depression

THIS CHAPTER AND THE SUBSEQUENT THREE CHAPTERS; PRESENT several clinical cases to illustrate how the gyroscopic principles and theory can be applied. Each case presented is an amalgam of several patients that I have treated over the years. Thus, each case presented is a composite of several patients rolled-into-one, this for the purpose of anonymity and clarity of illustration to highlight the key clinical concepts involved. No case presented refers to any one specific individual. The names used are fictitious. The following passages concern 'Linda' and her depression, but first a few general facts about depression.

Who suffers from Depression?

Depression affects more than 17 million Americans each year.

Less than 35% of those people will seek treatment for their symptoms.

1 of every 5 adults will experience major depression during their lifetime.

Twice as many women as men experience depression.

What causes depression?

Depression is felt to result from lowered brain levels of three major neurotransmitters: serotonin, norepinephrine, and dopamine. Genetics and the environment are felt to play a role in its development.

Depression is a biological illness and may require both medication and therapy.

Antidepressant medications are felt to work by raising either serotonin, nor-epinephrine, dopamine, or a combination of these neurotransmitter levels back to normal. There is also very strong evidence that neuronal healing in the presence of antidepressant medication occurs over the course of several months after an antidepressant is initiated.

The following is a list of the common symptoms of depression:

Sadness, the world often looks negative and gloomy

Psychomotor retardation, one's mind and body slow down

Tiredness, low energy, decreased motivation

Anhedonia (lack of interest in pleasurable activities)

Decreased desire for sex

Poor concentration and memory, indecision

Decreased or increased appetite

Poor sleep, insomnia

Diurnal (twice daily) major mood swings, restlessness

Feelings of hopelessness, helplessness, guilt

Low self-esteem

Preoccupation with death

Thoughts of suicide

Facts regarding suicide in the U.S.:

A rare but tragic event, about 30,000 Americans do so every year. This number compares with fewer than 19,000 U.S. homicides each year.

About 500,000 Americans attempt suicide each year but survive.

Suicide: Male / Female ratio 4:1

Women more likely to attempt, men more likely to succeed.

Men tend to use more violent means, firearms and car exhaust.

Women tend to use pills and drowning, but this is changing.

Now for Linda's story. Linda was a 48-year-old woman who entered my office in search of help with her increasing symptoms of severe depression. She was quite tearful and appeared to be in great distress. She spoke slowly and deliberately as she revealed that she had been suffering silently with depression for many years. She was working as a secretary for a local small business and had become overwhelmed by her many personal and job-related responsibilities.

She noted that times are changing and that the demands of life had become increasingly complex over the preceding years. That technology has been changing and has been hard to keep up with. She recalled being depressed as a child and then again as a teen. She noted that she never really felt fully happy for most of her life.

She confided that she had been having frequent feelings of sadness, hopelessness, helplessness, and low self-esteem which she kept secret from those around her. She often felt a strong sense of emptiness. She frequently had negative thoughts concerning her abilities and her accomplishments. She had been experiencing frequent hidden feelings of guilt connected to her inability to function well enough to meet the demands of her job, her husband, her children, her other family members, and her friends.

She complained of having very low energy which was accompanied by a pervasive sense of constant tiredness. She described herself as having poor motivation and poor frustration tolerance when attempting to complete her daily tasks. She had experienced frequent bouts of irritability when dealing with the people she interacted with. She reported having an erratic appetite and had often skipped eating breakfast and lunch only to substitute high calorie items for her meals.

She said that during the preceding months she had been drinking more sodas and would eat candy, cookies, cake, and ice cream instead of eating healthy balanced meals. She began drinking nightcaps to get to sleep. She had started to gain weight which greatly disturbed her. She began to feel that she was unattractive and worried about the status of her marriage. She noted that all of this was highly atypical behavior for her.

Linda had been experiencing frequent crying spells, and in fact openly wept at several points during our initial sessions. Linda confided that she often thought it would be best if she simply didn't exist. That she sometimes felt that she'd be better off dead. That she would be less of a burden to her family and friends if she were dead and gone. In fact, she had frequent thoughts of suicide over the preceding years and once took an overdose of pills for which she was hospitalized. She noted that she was so embarrassed about taking the overdose that she never followed-up with recommended outpatient mental health treatment. That she didn't want to appear 'crazy' in front of her husband and children.

She reported a disrupted sleep pattern with difficulty falling asleep and many middle-of-the-night awakenings where she would lie in bed for what seemed like hours, thinking about her problems, unable to sleep. Several times she had been awakened by intense distressing dreams where she was being chased, or where she had found herself in danger, abandoned, alone, and lost. Occasionally, she would drink wine or hard liquor in an attempt to fall sleep. She soon discovered that she would have to drink large amounts of alcohol to stay asleep through the night. She discovered that this approach didn't work for her, so she began using over-the-counter sleep medications that had variable effectiveness.

Linda noted that she had always been told that in times of adversity one just needed to 'pull themselves up by their own bootstraps'. However, thinking of that phrase only intensified Linda's feelings of failure, isolation and abandonment. She knew that her friends and family just didn't get how badly she was feeling. She simply didn't have the strength to go on! By the time she entered my office Linda only saw herself as a depressed failure of a person. This transformation had in fact occurred very slowly over many years.

She could not remember the last time she had felt happy or had experienced joy. She had long lost interest in all the hobbies and activities she once cherished. The thought of being happy had truly become an alien concept to her. To put this in the context of the gyroscopic model, Linda had suffered from depression for so long that she developed the major staxis of being a 'depressed person'. It had supplanted her previous major staxis of being a happy and productive functioning person. Reinforced by negative thinking and experiences she sunk further and further into her depression.

Linda noted that she had been treated with antidepressant medications for short periods by her primary care physician over the preceding years, with some mild-to-moderate improvement in her symptoms of depression. However, she confessed that she had taken her medications inconsistently, and sometimes not at all, and had never attended the psychotherapy sessions that had been suggested. She said that she did not want to feel dependent on medications, and didn't feel she was 'crazy' enough for therapy. She noted that with her low energy, poor motivation, and poor memory it was difficult for her to follow through with treatment. At the same time, she also acknowledged that she often really didn't give her treatments a chance to work for various unclear and seemingly poor reasons.

When discussing depression with someone for the first time I go over the typical symptoms associated with depression (as noted during the opening of this chapter). As I began educating Linda, I noted her confirmation of the presence (or absence) of the target symptoms I had presented. The reason I cover all the symptoms of depression is to establish a connection with the person. To enter their world of experience so that they know that I am aware of their experience and that I care enough to ask. This while verifying that their symptoms are consistent with the typical depressive experience and worthy of a presumptive diagnosis of major depression. If they are, I let them know that their symptoms are fully expected, are not bizarre, that they are not 'crazy', and that they should not feel fearful of their symptoms.

After confirming her diagnosis of major depression, I began the essential process of educating Linda about her depression and its treatment. I then let her know that she was not alone, that depression is very common, and that I will be by her side until she got better. We discussed the topic of the need to conquer one's own anxiety and fear (as I had discussed during an earlier chapter). That this helps to lessen one's feelings of isolation and dread. I also discuss how her various symptoms fit together, and just how they might be impacting her daily.

She was surprised by what I had to say. She stated that it's as if I had known her, her whole life. Using the gyroscopic model as a construct the objective is to provide an individual with information with which to populate their inner wheel to serve as a basis for the formation of a new perspective. This allows for the instillation of hope that things will get better. I informed Linda that many people equate the term sadness as being synonymous with the term depression. However, they are not one and the same.

That the sadness associated with depression usually lasts for only a few days or weeks and then it tends to 'fizzle-out'. What sadness then leaves in its wake is a feeling of emptiness with no feelings. The experience of emotional numbness. This inability to fully express or feel one's emotions can leave one feeling detached from others and from the world at large. The core mood of depression is not so much a feeling of deep sadness, as it is emotional detachment and apathy. The inability to truly feel anything.

I informed Linda that lack of energy is a major symptom of depression. That I believe this lack of energy causes the person's body to crave and seek high energy sugar containing foods such as cookies, candy, cake, soda, and ice cream in a futile attempt to restore its energy levels. Thus, this frequently causes a shift in one's diet away from relatively lower energy foods such as vegetables and meats to higher energy foods such as sweets.

The body's attempt is often futile because the temporary energy derived from eating high sugar content foods, is often short lived. Especially, when considering insulin's role in locking away excess sugar in response to increased blood glucose levels. Insulin 'over-shoot' (excess release of insulin in response to glucose) eventually leads to a lower blood glucose level with its associated 'slump'. This accounts for the post-prandial (post-consumption) snooze that is often seen after the consumption of large meals. Thus, a person may feel even more tired and less energy in the long run.

Thus, one can feel somewhat worse in terms of their energy level and mood after eating high sugar content foodstuffs. A depressed person may then eat sweets multiple times a day to achieve higher blood glucose levels and the temporary energy derived. But the body releases insulin that locks up the sugar and a vicious cycle is formed. The obvious undesired outcome being unwanted weight gain. This weight gain can occur gradually over periods of months and years. This unwanted weight gain can then lead to a further erosion of one's self-esteem.

Due to their low energy level, one of the last things a depressed person wants is for someone to place a steak dinner in front of them. Just the thought of having to chew a steak can be overwhelming in terms of the anticipated energy expenditure and the focus that would be required to do so. Especially if it's a tough steak. It is often perceived of as an exhausting task by a person who is depressed. Families sometimes cook full meals for a depressed person thinking that it will make them feel better. Often the depressed person will leave a partially eaten full plate at the dinner table.

A direct result of depression stealing one's energy is that it becomes increasingly hard to complete daily routine tasks. As discussed elsewhere in this book, the failure to achieve one's goals can lead to a lowering of one's self-esteem. We typically begin to criticize ourselves when we fail to complete our daily tasks. A person with depression may also experience what is termed psychomotor retardation. This is where things slow down and it becomes physically hard to move and to think quickly. One's memory can begin to fail them. They frequently may walk from one room to the next and forget why they did so. They may begin to forget people's names, scheduled appointments, and important events. Feelings of guilt may set in as they fail to complete tasks and to meet their responsibilities.

I like telling my patients stories. I use several stories when educating patients about their problems and illnesses. People tend to remember stories much better than lists and bits and pieces of information. More than lists and bits and pieces of information, stories provide a global picture which people can absorb and hang on to. For each symptom I have a story to tell. In keeping with this perspective, when I discuss the impact of depression on our energy level, I use a story format.

I asked Linda if she remembered the old science fiction television series Star Trek. She answered, yes. If you are familiar with the older television version of Star Trek, or even if not, this story may help to clarify the point I wish to make. In the Star Trek television series, very often we would find the Star Ship Enterprise traveling through space on an audacious mission. Occasionally, they would run into aliens such as the 'Klingons' or the 'Romulans' who would fire 'torpedoes' at their ship. A scene of the ship's bridge would then be shown with Captain James T. Kirk, Mr. Spock, and others standing there watching a screen as missiles brazenly struck their ship's defense shields. The bridge would shake violently with each explosive impact. In retaliation, the Enterprise would prepare to fire back at the enemy ship.

Purposely, written into most of the series' scripts, the Enterprise would somehow lose its power, and its protective shields would then fail and disappear. The ship would then become a helpless and defenseless 'sitting duck' during the assault. This would dramatically increase the sense of drama and suspense. The first thing Captain Kirk would say is 'call down to engineering and get Scotty...we need the power back for our shields'. When they finally reached Scotty, he would say something to the effect 'We're operating on half power, we have a power inversion problem, we have no energy to power the shields...and we've got to reverse the flux of the di- lithium crystals before we can fix it'. Or something like that. Whatever!

The point being that as Scotty worked on the power problem the ship would remain highly vulnerable and continue to sustain more direct damaging hits. The ship would continue to shake helplessly as it suffered further insults to its integrity. Eventually, after great heroic efforts the power would be restored, and they would put up their shields to protect the ship. At that point, they would either fight-off the aggressors or they would simply go to 'warp speed' and evade their enemies by disappearing into deep space.

I highlighted the point that the force field in the story is powered by a central power (energy) supply. I had visualized for Linda what would happen if the spaceship's power supply were to be drastically reduced or lost. The force field would weaken and fail, and the spaceship would be left highly vulnerable. I noted that the same thing happens to people when they are depressed. Normally, we each have a 'force field' (or boundary) around us. It protects us from the potentially damaging things in our immediate environment. It keeps out environmental noises, negative comments made by others, etc. It blocks them from 'getting to' us. But when depression steals our energy, that 'force field' drops and those things can get right through.

It then becomes very hard to filter things out. Things that would normally 'bounce-off' of our 'shields' go right through us. Negative comments and insults can painfully shoot through the core of us. Sometimes one can feel as if they've literally 'been shot' or like something went through them like 'a hot knife through butter'. Traffic, phones ringing, people making demands, long meetings, noise and activities at malls and the grocery store, crying children, dogs barking, and so on, flood the person who is depressed. These things drain a person's energy as they attempt to filter them out. This often leaves the depressed person feeling totally exhausted at the end of each day.

If you have no energy left to put up your shields, all you can do is remain a motionless 'sitting duck' as with the Star Ship Enterprise example. Eventually, all you may be able to do is to fire back in self-defense or make seemingly futile attempts to run for your life. If you decide to use what little energy you have left to fire back at the direct hits coming in you are likely to be seen as being irritable. If you choose to run you risk being seen as weak, cowardly, or avoidant. If you can run, it's usually to an office, your home, or to a restroom where you can escape to cry. A depressed person's home bedroom or isolated office can often become a place of refuge.

Depressed people often go straight home to get away from the stressors of the day. Upon reaching home they may even hop into their bed and pull the covers over their head to shut out the stresses of the world around them. They may close their blinds, unplug or turn-off their phones, and not answer their doorbell; all to get away from stress. This often compounds their feelings of loneliness and isolation.

Thus, they become trapped in a recurring dilemma. To either go out into the world and risk feeling stressed out and emotionally drained to the point of exhaustion, to be with other people (and thereby avoid loneliness and isolation) versus having to sit at home in loneliness and isolation to avoid overwhelming stress. The realization that they have no more energy often leads the depressed person to choose loneliness and isolation. The depressed person concludes that to avoid 'stress' and at least partially 'recharge my batteries' I have to accept being alone.

Without defenses in place this state of being can be quite a traumatic experience which serves only to worsen one's depression. In response, as the depression worsens the depressed person begins to avoid situations that involve a lot of people or a lot of activity. If they were to attempt to go to a mall for instance, they would quickly become overwhelmed and feel drained by the noise and the masses of people moving about in a seemingly aimless fashion. That drained feeling they develop comes from using the little energy they have to track the activity of the mall and to power their 'force field' to filter out unwanted intrusions on their inner world. Depressed people Thus, often learn quickly to stay away from malls and large events. Even small family centered events can be severely draining to a person who is depressed.

As noted earlier the depressed person's mood can severely distort their view of the world. I previously discussed this with my story about an old man sitting on a park bench which I presented in my earlier chapter on mood. I explained how that with a shift of his mood the old man's view of the world became radically distorted, changing all things for the worse. That his anger and pain had not only strongly affected his perception of the world but had changed his behavior as well. That a significant change in his mood had caused him to behave in a highly uncharacteristic fashion.

I reminded Linda that her depression had grown over many years. I asked Linda if she was familiar with the story "A Christmas Carol". In that story the ghost of Jacob Marley comes back to visit his old business partner Ebenezer Scrooge. As he arrives, Jacob is carrying many heavy loudly rattling chains that are attached to him. The rattling clanging noise of the chains both startled and greatly upset Ebenezer. Jacob noted that the chains he wore were made of all the bad things he had done in life and that Ebenezer too had forged similar chains in his own life. He came with the warning that

Ebenezer, since he was still alive and had time, should change the errors of his ways and rid himself of his chains and thereby save himself from eternal suffering and damnation.

I shared with Linda my belief that the symbolism of the chains in the story holds true in depression as well. Not that we have done anything bad, but that we carry our past life events with us. In that as we go through life from early childhood on, we experience multiple life stressors and traumas each of which serves as links on our own personal set of chains we must bear. When we are younger the chains are short, so they are light in weight and we are thus able to bounce back from stressors and traumatic situations with relative ease. However, as we age the chains get longer and heavier. Eventually they become so heavy a burden that it becomes more difficult for us to bounce back from stressors and traumatic events. At some point the chains can become so heavy that they just stop us dead in our tracks. Unable to move, we just stand there frozen. It is at that moment when the full weight of our depression hits us.

While attempting to complete tasks depressed people will often stop and question themselves. What's wrong with me? I feel exhausted…so tired! So, they stop to rest and eventually regain some energy. Then they move on to complete a task. But once again, they become exhausted and tired and stop to rest. This is the life of a depressed person. It is a continuous series of forcefully pushing themself to move forward alternating with periods of stops to rest. The goal for the treatment of depression is the total removal of all its debilitating symptoms. Complete long-term resolution of depression is now considered to be the expected optimal clinical target of treatment.

In parallel to the Christmas Carol story, I believe that the goal of treatment is to somehow erase some of the links on the chain to allow for complete freedom from depression. I believe that the process of erasing those links has biological underpinnings in that stress and trauma over time directly impact the neurotransmitter levels and neuronal networking in one's brain which then produces the foundation for depression. The promising work of psychiatrist Charles Nemeroff, MD has shown that the physical damage done to nerve cells evident in affective disorders heals in the presence of antidepressant and mood stabilizing medications.

I shared with Linda that it is important to understand the biology behind depression. That our brains are made up of billions of nerve cells that are connected by trillions of synaptic connections. The nerve cells of our brains are in constant communication with each other via trillions of nerve cell 'firings' that occur at our synapses each second. Those 'firings' are mediated through chemical neurotransmitters that travel from one nerve cell to the next. The major neurotransmitters that we currently focus on are serotonin, norepinephrine, and dopamine. All antidepressants raise either serotonin, norepinephrine, or dopamine, or a combination of these, back to normal levels.

The brain has many centers that regulate various functions such as our sleep cycle, appetite, memory, mood, energy level, libido, and pain threshold. When the levels of neurotransmitters fall below a given level those centers malfunction. People may then develop some or all the symptoms associated with depression. They may experience sadness, low energy, an increased or decreased appetite (with an associated weight gain or loss), decreased sex drive (with loss of interest in intimacy and sex), sleep disturbances (sometimes with intense dreams or nightmares), psychomotor retardation (mental and physical slowing), problems with memory, loss of caring about one's appearance and dress, and feelings of hopelessness, helplessness, and guilt.

They can experience a lowered pain threshold, and begin to have joint pain, back pain, frequent headaches, and frequent diffuse non-specific aches and pains. Pain associated with old injuries can arise. There is a television commercial which asks Where does depression hurt? And the answer is Everywhere! Truly, depression can present itself as being more involved with physical pain than with emotional pain. The person can become swallowed in a cloud of negativity. Due to the negative shift in their perspective of life the depressed person can become preoccupied with thoughts of death and sometimes will contemplate committing suicide.

In my role as the medical director of an acute care inpatient psychiatric unit, I have treated many people who were either experiencing suicidal thoughts or had made a suicide attempt. Sometimes the attempts were quite severe. After hearing their presenting stories, I often asked them a question. If I had a magic wand and I could tap your shoulder and all of your problems would disappear...if you had everything you wanted, your relationships with your significant other and family members were great, you loved your job, you were able to get great pleasure from your hobbies and interests, you felt fully satisfied with where you live, would you want to commit suicide then?

They most often answered "Of course not...why would I want to kill myself then?" I then noted that the point I was attempting to make is that when people feel suicidal or attempt suicide it is rarely simply a matter of whether they want to exist or not. It is usually a matter of whether they want to exist under their current circumstances feeling the way they do. However, I pointed out that a person's mood and circumstances can be changed. They can be changed for the better to the point where the person would rather live.

I started Linda on an antidepressant medication for her severe depression. Again, the target of antidepressant medication for depression is to raise the neurotransmitter levels back to their normal levels. Due to the deficit of the targeted neurotransmitters the brain centers malfunction and directly cause the physical symptoms of depression. I then likened this process as being roughly analogous to what would happen if one were to reduce or cut the power supply of a computer.

As the power level drops the computer screen begins to flicker erratically as the computer programs began to fail. When the power is restored the computer then reboots itself. The functions are restored, and the computer programs and screen remain stable and clear. Once 'rebooted', the brain centers begin to function again. This is of course a gross over-simplification of what transpires but the end result is that bodily functions and abilities return to normal.

I then provided Linda with an education concerning the gyroscopic model and how we would apply it to the structure our therapy sessions. We discussed the many events that had resulted in the shift of her previously, mostly healthy major staxis, to her then current staxis of being a totally 'depressed person'. She had fully developed the identity of being a depressed person and couldn't see much beyond that. The goal of therapy was to return her as much as possible to her former self. To a time, years before she had become depressed.

In order to help her, I first had to take a stroll down memory lane with Linda to get an idea of just who she was prior to becoming severely depressed. This to establish a relatively targeted endpoint for her therapy. She proceeded to tell me her life story. We then discussed how her depression had affected her life and had stood in the way of her life goals. How it had affected her marriage, her family life, her friendships, and her work life. As we proceeded, Linda was able to grasp what I was attempting to do in her therapy. I was attempting to weaken her 'depressed person' staxis (identity) and to re-strengthen her previously dominant healthy major staxis. The technique of cognitive therapy can be superimposed here.

I pointed out many of the strengths and positive attributes of her previously dominant staxis. I paid particular attention to reinforcing the fact that depression has nothing to do with a person's character or personality. I reminded her of the story I told her about the old man sitting on the park bench to address her feelings of guilt. The old man when he felt better noted that his was acting out of character due to the pain in his foot. That he was prevented from being his true self due to the pain. That no one would hold him accountable for acting badly while he was in extreme pain. That the pain and anguish of depression is no different.

Depression is a biochemical illness that affects all the centers of our brain that regulate our emotions and our thinking. The symptoms of our depressed state are forced upon us by our brain chemistry which is heavily impacted by environmental stressors. Thoughts can induce a negative mood that persists in the absence of the thoughts that generated it. Our thoughts can then shape our enduring mood. Cognitive therapy gets at the way we think to undo negative thinking and put us in a more positive frame of thought. As a result, our mood tends to be good.

I am now going to repeat a saying from Buddhism that I had presented earlier. Consider the following quote from Buddhism which was cited by Mahatma Gandhi:

> "Keep your thoughts positive, because your thoughts become your words.
>
> Keep your words positive, because your words become your behaviors.
>
> Keep your behaviors positive, because your behaviors become your habits.

Keep your habits positive, because your habits become your values.

Keep your values positive, because your values become your destiny."

- Buddha

Your values also become your character. With medication and the work of therapy Linda fully recovered from her depression. At first, it felt strange to her as she experienced having feelings again, but she quickly got used to the idea. Linda entered my office one day with a wide grin and then began tearfully thanking me for helping her with her depression. She was shocked that she was able to feel happy again. Her tears were tears of joy. She had previously lost all hope that she would ever be able to feel as good as she did. It has been and always will be for me a spectacular and wonderful thing to witness the emotional and mental rebirth of a person saved from the heartless grip of depression.

I couldn't get her to stop smiling and shedding tears of joy as she realized that she was fully out of her depression. I reminded her that she would need to continue her antidepressant for at least one year as her brain was continuing to heal from her depression. Research has shown that the nerve cells physically reconnect (heal) in the presence of antidepressants. Linda had reclaimed her life, much to her surprise and to the surprise and happiness of all of those who loved and cared about her. I reminded her that personal growth and change is best viewed as a lifelong task.

18

Mark's Battle with P.T.S.D.

IT IS THE HOPE OF MILITARY TRAINERS THAT AS THEIR RECRUITS PROCEED with their training, that they will develop both an individual and group based military identity. It is also the hope of trainers that recruits will share a common purpose, direction, and ethic. Thus, during boot camp recruit's staxes are intentionally shifted and transformed to prepare them to do multiple jobs as soldiers and to remain as safe as possible while doing their various jobs. Their lives are literally on-the-line and emotions run high. Their ideas, priorities, beliefs, feelings, emotions, and perspectives are intentionally shaped, re-shaped, and focused on keeping them alive and productive.

This very same military approach to the training process also applies to the "indoctrination" or "shaping-up" of police officers, prison guards, athletes, martial artists, pilots, doctors, nurses, lawyers, accountants, boxers, and essentially any discipline that requires cohesive action and a common purpose. In fact, it is easy to find everyday examples of the widespread application of military-type thinking used to train employees. For example, it is not uncommon to hear the phrase 'training the troops' used by commercial job sites during their employee orientation programs.

Some basic information about Post-Traumatic Stress Disorder (PTSD):

Post-Traumatic Stress Disorder (PTSD) is a disorder that can develop following a traumatic event that threatens one's sense of safety or makes one feel helpless and vulnerable. Many people associate PTSD only with the battle-scarred soldier. In fact, military combat is the most common cause of PTSD in men. However, any overwhelming traumatic life experience can trigger PTSD, especially if that event is perceived as unpredictable and uncontrollable. PTSD can affect not only those who personally directly experience a catastrophe, but also those who witness it, and those who pick up the pieces during the aftermath. This includes emergency medical workers, support crews, reconnaissance crews, and law enforcement officials.

It can even occur in the friends or family members of those who went through the actual trauma. Traumatic events that can lead to post-traumatic stress disorder (PTSD) include war, natural disasters, rape, robbery, violent assault, intimate partner aggression/violence, kidnapping, child abuse (physical and mental), motor vehicle accidents, plane crashes, gang violence, drive-by shootings, bombings, riots, political coups, mass murders, medical procedures (especially with children), etc... Please refer to a copy of the DSM V (Diagnostic and Statistical Manual of Mental Disorders, V) for the set of specific diagnostic criteria for PTSD.

However, PTSD can present with some or all the following symptoms:

- Intrusive, often upsetting memories of the traumatic event
- Flashbacks (acting or feeling like the event is happening again)
- Nightmares (either of the event or of other frightening things)
- Feelings of intense distress when reminded of the trauma
- Intense physical reactions to reminders of the event (e.g. pounding heart, rapid breathing, nausea, muscle tension, sweating)
- Avoiding activities, places, thoughts, or feelings that remind you of the traumatic event
- Inability to remember important aspects of the trauma
- Loss of interest in activities and life in general
- Feeling detached from others and emotionally numb
- Sense of a limited future (you don't expect to live a normal life span, to get married, have children, or have a career)
- Difficulty falling or staying asleep

- Irritability or outbursts of anger
- Difficulty concentrating
- Hyper-vigilance (on constant "high alert")
- Feeling jumpy and easily startled
- Anger and irritability
- Guilt, shame, or self-blame
- Substance abuse
- Depression and hopelessness
- Suicidal thoughts and feelings
- Feeling alienated and alone
- Feelings of mistrust and betrayal
- Headaches, stomach problems, chest pain

Our brains are composed of two hemispheres (halves). The left-side of our brain deals with logical functions such as the "Three R's" we are taught in school (i.e., reading, writing, and arithmetic), problem solving and logic, memory, interpretation, speech, syntax, to name a few. The right-side of our brains deal with our spatial sense, artistic ability, timing and rhythm, and with our emotions, to name a few. When we are faced with a traumatic event, the event provokes a physiologic response. Our adrenal glands release adrenaline (epinephrine) in response to a perceived provocative threat and we experience that "flight-or-fight response" we all learned about in high school.

The emotional right-side of our brain then gets activated and in response we fight-off the attack, we run for safety, and/or less adaptively we freeze (much like a deer caught in the headlights of a car). However, this "freezing" may adaptively allow us as animals to 'fall-off the radar' of the active movement-tracking senses of predators. It is important to keep in mind that these responses are all natural biologically driven-and-directed adaptive physiologic responses to stressful or threatening situations. It is felt by many scientists and clinicians however, that this basic physiologic response we have to stress (which is based in our early evolution to deal with risks to our lives from predators) is somehow maladaptive in every day modern society.

As a traumatic event continues to unfold and the right side of our brain gets activated, our bodies also respond by shutting down of the left-side of our brain. The left-side of our brain normally tracks and records the events of our immediate environment as they occur around us. It is as if it has a constantly running video camera that records the events of our environment. Forced to shut down during traumatic events it doesn't record the events well. The "camera" slows down and becomes faulty.

This is why victims of trauma will often report that during the traumatic event they felt as though things were happening in 'slow motion' and as if they were in 'a dream'. The "video" camera becomes a single shot camera. The faulty recordings of events made by the left side of the brain are riddled with 'holes' (i.e., memory deficits with missing frames). This is why victims often find it difficult to recount all of the events and details of their particular traumatic event.

As the traumatic event ends, and as time passes, the left-side of the person's brain begins to re-awaken (turn back on) and resumes recording events. The person's mind then attempts to piece-together what had just transpired to 'make sense' of things. This is often a difficult task, as the person's memory of the event is often spotty. They must piece together single photos in an attempt to recreate the video. Treatment for post-traumatic stress disorder focuses on relieving PTSD symptoms by helping the victim to deal with the memories and emotional responses they have had in response to their traumatic event.

Rather than avoid memories of the trauma or any reminder of it, the victim is encouraged during treatment to recall and process the emotions and sensations they felt during the original event. Besides offering them an avenue to express deeply felt emotions that they likely have been 'bottling-up' ever since the traumatic event, treatment for PTSD can help to restore their sense of balance and control. It helps to reduce the powerful feelings and emotions that memories of the traumatic event may trigger.

However, the hardwired neurophysiologic response (i.e., fight-or-flight response) can continue to give the person physiologic symptoms in the presence of provoking thoughts. The hope is that by doing so the power that PTSD symptoms have over the person's life is greatly reduced. This too must be dealt with in psychotherapy and very often in combination with medication.

Now for Mark's story. At the age of twenty-nine Mark had seen more horrific events than any person was meant to see in a lifetime. There he sat with an exhausted and bewildered facial expression after having been admitted to our acute care psychiatric unit. He sat with clenched teeth while holding his head tightly in his tensed hands. His cold fixed stare and unmistakable look of anger betrayed the inner emotional turmoil that had gripped his very being. I had seen that stare before in the eyes of other returning war veterans.

Mark had been arrested during a wild bar room brawl while he was intoxicated. Instead of bringing him to a detention center the officer who arrested him brought him to an emergency room for help. Mark stated that another patron at the bar had directed negative comments towards a friend of his. This made Mark very angry. In fact, it had totally enraged him. Mark had been drinking most of the day which helped to lower his inhibitions. His anger then caused him to confront and to strike the obnoxious patron. Mark had thrown the first punch and therefore he was arrested. As Mark saw it, he was defending his friend.

A year earlier Mark had spent two years serving as a combat soldier in Fallujah, Iraq. Fallujah is a city in the Iraqi province of Al-Anbar, located roughly 69 kilometers (43 miles) west of Baghdad. It was one of the hottest battle zones during the Iraq war. He had witnessed several of his fellow soldiers and many Iraqi civilians die in horrific ways. He had seen many people with gaping wounds, drenched not only in their own blood but in the blood of others as well. He had heard their screams of agony as their lives slipped away. He saw many children and fellow soldiers with missing limbs and other truly devastating often lethal injuries. He saw many traumatized families mourning the loss of their loved ones.

He openly admitted that after finishing his third tour he saw the world in an entirely different way than he did before he had left home. When his final tour was done, he felt deep down that he was not fully prepared to face the challenges of returning home. Prior to leaving for war, he had been trained as a combat soldier to "control, attack, and defend". He held the belief that being back in combat in Iraq was probably the best and only place for him to be.

He confided that he felt as if he had deserted his fellow soldiers by returning home to the U.S. after his most recent tour of duty. He stated, "I feel safer with a rifle in my hands and people backing me up than I do weaponless on the city streets". Following his return to the U.S. Mark had been diagnosed with Post Traumatic Stress Disorder (PTSD).

As a child, Mark loved celebrating the Christmas holidays. He would always get excited about buying presents for all his family members. Then he would watch with great anticipation for their facial expressions of surprise and appreciation as they opened their gifts. He was a typical American kid from a typical American town. He wasn't a straight-A student but was able to get fairly decent grades. He did well enough to make his parents feel proud of their son's accomplishments. He would glow with pride and delight at their praises for his academic successes.

He grew up in a loving family with two siblings: a brother and a sister. Mark was the oldest of the children by five years. He was taught to say his prayers each night and to acknowledge and respect the burdens of others. He was taught to care about those less fortunate and to be fully courteous with those whom he met. He taught by his family to live and let live. His father was also an avid outdoorsman and taught his children to respect nature.

Mark always greeted his siblings with huge hugs as he loved them dearly. He had been taught never to take a day of life for granted. He especially loved his younger sister who was often shy and timid around strangers. She would always run to her big brother Mark for comfort when she was upset; especially when their mom or dad weren't available. Mark loved his hometown. He was well liked by the shop owners of his town and had worked for a few of them over the years.

During the summer months he would clean their storeroom floors and bag purchased goods for their customers. Sometimes he would work on Saturdays during the school year to earn extra money. He used that money to take his brother and sister to the movies and to buy extra toys and candy for them. He would save a little money for the few things he wanted as well. He also made sure that he put some of his money in the collection plate at their church on Sundays.

As he grew, he developed a strong sense of patriotism for our country. He would proudly place his hand over his heart and say the pledge of allegiance at the baseball games he attended, side-by-side with his father and his siblings. He was a proud American boy. When he graduated from high school Mark joined the National Guard with the hope of serving his country and helping to pay for the cost of his college education.

Following his second year of college he decided to take a break from school and volunteered for deployment to Iraq. Part of his motivation was to fight alongside several of his friends who had already entered the military to serve. Mark left the U.S. feeling 'gung-ho' about serving as a combat soldier for our country. Upon his arrival in Iraq Mark was struck by the vast size of the desert before him. He had never experienced anything like it before. The desert seemed to swallow him, his platoon and all their equipment whole.

The year was 2005, and the war had just picked up in its intensity. There was a daily sobering number of casualties being reported by the news media back home. This made many Americans question why we were there in Iraq. Concerns arose both in the media and in daily public dialogue as to whether the American people had been lied to about the reason for our involvement in Iraq. This public reaction and level of suspicion proved to be like what had happened during the Viet Nam War. It caused many citizens and people serving their country to privately and publicly debate their various concerns, impressions, and negative perspectives of the war.

While serving in Fallujah, Mark had learned of the deaths of two of his close friends who had been killed in combat in nearby Baghdad. Learning of their deaths tore deeply at his heart and soul. He had always believed that they all would make it back home alive. That one day they would discuss their wartime experiences over a glass of beer or a cup of coffee. However, this was not to be. His friends were gone forever. His many gut-wrenching experiences in Iraq made him question the very existence of the God he once loved and worshiped. He privately wondered how there could actually be a God that would allow for such horrific things to happen and not intervene. This was a huge blow to his spiritual self.

Mark fit the criteria for a diagnosis of PTSD. In support of that diagnosis, he had been having frequent intrusive highly distressing recollections of the many traumatic events he had experienced while serving in Iraq. During his therapy, he revealed the intense fear, horror, and sense of helplessness he felt while experiencing many of the dreadful events he had witnessed. Where is God? He asked himself multiple times. How can people let this happen? He described many of the events as having a surreal quality at the time they occurred.

He felt as though he was in a dream at times as he watched things move about him seemingly in slow-motion. His memory was somewhat spotty for events. So, at times he had difficulty recalling the actual specifics of each event. I explained to him that our brains act differently during traumatic events. I shared the information I had covered earlier in this chapter. That this change in our brain often makes having a clear recollection of traumatic events quite difficult.

Mark recalled an extremely traumatic event where his lieutenant was killed by a roadside bomb. This event occurred as his lieutenant sat next to Mark in a jeep. As the shrapnel struck his body the lieutenant's blood and brain matter had splattered across Mark's face and hands. Mark sat there stunned in deep shock and horror as he attempted to process what had just happened. While looking at his bloodied hands and uniform and having come to fully realize what had just happened, Mark began to scream in dread. Nothing had prepared him for that moment and that moment changed his life forever.

Mark discussed his highest regard for his lieutenant who had left behind a wife and two young children. He noted that his lieutenant was "like a big brother" to him. He further revealed that not only was his lieutenant killed, but so were the driver and the soldier sitting next to the driver. Mark explained that he was sitting in the rear of the jeep on the right passenger-side while his lieutenant sat to his left on the driver's side. The roadside bomb exploded from the left side of the road so that Mark was shielded from the blast by his comrades.

He had been struggling with the painful memory that they all had exchanged seats with each other several times that day and that only by fate was he not sitting in one of the other seats when the bomb exploded. Mark wondered why he wasn't one of those killed instead of his lieutenant. In fact, he often felt and wised that he too would have died that day so that he could avoid his painful memories.

He then revealed an incident where he shot a teenage Iraqi boy. He stated that he has felt extremely guilty ever since that day. He noted that he thinks about that event whenever he sees teenagers. He stated that he used alcohol and drugs to drown out his guilt and shame. He asked if he would ever forget the events that now plagued him. He asked, "Is there is any drug that can erase the bad memories". I noted that he had horrific experiences and that there are no drugs available at this time that can selectively erase our bad memories.

Shortly after returning from Iraq, he began to feel detached from his friends and family members. He quickly lost interest in participating in family events. Soon he began to realize that he was unable to feel the love he once did for his friends and family members. He had a young son by his former girlfriend whom he visited out of a sense of duty rather than out of any overt sense of love for or bonding to his child. He began to drink alcohol heavily and started experimenting with marijuana, cocaine, and other street drugs. He felt that he would not live long and that he had no real future anyway.

He had forgotten about college and his friends and family members were at a complete loss as for a way to help him. Mark was having frequent nightmares. He had been experiencing mental 'flashbacks' to Iraq which involved intense feelings of anxiety. He frequently relived the traumatic events of Iraq in his mind until he would agonizingly force them from his consciousness. At times he felt he was back serving in Iraq. He was easily startled by unexpected sounds. Loud noises and driving down certain roads of his hometown would trigger memories of combat situations in Iraq. At times he would become hyper-aroused and hyper-vigilant.

He kept a loaded gun in his apartment for "protection". He had experienced several episodes where he had become highly irritable and combative with others as exemplified by his previously mentioned bar room brawl. In fact, he had gotten into several bar room fights and had been arrested several times. There was great concern for his safety. His family members and friends worried about the risk of his being shot by the police or by others during his episodes of anger and rage. He began avoiding people and the places that would trigger his flashbacks. As he walked the streets, he would avert his gaze when approaching crowds of people and would sometimes change his path in response to individuals.

He resented the many times that 'well meaning' people wanted him to recall the events of his tours in Iraq. They would slap him on his back and say 'great job...you're a hero'. They failed to understand the degree of distress and inner turmoil that such questions and comments had caused for Mark. Mark was a completely different person than he had been in the past. As such, he now saw people and their comments differently and from a negative perspective.

Mark had undergone the process of military training with the creation of a new military subordinate staxis as I have described earlier. This was my starting point for Mark. How could I undo the intentional shifting of his previous major staxis to a military-based subordinate staxis? And thereby return him to his true dominant staxis; back to his 'true' former 'self'. His new military subordinate staxis, given its underlying nature and intent, simply did not fit into everyday society. It is what causes many veterans to avoid society and, in some cases, to live in isolation.

Mark once made a statement that I have heard from many other veterans returning from Iraq. "I'm not the same person I was before I went to Iraq". As returning soldiers attempt to readjust to civilian life, they are met with the challenge of shifting back to their former dominant staxis. When veterans return home, they are not fully informed of the need to re-adapt to society. They are often left to do so on their own. No one ever openly and fully discusses with recruits the changes that they are about to undergo during their basic training or when they return home. It is expected that they just adapt.

When the elements of their military subordinate staxis collides with their former dominant staxis (true self) it causes a state of cognitive dissonance which is accompanied by great confusion, anxiety, and mental pain. This often leads to feelings of alienation, isolation, anger and distrust. Those dysphoric feelings very often can lead to substance abuse, with a general emotional and physical retreat from life. Indeed, it has pushed some to commit suicide. Mark had once cut his wrists in a suicide attempt, but after a few minutes of soul searching he decided to seek help through a local emergency room. However, once released from a community emergency room he failed to follow-up for further treatment.

I believe the gyroscopic model both predicts and explains why there is a higher suicide rate observed among younger Iraq veterans as compared with older Iraq veterans. I believe that the older veterans have had the benefit of a greater number of years to develop and solidify their non-military major staxes. The transition back to their "old selves" Thus, at least theoretically can be easier; with them having more to 'grasp' onto as they transition back. Younger veterans are often just several years post-adolescence and Thus, have less life experience to 'grab onto'.

I provided Mark with a full education concerning my gyroscopic model. I also discussed the process of military training that had resulted in a shift of his major staxis to a subordinate military staxis. Thus, as we proceeded, Mark was able to use the model to grasp what I was attempting to do in his therapy. The goal of therapy was to return him as much as possible to his former self. This, by weakening the strength of his military subordinate staxis, thereby allowing for his former major staxis to again take center stage.

In order to help him, I first had to take a stroll down memory lane with Mark to get an idea of just who he was prior to his military service. This involved exploring the events of his childhood and his adolescent years as noted above in the opening paragraphs of this chapter. I explored his relationship with his family members and friends. We discussed what his hopes and dreams had been prior to his military training. What his usual activities had consisted of, to get a general sense of his daily life, goals and aspirations.

This process had the added benefit of awakening his displaced major staxis which had purposely been suppressed and supplanted by his military subordinate staxis. By directly confronting each major area of conflict with him, I laid the groundwork for the challenging process of returning Mark back to his former self. As we proceeded to explore his past beliefs, ideas, memories, and perspectives, it would sometimes lead him to experience some anxiety and distress. Sometimes this was due to the uncovering of repressed memories that ran counter to his still mostly dominant military subordinate staxis. He still for the most part identified himself as being a soldier, who was out-of-place, like a fish out-of-water, and not his former self.

As mentioned previously, the effective therapeutic process often leads to episodes of cognitive dissonance. As our sessions proceeded, we explored issues such as: Was he a person of peace or a killer? Was he truly a religious person or had he by his wartime actions and experiences somehow lost that possibility? Did his family, friends, and for that matter, society at large really care about him, or not? Among others.

How did he feel about the people in his life before Iraq versus now? Occasionally, I would have to push Mark to confront the issues at hand and to define where he truly stood. For Mark that was the hard work of his therapy, dealing with his emotions as he attempted to reclaim as much as possible his former self. He was eventually able to get in touch with his true feelings and to make sense of them.

He struggled through his evoked feelings of anxiety, anger, guilt, grief, helplessness, and hopelessness as we proceeded with his therapy. Several times he questioned whether he was getting any better, if he had what it took to get better, and each time I assured him that he did indeed have what it took. Fortunately, as we proceeded with his therapy Mark began to feel better and agreed to begin the process of reclaiming his former self. He began to understand that he did have what it took to reclaim himself and he discovered how to do it.

He became his own therapist with a structured model to guide him through his life's journey. He understood that he could never become one hundred percent his old self, because he had new experiences and memories that were now a part of him. But he also came to understand that as people grow older, no one can ever become one hundred percent of what they used to be. This is true because new experiences and memories change us all. That if we are flexible, we can experience emotional growth.

Mark continued to struggle with his feelings of guilt concerning having shot an Iraqi teenager. I pointed out to Mark that sometimes we must take the painful and negative events of our life and turn them into positive responses to those negative events and thereby into positive outcomes. I gave Mark the example of John Walsh whose son was abducted, sexually assaulted and murdered. Rather than be destroyed by his pain and tragic loss, and become bitter and live mental anguish, John became a national advocate for missing and exploited children. He founded the show "America's Most Wanted". It was the first time in history that the issue of abused, missing and exploited children got such national exposure. It has influenced law enforcement and multiple other agencies across the nation, and indeed around the world.

I then asked if he had ever seen the movie Gandhi and he noted that he had. I asked if he remembered the scene where a Hindu man approached Gandhi and stated that a Muslim man had killed his son. He asked Gandhi what he could possibly do to not feel hatred for Muslims. Gandhi answered that he should go to a village and find an orphaned child. But that he should make sure that the child was a Muslim and that he should raise the child as he would his own son. With the provision that he should be sure to raise his adopted son as a Muslim. Only then would he be free of his hatred towards Muslims.

The Hindu man looked at Gandhi as if in deep shock. He then began weeping uncontrollably as he began to understand Gandhi's point. That he should answer a negative event with the positive power of love in action. Realizing this message, he began kissing Gandhi's hands out of gratitude for the insight. In thanks for Gandhi's gift of that flash of lightning that has the power to illuminate our minds, to heal, and to change the very course of our existence.

I intentionally told multiple stories to provide Mark with the information with which could populate his new major staxis which lay somewhere between his former-self and his military-self. Mark was gradually able to reconnect with his family members and friends and was shocked by the intensity of his newly found feelings of love for his son. He now truly adores his son. He began proudly showing me pictures of his son and to people he met during his daily routine. He was able to re-establish his relationship with his son's mother and they now have a daughter as well. Mark achieved his sobriety, found gainful employment, and returned to college as a part-time student. He stated, "I'm not sure of what my college major will finally be... or what my future will be... but I'm fully certain that I now have the power to shape it"!

Of note, the technique of using cohort groups involves placing people with similar traumatic experiences into groups for the purpose of delivering therapy. It is a method that has become quite popular. While it offers group members the benefit of being brought together with people who can identify with each other around the issue of military trauma, it also runs the risk of reinforcing their military subordinate staxes through the process of group identification. Also, every veteran's experience and situation can be different. Thus, I feel that individual therapy, which granted is more labor intensive, should always be the mainstay.

19

Brenda's Treatment Dilemma

UNFORTUNATELY, BRENDA'S STORY IS NOT A RARE EVENT IN AMERICA OR for that matter the world-at-large. It reveals how the negative perceptions held by caregivers can prove destructive to those under their care. However, before exploring Brenda's treatment dilemma, I will first present a few words concerning psychosis. According to the Merriam-Webster dictionary, the word psychosis is defined in the following way:

Psychosis (from the Greek ψυχή "psyche", for mind/soul, and -ωσις "-osis", for abnormal *condition) means abnormal condition of the mind, and is a generic psychiatric* term for a mental state often described as involving a "loss of contact with reality". Psychosis: fundamental derangement of the mind (as in schizophrenia) characterized by defective or lost contact with reality especially as evidenced by delusions, hallucinations, and disorganized speech and behavior.

Thus, psychosis is defined as any severe mental disorder in which contact with reality is lost or highly distorted. It often prevents people from being able to distinguish between the real world and their own imagined world. During a psychotic episode an individual will often experience hallucinations (seeing, hearing, feeling, tasting, smelling, or sensing things that in reality don't exist). Their impaired perceptions may lead them to act in a seemingly bizarre manner.

While engaged in teaching rounds with medical students and residents, I will often ask if any of them ever have hallucinated daily. Often my question is met with several laughs and snickers. However, when they came to realize that I had asked them a serious question a wall of puzzled expressions would often fill the room. I then ask them if they think that they dream when they are sleeping. The answer is almost always a resounding, 'yes, of course... people dream, don't they?'

I then call to their attention to the fact that while they are dreaming that they see and hear people talking, see cars, trees, airplanes, and buildings. They hear noises, experience talking, walking and running, etc. Those things are not real and exist only momentarily for the purpose their dream. I go on to explain that that we can begin to understand both the dream state and the experience of psychosis more fully if we were to draw a horizontal line and let the space below that line represent the unconscious mind and the space above represent the conscious mind.

As noted previously our unconscious mind contains our thoughts (individual words and sentences), memories, perspectives, wishes, desires, hopes, fears, impulses, past experiences, etc. When we dream it is as if a projector appears and sits in the middle of our mind. It then projects our unconscious material onto an internal screen which then leads to the creation of our dreams. When we wake from our sleep in the morning, it is as if a door shuts in front of that projector. This essentially locks away our unconscious mind and shuts down our dreams.

Thus, we are allowed to enter and deal with the reality of our world, without total unconscious intrusion. However, when a person suffers from severe depression, bipolar disorder, schizophrenia, delirium, or other such disorders that door can become broken. When a person with such a disorder awakens each day, the door may only partially shut, allowing for unconscious material to escape. Instead of being projected onto a screen in their mind to create dreams the unconscious material instead gets projected onto the environment.

Thus, hallucinations are much like a daydream. However, they seem more real to the person experiencing them than just a typical (imaginary) daydream. The person may question their perceptions, much like we sometimes question ourselves upon waking from a vivid dream. When we are halfway awake, we may question ourselves if we really experienced what had occurred in our dream vs. it being just a dream.

Now for Brenda's story. Brenda was a 47-year-old woman who entered our acute care psychiatry unit in a highly agitated state. She was lying on her back strapped to a stretcher. She had been placed in what are termed four-point restraints, each of her limbs having been tied to the sides of her stretcher. She wore an angry scowl on her face and her eyes were set in a fixed stare straight ahead toward the ceiling above us. She made eye contact with no one as her stretcher rolled down the hallway.

She was immediately placed in locked door seclusion where she was tied to a bed. Her loud screams to be let go were heard throughout the unit. Her screams, however, were half-hearted as Brenda had grown to know the routine through many years of repeated hospitalizations. Brenda was a forty-two-year-old woman who had spent much of the preceding eight years hospitalized. Having been transferred from hospital-to-hospital she had fallen under the care of many healthcare providers.

She was felt to be quite psychotic and had been tried on multiple combinations of medications with little improvement in her condition. After she had quieted down somewhat, I entered her room to introduce myself as her new psychiatrist. She promptly asked me to leave the room in a loud hostile tone. I told her that I would do so in a moment, but that I had to inform her that I was there to help her. Then I stated, "my name is Dr. David Arnold".

She stated that she didn't trust me or anyone else for that matter. I replied that I didn't expect her to. That she would be 'crazy' to do so, so quickly. That she didn't know me and that if she trusted me right away, especially under the given circumstances, she would clearly be showing signs of very severe mental illness. I then stated that she had been in the hospital system for too long to just trust anyone. I reassured her that I was there to help her out of her situation, and to try to relax while I began looking at her chart and tried to figure things out.

Only then, did I honor her original request for me to leave the room. It is important to realize that I did not abandon her at her initial request for me to do so. As I left the room, I stated that she could have the staff contact me if she needed me for anything. "Whenever you feel like talking just let me know". This established a connection between us that she could feel free to use. She answered with her silence, a brief jut of her head, and a continued fixed angry stare at the ceiling above her.

By the next morning, she was calmer and out of restraints. I met with her to discuss how she was feeling and to discuss her concerns. She immediately began to complain about having been abused by all the staff members that had previously cared for her. Apparently, while on prior hospital units she had taken and hidden multiple contraband items from the staff. As a result, she had been forced to undergo several highly intrusive and demoralizing body cavity searches by staff seeking to find hidden contraband. She stated that she felt those staff members had physically and emotionally "raped" her. She felt that they all were surely "evil devils". That God would eventually punish them for their malicious deeds.

She felt that a previous psychiatrist of hers was a "witch" who could "cast spells" on people. She was certain that the staff members of the various hospitals where she had stayed during the previous years were all conspiring to kill her. She stated, "They all wanted me dead!" She revealed that she truly believed that people had been attempting to place "curses" on her using "witchcraft". She recounted having seen "a snake…and then a woman's head on a stick" in her bedroom at a previous hospital. She stated "I'm not making that up…it's true! I'm so afraid of snakes that I run out of the room when they come on T.V.".

She then stated that in the past she has asked God why he made snakes; "especially when they're so ugly". She noted that a therapist once informed her that the snake symbolized a man's penis. No further interpretation or significance was given. This caused Brenda great concern and torment for many years thereafter as she attempted to interpret what that could mean for her. Clearly, giving bits and pieces of charged information without it being addressed within the context of a cohesive structure of true psychotherapy only leads to information that may cause cognitive dissonance and possibly lead to great distress on the patient's part.

I started a walk down memory lane with Brenda to get a better sense of the person sitting before me. I had to get a sense of what things had populated her inner wheel over the years of her life. Brenda grew-up in a mid-sized city with her parents, her two younger brothers, and a younger sister. Her father worked long hours as a laborer to provide for their family. Through his hard work he was able to provide a simple but comfortable home environment for his family. What their home lacked in material goods was replaced by the family's love for each other. Her father truly loved her mother dearly. Brenda's mother would earn extra money for the household by cleaning the homes. They were a simple people but loved a wide-range of music and the arts. They felt that the arts were an important aspect of our lives. Brenda's family would faithfully attend their local church each Sunday.

Brenda was a good student and often helped her siblings with their homework and school projects. She loved her brothers and sister dearly. She spent many hours helping her mother with the household chores and loved cooking with her grandmother who had come to live with them following the death of her husband. She recalled numerous stories of her childhood that revealed the normal challenges of growing up with three siblings. There were times they competed for their parent's attention. Sometimes they would quarrel among themselves, but in the end, they knew that they loved each other just the same. Their family placed loyalty above all things; except God.

Upon leaving high school Brenda decided to enter the military to serve her country, get an education, and earn money. Brenda was met by the biases and fixed perceptions of her trainers as she entered basic training. However, by the first month of her training she not only exceeded her trainer's expectations but did well enough to earn the respect of higher-ranking officials. She made her father, a former WWII sergeant, quite proud of her accomplishments. She later encouraged one of her brothers to enlist, and he too did well in the military. Making their father and mother prouder of their children.

Brenda spent much of her time learning basic drills and army protocol. She felt as if she had found a second home in the military. She fully identified with being a soldier in the military. However, on one very dark day Brenda was sexually assaulted by another soldier in her barracks. She felt devastated by what she felt was the worst type of betrayal imaginable; an assault perpetrated by a fellow soldier. That soldier was eventually court marshaled, but eventually was only reprimanded for his crime. However, the damage had already been done to Brenda. She also felt betrayed by the military system that failed to provide adequate justice on her behalf.

Following the trial, and totally beguiled by her experience, Brenda fell into a deep depression. She soon began to experience disturbing nightmares. Several months following this she started to experience auditory hallucinations. She heard "voices" telling her what a "bad" person she was. She received some counseling, but eventually left military service on the basis of a medical board discharge, referred to as "boarding-out", under honorable conditions. Brenda had become unable to keep up with the demands of military life by that point. Following her discharge, she chose to re-enter her hometown community in search of work.

After several months of trying earnestly, Brenda found that she couldn't seem to hold a stable job. She began to experience more frequent auditory hallucinations which she hid from others. She soon fell into deep despair. She was hospitalized, which began her ten-year journey through hospital systems leading to our acute care unit doorstep and me. During her continuous hospitalizations various contrived stories concerning Brenda's condition arose. In fact, word of Brenda's negative reputation and her many supposed shortcomings had preceded her arrival to our unit.

Brenda had been portrayed as an irritable, often combative, horrible, manipulative, and mean-spirited person. The truth, however, was that over the preceding years Brenda had been transformed from her previously healthy major staxis to a pathologic major staxis. That pathologic state had been created by the anger, stereotypes, distorted perspectives, personal and racial biases of the preceding staff members who were supposedly there to treat Brenda. When others repeatedly flood us with negative thoughts, ideas, and perspectives about ourselves, this can cause a shift of our energies from supporting a preferable dominant staxis toward supporting a less preferable weaker pathologic minor staxis.

This is accomplished through an actual fracturing of one's ego (i.e., breaking down the ego defenses). As time passes, we can become trapped in that induced pathological state of being. Thus, one's staxes can be manipulated by others to create an enduring and completely pathologic state. After discovering what had transpired it then became clear to me that my job was to shift her back to her true formerly healthy major staxis. In order to help her I first had to take a stroll down memory lane with Brenda.

Again, I had to get an idea of just who she was prior to her entrance into military service. As it turned out, her true major staxis was that of a kind, caring, and sensitive person. A fact that was fully supported by her life history and yet was totally ignored and dismissed by her previous treatment team staff members. During the preceding paragraphs I have revealed some of Brenda's significant history.

I first employed the use of medications to deal with Brenda's core symptoms of psychosis and intense anxiety. I reviewed with her the multiple medications she had been tried on in the past and asked her what worked best for her. I then started her on those medications with good effect. Prior to starting with her psychotherapy, as I did with Mark and Linda, I provided Brenda with a clear and full education concerning my gyroscopic model. I reviewed the events of her previous psychiatric treatment experience and how that had resulted in a shift of her healthy major staxis to a negative subordinate staxis. Thus, as we proceeded Brenda was able to grasp what I was attempting to do with her in her therapy.

The goal of therapy was to return her, as much as possible, to her true former self. To undo what had been done to her, Brenda and I had to systematically confront the highly negative and destructive information placed in her mind. This by eliciting and then countering each individual item as it arose during therapy. This process was the challenging hard work of her therapy. It led to many emotions for Brenda which she had to tolerate to get better.

She sometimes cried profusely as we uncovered and then removed each negative thought and label that had been applied to her. This therapy was done in conjunction with the careful administration of medications to control her symptoms of intense anxiety and symptoms of psychosis, such as her auditory hallucinations and her inability to think clearly. The span of her therapy covered several months of restructuring work.

After several months of therapy Brenda began to do well. She began to regain her self-confidence as we proceeded. She soon began to feel good about herself. Something she hadn't felt for several decades. When it came time to discharge her from the hospital Brenda initially became terrified of re-entering the outside world. She felt that she was too unsafe and emotionally vulnerable to return to the community.

Through the venue of a transitional housing program, Brenda was gradually able to return to live in the community in her own apartment. She was thrilled with being able to do so. She was soon able to find a stable job. I met with her one day for lunch at the University hospital's café to see how she had been doing. When we met, she informed me that it was the first time in fifteen years that she had eaten in a café. It then struck me how very far removed from life Brenda had been for the preceding decades.

Final confirmation that I had been on target with my therapeutic assumptions came when Brenda made the following comment: "They locked me up and threw away the key, and you found the key and freed me...you saved my life". Her comment confirmed for me that our work had not been in vain. That she had a good understanding of what we had accomplished. This was very much like what I had accomplished with Mark and Linda.

Brenda has continued to flourish ever since and as of the writing of this book, she has not been re-hospitalized for the past eight years. In final analysis, Brenda first needed someone she could connect with and someone who would believe in her. This needed to happen before she could begin to believe in herself again. She needed someone who understood what had happened to her and had a systematic way to undo that which had been done to her.

20

Roger's Substance Abuse

ROGER WAS A 28-YEAR-OLD MAN WHO ENTERED THE COMMUNITY
mental health clinic where I worked. He brought with him a long history
of substance abuse. He was highly distraught and in search of help when
he first spoke with me. He presented with an intense desire to change his
life. However, it became quite apparent as we spoke that this was just one of
many such visits Roger had made to community outreach clinics over the
preceding years. Even with all those visits, things had somehow remained
unchanged in his life. He had continued to use substances in the context of
a chaotic lifestyle in spite of multiple drug rehabilitation programs.

Roger was becoming increasingly fearful of losing his job as a floor
manager at a local hardware supply store. He was having problems staying
focused at his jobsite. His use of alcohol and drugs had recently increased
and was causing him to call-out 'sick' from work more frequently than he had
in the past. He had gotten several warnings about his time and attendance
from his supervisor. He had worked that job for eight years and hoped to
eventually earn a pension and retire one day. Roger was seeking help for his
multiple substance addictions in an attempt to save his job and his future life.

Like most substance abusers Roger had islands of optimistic clarity
floating in a sea of confusion and despair. For most of the years of his life
Roger had used alcohol, marijuana, cocaine, and heroin, and had tried
various prescription drugs as well. He had gotten to the point where he would
use benzodiazepines (diazepam, clonazepam, alprazolam) to counteract the
emotional and physical effects of alcohol and cocaine. He would counteract
his withdrawal from opiates with Suboxone he bought on the street. He felt

quite adept at dosing himself with one substance or another. He felt quite strongly that drugs were necessary not only for him to stay "stable", but to stay alive as well.

Roger noted that he began his substance abuse at an early age. When his parents held parties for their friends several of their guests would leave half-empty cups of alcohol containing beverages scattered about the house. At the age of nine Roger began to sneak sips from their unattended cups. Pretty soon he began sneaking drinks out of his family's unlocked liquor cabinet. By age eleven, he would attempt to conceal his use of liquor by adding water to the bottles. He drank mostly at night to avoid detection. He noted that his parents never seemed to notice.

He felt some degree of pride at being able to be so artful and stealth with his use of alcohol. He would fill the bottles with small amounts of water to avoid detection. As a teen he began to "experiment" with his parent's various medications to feel their differing effects on his body and on his emotions. He would often trade them with his friends who got hold of their parent's medications as well. They would look-up their effects and side effects when 'studying' in the school library. Roger laughingly stated that it was a good use of the school's educational resources.

When Roger entered high school, he was introduced to marijuana. He began to socialize with individuals that supported his substance abuse lifestyle. He started to do quite poorly in school as his focus switched away from his schoolwork and towards his deeper use of alcohol and drugs. As time progressed, he became increasingly frustrated with school and felt highly discouraged by his poor grades. He stated that he just couldn't "get" the subjects he had to study. He was often directly or indirectly called "stupid", "pot head", or "lazy" by several of his classmates who had become increasingly aware of his academic failures. His father reinforced the idea that he was "stupid" through his frequent scolding and admonishments.

His father, who was fully immersed in his long hours at work had no idea of the severity of Roger's substance abuse problem. His mother had her suspicions but found it too difficult and anxiety provoking to confront Roger. Eventually, Roger quit high school to get a job and to avoid the criticism of others. As he continued with his substance use it eventually escalated to his use of cocaine and narcotic painkillers. Roger felt that without drugs he was an incomplete person. He felt that he absolutely needed substances to exist in our world. That he would surely fall apart and die a slow death without them.

After hearing his story, it soon became apparent to me what had happened to Roger. Over the years of his life Roger had built a major staxis that included alcohol and drugs as its chief component. As a result, his very identity was that of a substance user. With gyroscopic forces at play he had developed several strategies to defend that major staxis from being shifted. He knew well, and was quite skilled at, using the various games that substance abusers play to defend their continued use of substances.

Since early childhood he had practiced concealing his alcohol and drug use from others. But now, he was spiraling out of control. His drug use was beginning to affect his health and judgment. He wasn't as effective at maintaining his emotional stability with drugs. He had become less able to rebound from his alcohol binges as compared to his past use. He was stumbling. In that Roger's pathologic major staxis was that of being a substance user and this had been his major identity since childhood a lot of work had to be done.

The obvious question at that point was How could Roger be helped? It was clear to me that Roger would need to develop a new subordinate staxis of having a substance-free identity. That new substance-free identity once established and strengthened would ideally take center stage as his major staxis. I provided Roger with some education concerning my gyroscopic theory and model. I then spoke of how his early use of alcohol and drugs had eventually led him to the creation of a truly self-destructive major staxis. He laughingly stated, "I know doc".

As we proceeded, Roger was able to grasp what I was attempting to do in his therapy. The goal of therapy was to create a new 'non-user' subordinate staxis and then eventually have it take center stage. Supplanting his existing dominant major staxis identity of being a 'substance user'. Typically, substance users most often see themselves as substance users not abusers. To help him I first had to take a stroll down memory lane with Roger to get an idea of just who he really was under that 'substance user' mask. Surely, there were things other than his substance use. This process involved exploring the events of his early childhood and his adolescent years.

I explored his relationship with his family members and friends. What his usual activities consisted of prior to and during the onset of his substance use. I did this to get a sense of how he saw his pre-substance self. We then discussed what his hopes and dreams had been for his future, prior to his leaving high school. What his 'idealized self' was. These were the existing elements that could be used as a foundation to build his new 'non-user' subordinate staxis.

As we proceeded with his therapy, I made it clear to Roger that the only way he knew to deal with anxiety and frustration was through his use of substances. That he would need to attain his sobriety for our work to be of any long-term use. To that end, he would need to be actively involved with a substance abuse program. That additionally, he would need to have a sponsor who would be available 'twenty-four-seven' to help him maintain his sobriety. With those things in place, we began the arduous work of transforming Roger's life.

First, we had to deal with his initial disbelief that he could make such a change. He highlighted the fact that he had been using substances for such a long time that it was all he knew. I pointed out that his initial disbelief in his ability to change was a natural reflexive response. It was a reflexive and defensive rejection that stemmed from his underlying gyroscopic forces that were fighting to resist change. Those forces naturally resist any attempts that are made to change his predominant staxis. That it would challenge his sense of stability and sense of security.

I then revealed the immense power this gave his major 'substance user' staxis. I also pointed out his very active and long-time role in constructing that type of existence. That he had actively worked on creating his own self-destructive self. The time and energy he had put into such a process. Upon hearing this, he went through a grieving process as he began to realize how much he had contributed to the construction of his own pathologic major staxis. A major staxis that included alcohol and drugs which then had a huge negative impact on his family and indeed on his entire life in general.

During the course of his therapy, he had to deal with many emotions that he had buried for years with his substance use. Feelings of guilt arose that stemmed from the many negative effects that alcohol and drugs had on his past and current relationships. We discussed how he had made alcohol and drugs higher priorities than his friends and family members. He had ended most of his relationships with former girlfriends due to problems arising from his substance use.

Roger began to realize how quickly and reflexively he used substances to deal with his uncomfortable emotions as they arose rather than to work through his various emotions and life issues. This had resulted in his being less emotionally mature, resilient, and effective in life. I pointed out how he had spent many years creating positive images of substances and what they could do for him. This further strengthened his substance user major staxis.

However, he spent little time building any negative images, thoughts or perspectives (elements) of what substances did to harm him. I suggested that he spend time each day thinking of all the negatives associated with substance use. That he should begin to create a negative mental image of substances that he would then reinforce daily. I suggested that when he thought of alcohol, he should use imagery by envision a bottle of poison with a skull-and-crossbones and poisonous fumes pouring from the bottle spout. Those thoughts and images could then serve as elements for his new subordinate staxis.

At one point it became apparent that his parents also used alcohol and drugs to deal with their uncomfortable emotions. I informed him of my continued surprise with people who use substances. The fact that substance users can always see their next drink, their next joint, their next 'hit' of a substance and at the same time become totally blind to the many things they are losing in the process. They can lose their jobs, their homes, their relationships, their health, their families and friends, but still feel they can continue to use substances to solve their problems.

As we proceeded, Roger began to get a sense that a part of him truly didn't want illicit substances to be a part of his life anymore. I informed him that if he wanted to see his very best friend and his very worst enemy on this earth to look in any mirror. I asked him to look at himself in the mirror each morning while he got ready for the day and to ask himself one question while no one else was around. The question is, Do I love myself enough to be my very best friend today or will I be my very worst enemy?

At some point he began to realize that he once strongly desired to become a graphic artist. He had made several graphic arts drawings over the years and felt that he indeed had talent. He had gotten positive feedback from those who viewed his work. Substance use had stolen this from him. It had taken it all. All his potentially great works of art gone. Lost or stolen in his many moves during his substance use. He mentioned a high school teacher who had once been impressed with his work. He stated that remembering this made him feel inspired to pursue his initial interest in becoming a graphic artist.

We next examined who this 'graphic artist' was. And what his life would look like. This process of crafting a new potential major staxis involves the process of self-creation. Roger laughed at the need to not prematurely quit his day job and avoid jumping 'foot-first' into the art world. Though clearly a practical stance for Roger to take, this too was a defensive resistance toward any change: that stemmed from underlying inertia of his gyroscopic forces. He wasn't quite ready yet, but clearly this was a motivating goal for him to consider.

This case was presented in a simplistic manner to get directly at the core principles I wished to cover. Mark's actual recovery process took place over the span of two years with occasional relapses into substance use, before he was able to attain his longer-term sobriety. Such an accomplishment is never an easy process and requires tremendous commitment on the part of the individual involved. The mantra of one day at a time is a mainstay of sobriety. Roger was able to obtain his sobriety during our sessions, and when I last saw him, he had achieved four years of sobriety had obtained his GED and had enrolled in a school for graphic arts. He continues to work on shaping his new life and now has a clear mental model to work with. He is truly happy with his new 'substance-free' life and identity and lives his life one day at a time.

21

Karen's Bipolar Challenge

KAREN WAS A 36-YEAR-OLD WOMAN WHO ENTERED MY OFFICE ONE DAY stating that she had been feeling quite depressed for several weeks. She noted that she was very unhappy with the way her life had been going over the preceding years. She felt especially down because she had recently gone on an impulsive shopping spree and as a result, she was unable to pay her monthly bills. She felt highly embarrassed by having to return the multiple items she really couldn't afford to the stores where she had purchased them. She stated that she knew she needed some form of help.

She had been drinking more alcoholic beverages which she noted was really not typical for her. She stated that the drinks did help to 'calm her nerves' and helped with her "bitchy" mood. Karen's supervisor had once informed her that he felt Karen had an "attitude problem". She admitted that when he made the statement, she knew that he was right but was feeling too irritated to process his comment. She had already been feeling highly embarrassed by the many angry and inappropriate things she had been impulsively saying to her co-workers, friends, and family members.

She revealed that she had experienced multiple problems over the five years preceding her initial visit with me. She had broken up with her boyfriend of three years. She had lost her apartment because she failed to pay her rent and as a result had to move in with her sister for several months. She eventually found a new apartment, but worried that she may again be evicted someday. She had also changed jobs several times, and felt unstable in terms of her employment. She was uncertain if she had the potential for a career at all.

She then confided that she had had a 'fling' with a co-worker, although she had previously made a vow never to date anyone that she worked. She noted that she attempted to resist having the fling, but her sex drive was just too intense at that time. She found herself flirting with men that she normally wouldn't approach or typically find attractive. She was fearful of her own sexual impulses and felt that they would eventually cause her severe problems. She began to avoid social events out of fear that she might act on her sexual impulses.

She noted that she had a very stressful job working for a collection agency. Her job was to call customers about past due accounts. The calls were continuously monitored by her supervisors who would critique her performance daily. They would frequently comment that she needed to slow her speech when talking to customers on the phone. She had worked at her current jobsite for just under two years. She had always found her work there to be very stressful but found it even more so during the previous year.

She recalled that she was once interviewed for a management position and was told by the interviewer that she had gotten the new position. She was later informed by upper management that the interviewer had misspoken and that she didn't get the promotion. She began to feel "worthless" and "depressed" at that point. She attempted to contact the interviewer, but he didn't return her calls. So, she stopped calling him out of the fear of seeming too pushy or inappropriate.

Several months later she switched her position at work, thinking that her problems were mostly due to job related stress and to office pressures. She had found the new position with the assistance of her human resources department. She felt that due to her 'superior skillsets' she wouldn't need much secretarial support which was sorely lacking at her jobsite. As a result, she optimistically accepted the more demanding position. After starting the new position, she found it to be more taxing and stressful than her previous position. Though it was tough to achieve, she was able to get by in terms of her overall performance. She constantly questioned if she had made the right decision.

She had been feeling moderately depressed and highly anxious. She confided that she was worried about eventually being fired from her job because she sometimes just puts the work aside and calls her friends and surfs the internet to relieve her stress. She had also been having problems with her sleep due to worry about her job security. She stated that when she laid down at night her mind would 'go wild...thinking about anything and everything'. She stated she had been that way ever since her teen years. However, she was unsure as to why she had experienced those symptoms for so many years.

She also had experienced periods of time where she slept excessively, usually after experiencing 'emotional crashes'. She noted that just prior to her crashes she was usually feeling 'really great...the best I ever had'. During those times she felt nothing was impossible and had started multiple projects which eventually failed or she simply 'just lost interest in'. She then moved on to new projects. However, following the crashes she felt just the opposite; that nothing was possible.

After hearing her entire story and list of symptoms, I informed Karen that I felt she was suffering from bipolar disorder. I then began to educate Karen about Bipolar Disorder. I covered the symptoms of the disorder and used several stories and analogies to help clarify specific points of importance. The following three paragraphs describe the various symptoms and general nature of Bipolar Disorder.

Bipolar Affective Disorder, aka Bipolar Depression, formerly known as Manic-Depressive illness, is a disorder of mood characterized by wide swings in one's mood. The person affected by this disorder is subjected to intense periods of depression alternating with periods of mania (the opposite of depression) or hypomania (less intense mania). The symptoms seen in bipolar disorder arise from periods of depression alternating with those of mania. The following two paragraphs cover the specific signs and symptoms of both depressive and manic episodes.

Depressive symptoms may include feelings of sadness, low energy, persistent tiredness, decreased motivation, poor frustration tolerance, increased irritability, an increased or decreased appetite, disrupted sleep pattern with insomnia, decreased sex drive, feelings of helplessness, hopelessness, low self-esteem, and feelings of guilt.

Manic symptoms may consist of the following: experience of racing thoughts, periods of rapid speech, inability to get all of one's ideas out via speech, people frequently commenting on need for the affected person to 'slow down', frequent periods of irritability, experience of having an expansive mood, of having endless power, increased sense of energy, awake for extended periods of time (sometimes for days with a lack of tiredness or need for sleep), increased spending, multiple shopping sprees beyond means, increased sex drive with more frequent flirting and sexual activity, sharp increase in number of projects started during these periods, and multiple project failures.

A person with bipolar disorder may feel as though their life course is much like riding on a roller coaster. With extreme highs and lows with no true control over where their extreme emotions eventually will take them. They often love the high-energy highs of mania and dread the low-energy lows of depression. They can often feel helpless as their intense mood-shifts push them in one direction or another. When discussing bipolar disorder with my patients I actually use the analogy of them being on an emotional roller coaster. I believe that such an analogy helps to provide a good foundation for understanding the experience of having bipolar disorder.

I noted that ordinarily when people line-up to get on a roller coaster ride, they are often filled with mixed emotions and prominent among those emotions is a feeling of excitement. As they pile into their seats and then wait for the ride to begin, they often experience a sense of thrill mixed with a sense of fear. All-in-all, they most often have a charged state of emotion that supports an overwhelming sense of excitement which momentarily overrides their anxiety, fear, or dread. As the roller coaster cars begin to move up the initial incline the riders often begin to cheer and sometimes wave their arms in the air. There is a feeling of fun and excitement going up the incline.

However, as they approach the top of the incline, a feeling of dread soon sets in. This is very often because they know that once they reach the top, a rapid plunging descent awaits them on the other side. This they fear! Fear, as I noted in the section on mood, is the extreme form of anxiety. This can be experienced as the emotions of panic and dread. With each course of track the riders begin to experience feelings of helplessness over their condition. They are powerless to stop the ride. Even if they feel, sick to their stomachs. People who have experienced the severe the ups and downs of bipolar disorder for many years; often feel helpless and begin to fear the other side of their manic episodes (i.e., severe depression).

After describing the symptoms of Bipolar Disorder and the goals of treatment, I described my gyroscopic model and theory to help guide the therapy portion of the treatment process. I noted the powerful role that mood regulation plays in bipolar illness. As noted previously, our mood has the power to drive our behavior and to distort the way we see our environment. I used the example involving an old man sitting on a park bench, that I presented earlier in this book, to clarify this point for Karen.

I then informed Karen that one of the major goals of treatment was for Karen to take back control over the regulation of her mood. And by doing so, hopefully prevent future manic and depressive episodes. That until this was accomplished, Karen would be subjected to the ups and downs of bipolar disorder. In such a state it would be quite difficult for her to do any productive or lasting psychotherapy.

She would find it extremely difficult to work on restructuring her major staxis as her ability to focus her thoughts would constantly shift at the dictates of her extreme moods. Not to mention the distorted thinking she would likely experience. Intense moods can severely distort reality and Thus, one's interpretation of both intra-psychic and extra-psychic events.

When we experience the extreme emotions of despair, euphoria, rage or fear for prolonged periods of time we can begin to distort reality. We are highly prone to enter a state of irritability and agitation the longer these intense emotions continue. Figure 22 (below) shows a representation of our moods and emotions graphed over time. By referring to this illustration one can begin to get an idea of the range of moods and their extremes.

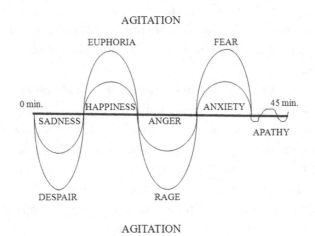

Figure 22: Moods and Emotions Graphed over Time.

To stop Karen's cycling negative moods and emotions medications were necessary. The medications block-out the occurrence of extreme moods (i.e., mania or depression). Normally our moods fluctuate over time around a mid-line. Each of us has our own unique bio-rhythm.

Figure 23 (below) illustrates the effect of Lithium, Lamictal, Trileptal, Depakote, and other such medications ("mood stabilizers") on mood regulation. Dosed properly, these medications block out the extremes of the mood spectrum (blackened areas) while allowing for a normal range of emotions (in-between the lines).

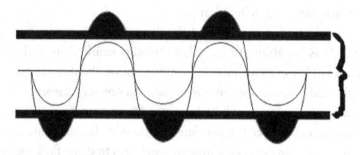

Figure 23: Effect of mood-stabilizing
medications on mood regulation.

After being placed on mood stabilizing medications that block-out the extremes of the mood spectrum (i.e., the highs and lows), Karen was able to experience a stable mood over time for the 'first time' in her life. Once she was affectively stable, she was able to begin examining the distorted picture she had of herself, of her loved ones, of her community, and of her life situation.

For the first time she was in control of her mood and emotions (via medications) rather than being ruled by them (in the absence of effective medications). This allowed for her to proceed with highly beneficial psychotherapy in both a stable and productive fashion. Using the gyroscopic method of psychotherapy, she was able to work-through many life-long issues and was eventually able to lead a stable and fulfilling life.

The next chapters deal with the application of the gyroscopic model and method to specific areas of interest and concern.

22

Application to Violence and Mass Murder

AMERICA IS A LAND OF FREEDOM AND OPPORTUNITY WHICH HAS NO comparison elsewhere in this world. However, we also live in a nation with a significant history of violence. In fact, we live in a nation that has experienced regular violence since its very inception. Our nation certainly has areas of needed improvement, growth, and healing when it comes to our long-standing culture of violence. Our citizens and government have become increasingly concerned about and focused on the alarming increase of mass killings that have recently occurred in some of our otherwise peaceful communities.

Unfortunately, prior to these recent traumatic events the importance of mental health in our communities sat on a back burner. People's mental health was often treated, quite simply, as a joke. However, by many it's no longer being considered a joke. People have become more outspoken concerning the need for our mental health to be taken seriously. This attitude was also highlighted by legislation that requires "mental health parity" by third party health insurance companies when processing their healthcare claims. Considering the powerful and enduring nature of gyroscopic forces this previous disregard for mental health awareness and general acceptance of violence has proven to be a very unfortunate, dangerous, and frankly deadly position for our society to have taken. This takes on an even more ominous tone when we view our critical role as leaders of the free world.

Democracy can easily fall in the face of an uneducated, emotionally unstable, narcissistic, violence driven and morally bankrupt public.

A major part of our culture accepts the idea of violence as a plausible answer to the problems and struggles we face. We are exposed to the use of violence as an option to solve problems daily through television, the internet, on radio programs, in newspaper articles, in casual conversations, etc. We incorporate violence as an option into our thinking. In fact, the foundation for a violence prone military-type subordinate staxis is being instilled in our children today. Their exposure to video games that involve the use of weapons to 'kill and destroy the enemy'. That require the active employment of military tactical strategy to fully participate. Games that use sniper rifles and show the blood of one's "enemies" splatter across the screen serve to desensitize our children to the act of killing others. Some say we've always played with guns as kids playing cops and robbers. Maybe we have but not at this graphic level and with such intense malice and exposure for hours at a time. This intense level of participation is very often coupled with a high level of emotional detachment from the players actions of killing others.

We hear daily news reports about violence in our communities. We are bombarded with episodic news reports of 'twenty-three people shot dead here...eighteen innocents massacred there...this just in, twelve people shot at jobsite...man shoots family and then takes his own life', etc. We are currently locked into the powerful gyroscopic forces of the violence of our past. Between 1982 and 2019 there were an estimated 167 mass shootings in the United States and the number has continued to rise during the past few years.

The following is a partial list of those previous shootings (provided by Mother Jones website). Visit their site to see all of the data they track including the number killed/injured and the specific details of the shootings. Please consider giving a donation for the hard work they do every day.

https://www.motherjones.com/politics/mass-shootings-mother-jones-full-data/:

> 101 California Street shootings: San Francisco, CA
> Accent Signage Systems shooting

Air Force base shooting: Fairchild Air Force Base, Washington
Alturas tribal shooting
Amish school shooting: Lancaster County, Pennsylvania
Apalachee High School shooting
Arkansas grocery store shooting
Atlanta day trading spree killings: Atlanta, Georgia
Atlanta massage parlor shootings
Atlantis Plastics shooting: Henderson, Kentucky
Aurora theatre shooting: Aurora, Colorado
Baton Rouge police shooting
Binghamton shootings: Binghamton, New York
Boulder supermarket shooting
Buffalo supermarket massacre
Caltrans maintenance yard shooting: Orange, California
Capital Gazette shooting
Capitol Hill massacre: Capitol Hill, Washington
Carthage nursing home shooting: Carthage, North Carolina
Cascade Mall shooting
Charleston Church Shooting
Chattanooga military recruitment center
Chuck E. Cheese's killings: Aurora, Colorado
Church potluck dinner shooting
Coffee shop police killings: Parkland, Washington
Colorado Springs shooting rampage
Columbine High School massacre: Littleton, Colorado
Concrete company shooting
Connecticut Lottery shooting: Newington, Connecticut
Crandon shooting: Crandon, Wisconsin
Dallas nightclub shooting: Dallas, Texas
Dallas police shooting
Damage Plan Show shooting: Columbus, Ohio
Dayton entertainment district shooting
Edgewood business park shooting
El Paso Walmart mass shooting
ESL shooting: Sunnyvale, California
Excel Industries mass shooting

FedEx warehouse shooting

Fifth Third Center shooting

Florida awning manufacturer shooting

Fort Hood massacre: Fort Hood, Texas

Fort Hood massacre: Fort Hood, Texas 2nd shooting

Fort Lauderdale airport shooting

Fort Lauderdale revenge shooting: Fort Lauderdale, Florida

Fresno downtown shooting

Garden State Plaza Mall Shooting

Gilroy garlic festival shooting

GMAC massacre: Jacksonville, Florida

Goleta postal shootings: Goleta, California

Greenwood Park Mall shooting

Half Moon Bay spree shooting

Harry Pratt Co. warehouse shooting

Hartford Beer Distributor shooting: Manchester, Connecticut

Hialeah apartment shooting

Highland Park July 4 parade shooting

Hotel shooting: Tampa, Florida

IHOP shooting: Carson City, Nevada

Isla Vista mass murder

Jacksonville Dollar General store shooting

Jersey City kosher market shooting

Kalamazoo shooting spree

Kirkwood City Council shooting: Kirkwood, Missouri

LA dance studio mass shooting

Las Vegas Strip massacre

LGBTQ club shooting

Lindhurst High School shooting: Olive Hurst, California

Living Church of God shooting: Brookfield, Wisconsin

Lockheed Martin shooting: Meridian, Mississippi

Long Island Rail Road massacre: Garden City, New York

Louisville bank shooting

Luby's massacre: Killeen, Texas

Luigi's shooting: Fayetteville, North Carolina

Maine bowling alley and bar shootings

Marjory Stoneman Douglas High School shooting
Marysville-Pilchuck High School shooting
Mass random shooting: Isla Vista, California
Mercy Hospital shooting
Michigan State University shooting
Mohawk Valley shootings
Molson Coors shooting
Nashville Christian school shooting
Navistar shooting: Melrose Park, Illinois
Navy Yard, Washington, DC
New Mexico neighborhood shooting
Northern Illinois University shooting: DeKalb, Illinois
Odessa-Midland shooting spree
Oikos University killings: Oakland, California
Orange County biker bar shooting
Orange office complex shooting
Orlando nightclub massacre
Oxford High School shooting
Pennsylvania carwash shooting
Pennsylvania hotel bar shooting
Pennsylvania supermarket shooting
Pensacola Naval base shooting
Philadelphia neighborhood shooting
Pinewood Village Apartment shooting
Planned Parenthood clinic
R.E. Phelon Company shooting: Aiken, South Carolina
Raleigh spree shooting
Rancho Tehama shooting spree
Red Lake massacre: Red Lake, Minnesota
Rite Aid warehouse shooting
Robb Elementary School massacre
Royal Oak postal shootings: Royal Oak, Michigan
Rural Ohio nursing home shooting
Sacramento County church shooting
San Bernardino mass shooting
San Francisco UPS shooting

San Jose VTA shooting

San Ysidro McDonald's massacre: San Ysidro, California

Sandy Hook Elementary massacre

Sandy Hook Elementary school shooting: Newtown, Connecticut

Santa Fe High School shooting

Santa Monica rampage

Seal Beach shooting: Seal Beach, California

Seattle cafe shooting: Seattle, Washington

Shopping centers spree killings: Palm Bay, Florida

Sikh temple shooting: Oak Creek, Wisconsin

Springfield convenience store shooting

Standard Gravure shooting: Louisville, Kentucky

Stockton schoolyard shooting: Stockton, California

Su Jung Health Sauna shooting

SunTrust bank shooting

T&T Trucking shooting

Texas First Baptist Church massacre

Texas outlet mall shooting

Thousand Oaks nightclub shooting

Thurston High School shooting: Springfield, Oregon

Tree of Life synagogue shooting

Trestle Trail bridge shooting

Trolley Square shooting: Salt Lake City, Utah

Tucson shooting: Tucson, Arizona

Tulsa medical center shooting

Umpqua Community College shooting

United States Postal Service shooting: Edmond, Oklahoma

University of Iowa shooting: Iowa City, Iowa

University of Virginia shooting

UNLV shooting

Virginia Beach municipal building shooting

Virginia Tech massacre: Blacksburg, Virginia

Virginia Walmart shooting

Waffle House shooting

Wakefield massacre: Wakefield, Massachusetts

Walmart shooting in suburban Denver

Walter Rossler Company massacre

Walter Rossler Company massacre: Corpus Christi, Texas

Washington Navy Yard shooting

Watkins Glen killings: Watkins Glen, New York

Wedgwood Baptist Church shooting: Fort Worth, Texas

Welding shop shooting

West Roads Mall shooting: Omaha, Nebraska

Westside Middle School killings: Jonesboro, Arkansas

Xerox killings: Honolulu, Hawaii

Yountville veterans home shooting

Since 2015, over 19,000 people have been shot and wounded or killed in a mass shooting. In 2022 alone, over 600 people were killed, with over 2,700 wounded. Both the number of mass shooting incidents and the number of people shot in them have increased since 2015, reaching a high of 686 mass shooting incidents in 2021. In 2021, the Gun Violence Archive recorded 692 mass shootings and found that gun violence overall killed 45,010 people. Since 1992 there have been over 400 school shootings. Sixty-nine percent of the shooters were between 10 and 19 years old. Seventy-five percent of the victims were between the ages of 10 and 29 years old. Between 1982 and 2013 these mass shootings rose to leave 543 people dead. Sixty-eight of those 543 victims were killed during 2012. During the recent revision of this book, we have seen 26 more mass shootings. The statistics seem to imply an increasing rate of both individual and mass killings. In 2022, the Archive recorded 647 mass shootings and recorded gun violence-related deaths of 44,287 people between 2018 and 2022. During January of 2023 there were 40 mass shootings leaving 69 people dead.

Let's take a closer look. On May 23, 2014, a killing spree occurred in Isla Vista, California. The killer, Elliot Rodgers, left a manuscript behind that is truly worth studying. Excerpts from his manifesto will be presented later in this chapter. I believe that the gyroscopic theory can be used to examine the various dimensions of this critical aspect of violence. It can be used to look at the perpetrators of these deplorable acts of violence as individuals living within the context of their families and their communities. It can be used examine how they systematically developed their staxis of hatred which eventually supported their killing rampages.

David S. Arnold, M.D.

We are strongly inclined to ask: What type of people would carry out such heinous acts of inhumanity? When examining their histories closely it is often easy to recognize a familiar pattern. It is the pattern of the perpetrator angrily adding multiple hateful elements to fuel and reinforce their gyroscopic inner wheel of hatred. They often feel wronged and feel entitled to justice and revenge. In a sense, over time they 'build a case' to justify carrying out their hateful killings. Most often these horrific atrocities have involved people who in retrospect had been identified as having "mental issues" earlier in their lifespan.

Examples of how one can apply the gyroscopic theory to case studies of mass murders will now be presented by examining the heartbreaking cases of the "Oklahoma City bomber"; Timothy McVeigh, the Columbine shooters; Eric Harris and Dylan Klebold, and that of the Isla Vista, California killer; Elliot Rodgers. The gyroscopic theory can be used to understand how the perpetrators of these mass killings transformed themselves into some of America's most notorious mass murderers.

It is my hope that by using the gyroscopic model to examine the many steps leading up to those dreadful days in our history, it might become clearer to you how things took shape and lead to such tragic events. The following paragraphs will take a more in-depth look at these mass murderers.

Timothy McVeigh developed a set of beliefs and perspectives that were fueled by many of his early life experiences and by his military training. He self-admittedly saw himself as being severely 'bullied' as a child. Of note, he later saw the government as a 'big bully' of the people. As he grew, he filled his head with thoughts, beliefs, ideas, and perspectives that supported his growing convictions of having been done wrong by people and by society at large. Mass murderers have a common habit of collecting mental lists of injustices and then developing a theme of revenge. He developed a very rigid view of what he considered to be "right and wrong" and felt that he was defending that perspective on the day of the Oklahoma City bombing.

The bomb's blast caused 168 deaths and injured more than 680 people. It totally destroyed or damaged 324 buildings within a sixteen-block radius of the blast site. It either destroyed or burned 86 cars and shattered the glass of nearby buildings in a 258-degree circumference. The bomb caused an estimated $652 million worth of damage.[8, 9, 10]

This same type of analysis can be applied to the Columbine shootings in Colorado. In that situation, Eric Harris and Dylan Klebold embarked on a massacre that led to the killing of 12 students and one teacher. They directly injured 21 other students, and 3 students were injured while attempting to escape the scene.[11, 12, 13]

Prior to the killings both Eric and Dylan were seen as "outsiders" at their high school. They had formed an outsider group identity known as the "trench-coat-mafia". They wore black trench coats which symbolized their solidarity. They began to build and incorporate their own distorted perspective of both people and institutions. The power of gyroscopic forces then allowed for the formation of a highly organized evil and lethal staxis. It is one of my hopes that the gyroscopic model can be used to better understand and prevent such atrocities in the future. Now I will present the Isla Vista mass murder to reinforce what has been stated Thus, far.

On May 23, 2014, Elliot Rodgers went on a killing spree through Isla Vista, California near the campus of the University of California at Santa Barbara. When he was done, he had killed seven people (including himself) and had wounded thirteen people. He began by stabbing to death three men in his apartment. He then drove to a nearby sorority house where he shot four people resulting in the death of two women. He then drove to a nearby delicatessen where he shot to death a male student. He then sped through Isla Vista shooting at people while striking four people with his car. He exchanged gunfire with police twice during his shooting spree. The killing spree ended when his car struck a parked car, and he ended his life by shooting himself in the head.

On the night before his shooting spree Elliot Rodgers posted a video on YouTube entitled Elliot Rodger's Retribution. There he described in detail his plan for a mass murder and his reasons for doing so. The video was removed by YouTube following the killings due to its' violating their policy regarding threats of violence. Just prior to his killing spree he emailed a copy of a lengthy autobiographical manuscript to approximately twelve acquaintances and family members.

The document which he entitled "My Twisted World" was made available on the internet and became known as his "manifesto". In it he chronicled his childhood experiences, his intense feelings of inferiority, his multiple family conflicts, his conflict with Soumaya (his step-mother), his having been bullied by schoolmates and others, the effect puberty had on his sex drive, his inability to get a girlfriend, his hatred of women, his hatred of minorities, his hatred of interracial couples, the role and effect video games had in his life, and his general anger and rage directed at the world. He projected his feelings of inadequacy and intense anger onto the people and the world around him.

Psychiatrist Alfred Adler noted that vain or prideful people usually attempt to keep their true outlook on life and people hidden, while noting that they are often seen as simply "ambitious" or "energetic". Adler's piercing observation that for a vain person; everything comes down to one question for them. "What do I get out of this?" Station: 'WII FM' (What's-In-It-For-Me?). Adler felt that "adaptation to the community is the most important psychological function". He noted that people may achieve much in life, but without this essential adaptation (to the community) they may feel like nothing and be perceived by others as such. Such people, Adler stated, are the "enemies of society".

The following significant sentences, words, and passages are taken directly from Elliot Rodger's manuscript: "My Twisted World". These served as the elements of his staxis of hatred. I feel it is worthwhile for all mental health workers and other concerned people to read the manuscript in its entirety to understand the process of how a person can construct such a destructive staxis.

Elliot used grandiose terms and language to describe himself and his family members such as:

> "wealthy, upper class, renowned, upscale, private school, world traveler, we traveled on Virgin Atlantic Upper Class, I always loved luxury and opulence, I am descended from British aristocracy, I *was* a superior gentleman. *Yes*, I thought. *I am the image of beauty and supremacy.*"

> He also used negative and debasing terms to describe both himself and the people around him. I've added bolded italicized words for clarity of reference:

"my lack of physical capability, short-statured, my mother's pregnancy *(with me)* was an accident, Mother's pregnancy with Georgia *(Elliott's sister)* was planned, I immediately went to the restroom to look at myself in the mirror a few times, just so that I can feel more assured of myself, I never understood the game *(football)* and I could never keep up with the other boys, Joey: a rotten little prick who I would always get into fights with...became my greatest enemy at the school, powerful and successful man *(regarding his father: at first)*, the cruelties of this world, twisted and cruel this "fascinating world" is, bitter brutality, I would harbor a great hatred for Riley, feelings of inferiority in me would only grow more volatile with time."

"I realized, with some horror, that I wasn't "cool" at all, I had a dorky hairstyle, I wore plain and uncool clothing, and I was shy and unpopular, I realized that I sucked *(re: skateboarding)*, *Why did I fail at everything I tried?*, I felt so defeated, I always felt like a loser compared to them, and I hated them for it, though I still wanted their approval, loneliness, I was extremely unpopular, widely disliked, and viewed as the weirdest kid in the school, I felt so ashamed of myself, this saddened me deeply, I was in a sullen mood, infamy is better than total obscurity, I was a complete dork, stuck in my own little world, Females truly have something mentally wrong with them. Their minds are flawed, and at this point in my life I was beginning to see it, I often fantasized about barging into their rooms while they had sex and slashing them to death with my knife."

Regarding his new roommates and others, in his own words from his manifesto:

* * * * *

"This was extremely disappointing, I was hoping I would get decent, mature, clean-cut housemates. Instead, I got low-class scum, I am a beautiful, magnificent gentleman and he is a low-class, pig-faced thug, I fantasized about capturing the two of them and stripping the skin off her boyfriend's flesh while making her watch. *Why must my life be so full of torment and hatred?* I questioned to the universe with turmoil roiling inside me. I screamed and cried with anguish that day. My housemate Spencer heard it all, but I didn't care, my hatred and rage towards all women festered inside me like a plague, how wicked and degenerate women really are."

"I realized that there were hierarchies, that some people were better than others.

My mother indulged in me more than my father and Soumaya ever did.

Mother always got me what I wanted, right when I wanted it.

At mother's house, all of my needs were met with excellent precision, whereas at father's house, there would always be a time delay because father and Soumaya had less time for me and paid less attention to me.

I was furious, and I threw a huge crying tantrum.

My first act was to ask my parents to allow me to bleach my hair blonde. I always envied and admired blonde-haired people, they always seemed so much more beautiful.

I always had the subconscious preconception that the coolest kids were mean and aggressive by nature.

The pleasures of sex and love will be denied to me. Other boys will experience it, but not me. Instead, I will only experience misery, rejection, loneliness, and pain.

Despite all of my attempts to be cool, I didn't feel as if the other kids respected me as such. I was still quite the outcast, as I always will be.

Girls were like completely foreign creatures to me. I never interacted with them… I wasn't expected to.

Only after the advent of puberty does the true brutality of human nature show its face. Life will become a bitter and unfair struggle for self-worth, all because girls will choose some boys over others. The boys who girls find attractive will live pleasure-filled lives while they dominate the boys who girls deem unworthy.

I will go on to be rejected and humiliated by girls. At that moment in time, we were just playing together as children, oblivious to the fact that my future will be dark and his will be bright. Life is such a cruel joke.

I thought all of the cool kids were obnoxious jerks, but I tried as best as I could to hide my disgust and appear "cool" to them. They were obnoxious jerks, and yet somehow it was these boys who all of the girls flocked to.

This showed me that the world was a brutal place, and human beings were nothing more than savage animals.

Connor was a true bully. I started hanging out with him during recess and lunch, and we made a few jokes with each other and had a few good laughs, but he would always push me around and act tough.

At this camp, an incident happened that would scar me for life. The first time that I was treated badly by a girl occurred at this camp. I was innocently playing with the friends I made, and they were tickling me, something people always did because I was very ticklish. I accidently bumped into a pretty girl the same age as me, and she got very angry. She cursed at me and pushed me, embarrassing me in front of my friends. Cruel treatment from women is ten times worse than from men. It made me feel like an insignificant, unworthy little mouse. I felt so small and vulnerable. I couldn't believe that this girl was so horrible to me, and I thought that it was because she *viewed me* as a loser. That was the first experience of female cruelty I endured, and it traumatized me to no end.

Playing video games with people over the internet invoked a whole new level of fascination in me.

My initially happy interest in the game Warcraft 3 had an ominous tone to it.

It enabled the player to build an army and battle against other players online. This was the beginning of a long relationship with the Warcraft franchise. In less than a year from that point, they would release their ultimate game, World of Warcraft, a game that I would find sanctuary in for most of my teenage years. World of Warcraft. I didn't think much of it at the time, ignorant of the effect it would have on me in my later life.

While I was playing WoW after dinner at mother's house once, I heard my sister watching the new show Avatar: The Last Airbender on the television. I decided to check it out. I soon found myself really enjoying it. It was a magnificent story set in a fantasy world where people can control the power of the elements. Once I watched the first episode, I was hooked on the story. Prince Zuko was my favorite character; he was a banished prince who was trying to regain his rightful place in the world. I always related to him. Avatar: The Last Airbender became my favorite T.V. show.

Finding out about sex is one of the things that truly destroyed my entire life. Sex... the very word fills me with hate. Once I hit puberty, I would always want it, like any other boy. I would always hunger for it, I would always covet it, I would always fantasize about it. But I would never get it. Finding out about sex was just the beginning of my horrific downfall.

The only time I did care was when a group of popular Seventh Grade girls started teasing me, which hurt a lot. One of these girls was Monette Moio, a pretty blonde girl who was Ashton's younger sister. She must have thought I was an ultimate loser. I hated her so much, and I will never forget her. I started to hate all girls because of this. I saw them as mean, cruel, and heartless creatures that took pleasure from my suffering.

I was extremely unpopular, widely disliked, and viewed as the weirdest kid in the school.

They teased me because I was scared of girls, calling me names like "faggot". People also liked to steal my belongings and run away in an attempt to get me to chase after them. And I did chase after them in a furious rage, but I was so little and weak that they thought it was comical. I hated everyone at that school so much.

I developed a very high sex drive, and it would always remain like this. This was the start of hell for me. Going through puberty utterly doomed my existence. It condemned me to live a life of suffering and unfulfilled desires. Even at that young age, I felt depressed because I wanted sex, yet I felt unworthy of it. I didn't think I was ever going to experience sex in reality, and I was right. I never did. I was finally interested in girls, but there was no way I could ever get them. *And so my starvation began.*

I told everyone that I wanted to commit suicide. Father, Soumaya, Alex, and Karina talked to me for three hours to cheer me up. I sank into a major depression. I started to question why I was condemned to suffer such misery. I felt completely powerless.

I disliked all of the degenerate, low-class students there. They repulsed me.

I spent more time studying the world, seeing the world for the horrible, unfair place it is. I then had the revelation that just because I was condemned to suffer a life of loneliness and rejection, doesn't mean I am insignificant. I have an exceptionally high level of intelligence. I see the world differently than anyone else. Because of all of the injustices I went through and the worldview I developed because of them I must be destined for greatness. I must be destined to change the world, to shape it into an image that suits me!

And I developed extreme feelings of envy, hatred, and anger towards anyone who has a sex life. I saw them as the *enemy*.

Soumaya returned from Morocco, and she was very angry with me due to the way I acted while I was there. She effectively kicked me out of father's house, and because I was eighteen, she was allowed to. Father didn't do anything to stop her, being the weak man that he is. This is how it has always been. Father has always given Soumaya free reign to impose her rules on the household. He gave her all the power. This caused any respect I still had for my father to fade away completely. It was such a betrayal, to put his second wife before his eldest son. What kind of father would do that? *The bitch must be really good to him in bed,* I figured. *What a weak man.*

I repeatedly took pleasure in killing James's, Steve's, and Mark's characters as they tried to level up, as a petty form of revenge for them leaving me out of their group meetings years ago, and because I was jealous that Steve and Mark were more skilled at the game than I was.

By the time dinner arrived, I had already consumed three glasses of wine, and I had a fourth glass with the meal.

Everything's better with some wine in the belly, as a famous character from Game of Thrones would say.

I wished he could be a friend that felt the same way about the world that I did. But he wasn't that kind of person. He was a weakling.

When I got home, I began to cry because of all the emotions I experienced that night. My mother heard me and showed some concern, as she always did. She was used to me crying a lot, but she never understood why I was so miserable. I always had to explain it to her – that I was a lonely, miserable, unwanted virgin who women treated with disdain – but she could never grasp how severe this was to me. After all, how could she? She was a woman herself.

I named it the Day of Retribution. It would be a day in which I exact my ultimate retribution and revenge on all of the hedonistic scum who enjoyed lives of pleasure that they don't deserve. If I can't have it, I will destroy it. I will destroy all women because I can never have them. I will make them all suffer for rejecting me. I will arm myself with deadly weapons and wage a war against *all women and the men they are attracted to*. And I will slaughter them like the animals they are. If they won't accept me among them, then they are my enemies. They showed me no mercy, and in turn I will show them no mercy. The prospect will be so sweet, and justice will ultimately be served. And of course, I would have to die in the act to avoid going to prison.

My deep depression lasted well into the summer. My life stayed stagnant and miserable, and my hatred towards everyone, especially women, for depriving me of a happy life only grew stronger.

I would be a God to them. They will be the mice, and I will be the predator. I briefly fantasized about being a god as I looked down upon them all. I imagined having the power to destroy everything below with destructive, supernatural powers.

My first act of preparation was the purchase my first handgun. I did this quickly and hastily, at a local gun shop called Goleta Gun and Supply. I had already done some research on handguns, and I decided to purchase the Glock 34 semiautomatic pistol, an efficient and highly accurate weapon.

After I picked up the handgun, I brought it back to my room and felt a new sense of power. I was now armed. *Who's the alpha male now, bitches?*

People having a high opinion of me is what I've always wanted in life. It has always been of the utmost importance. This is why my life has been so miserable, because no one has ever had a high opinion of me.

On the Day of Retribution, the tables will indeed turn, I mused to myself.

I will be a god, and they will all be animals that I can slaughter.

The house had a swimming pool and was located in a nice enough area, though I would have still preferred it if my mother had gotten married to a wealthy man and moved into a mansion. I still continued to pester her to do this, and she still stubbornly refused. I will always resent my mother for refusing to do this. If not for her sake, she should have done it for mine. Joining a family of great wealth would have truly saved my life. I would have a high enough status to attract beautiful girlfriends and live above all of my enemies. All of my horrific troubles would have been eased instantly. It is very selfish of my mother to not consider this.

Once they see all of their friend's heads roll onto the street, everyone will fear me as the powerful god I am.

I am not part of the human race. Humanity has rejected me. The females of the human species have never wanted to mate with me, so how could I possibly consider myself part of humanity? Humanity has never accepted me among them, and now I know why. I am more than human. I am superior to them all. I am Elliot Rodger... Magnificent, glorious, supreme, eminent... Divine! I am the closest thing there is to a living god. Humanity is a disgusting, depraved, and evil species. It is my purpose to punish them all. I will purify the world of everything that is wrong with it. On the Day of Retribution, I will truly be a powerful god, punishing everyone I deem to be impure and depraved."

*   *   *   *   *

One can clearly see how Elliot added multiple destructive elements to his 'god-like' narcissistically driven staxis of hateful retribution and how those elements were reinforced by his negative life experiences and his developing perspectives of hatred for the world around him. What I found quite interesting is the effect video games had on him. With particular focus on his playing with real-life friends in a virtual reality where he could feel powerful and practice killing them. This experience served to blur the boundaries between fantasy and reality. He states that he used video games as his "sanctuary" where he constructed his very powerful battle character. I believe that "character" he created represented his hateful and unforgiving staxis. He had consciously incorporated his video game experience and the movie Alpha Male into his staxis of vengeance. They served as a part of the matrix and breeding ground for his distorted sense of reality.

This system of analysis, employing the gyroscopic theory to understand the basic issues involved can also be applied to the 1927 Bath School disaster, the 1966 University of Texas massacre, the 2007 Virginia Tech massacre, the 2012 Sandy Hook Elementary School massacre, the violence seen with prison guards who are given absolute power over inmates, the violent reactions seen with crowds that get provoked, etc.

215

In some cases, it has been postulated that the perpetrators of mass shootings had an antisocial personality disorder or a narcissistic personality disorder. I believe that this may be true in many instances, but likely is not a requirement. In the field of psychology, the term "dark triad" is used to describe three highly destructive personality traits (types). The dark triad consists of Narcissism, Psychopathy, and Machiavellianism. I will now discuss this in more depth.

Psychopath and sociopath are two mental health conditions that often get confused. However, they have distinct characteristics and distinctions. Both conditions can lead to dangerous and destructive behaviors and can cause serious harm to both individuals and society. Psychopaths and sociopaths share some traits, including lack of empathy, callousness, and a disregard for societal norms. However, the two conditions are distinct, with psychopaths being more calculating and manipulative, and sociopaths being more prone to impulsive and aggressive behavior. Treatments for both conditions typically involve psychotherapy and medication, though the approach may differ depending on the individual. At the heart of all personality disorders is rigidity that can be explained by the gyroscopic model.

The primary difference between a psychopath and a sociopath is the presence of a conscience in the latter. Psychopaths lack a conscience and are more likely to engage in manipulative and calculating behavior, while sociopaths may be more impulsive and aggressive. For example, a psychopath may steal from someone and not feel any remorse or guilt, while a sociopath may do the same but feel guilty afterwards. Another difference between psychopaths and sociopaths is their behavior towards other people.

Psychopaths may be more likely to charm their victims in order to get what they want, while sociopaths may be more likely to intimidate or threaten their victims. For example, a psychopath may use words and actions to manipulate someone into giving them money, while a sociopath may simply take it by force.

Antisocial Personality Disorder (Sociopathic Personality Disorder) is characterized by certain specific signs. The signs of a sociopathic personality often occur during early childhood and include cruelty towards animals or people, fire setting, initiating fights with others, impulsive and irresponsible behavior, stealing, disregard for the feelings of others, irritability, lack of regard for the safety of others, bullying, threatening, or intimidating others, late bed wetting, and failure to learn from disciplinary actions and punishment.

The characteristics of an antisocial personality (sociopath) include: superficial charm, narcissism, self-centered and self-important statements and behavior, need for stimulation, prone to boredom, deceptive behavior and frequent lying, conning and manipulative behavior, show little remorse or guilt over their bad behaviors, shallow emotional responses, callous emotions with a lack of empathy, lack of regard for the safety of others, frequently live-off of others, predatory behavior towards others, poor self-control, promiscuous sexual behavior, early behavioral problems, lack of realistic long term goals, impulsive lifestyle, irresponsible behavior, blaming others for their problems and actions, short-term relationships, juvenile delinquency, breaking parole or probation, and various criminal activities.

A person with a sociopathic personality can lead what appears to be, at least superficially, an ordinary life. They can have jobs, get married, have children, attend church, attend sporting events, etc. They can also break the law like anyone else. But their jobs and marriages usually don't last very long. Their lives are usually unstable and are often on the verge of chaos. A sociopath is usually a callous manipulator. They manipulate others by playing to their emotions. They typically have high verbal intelligence, can be quite bright, but they lack what is commonly referred to as "emotional intelligence". Due to their lack of ability to fully appreciate the emotions of others they often become isolated.

There is always an observable shallow quality to the emotional aspects of their stories. They have difficulty describing how they felt, why they felt that way, or how others may have felt and why, when telling their tales. Sociopaths with low intelligence or a poor education often end up serving time in jail more frequently than ones with higher education. Their lack of emotional insight and true empathy is the first good sign you may be dealing with a psychopath.

Yet another sign is a history of criminal behavior in which a person does not seem to learn from their wrong deeds, negative experiences, and adverse legal repercussions. Instead, they often obsess about ways of not getting caught in the future. Even more surprising has been the observation that many adult sociopaths do not seem to benefit from traditional counseling or therapy and that they may in fact commit crimes again and sooner because of it. It can simply call-forward or provoke their underlying malevolent major or subordinate staxis.

Narcissistic Personality Disorder is characterized by a pervasive pattern of grandiosity (in fantasy or behavior), an intense need for admiration, and a lack of empathy for others which usually begins during early adulthood and usually presents itself in a variety of contexts. The narcissist has a grandiose sense of self-importance and often exaggerates achievements and talents, expects to be recognized as superior. They are usually preoccupied with fantasies of unlimited success, power, brilliance, beauty, or ideal love.

Narcissists believe that they are "special" and unique and can only be understood by, or should only associate with, other special or high-status people or institutions. They usually have a sense of entitlement, with irrational expectations of especially favorable treatment or automatic compliance with his or her expectations. Takes advantage of others to have own needs met. They are often envious of others and/or believe that others are envious of them. They often show arrogant, self-important behaviors or attitudes.

Alfred Adler noted that vain people are concerned with one basic concern: 'What's in it for me?' Adler once stated, "adaptation to the community is the most important psychological function". It is felt that communal life is necessary for our collective survival. Adler felt that vain people fail to meet that standard and are in fact "the enemies of society".

Another very important area of concern to consider when analyzing this topic is that of Machiavellianism. According to the Oxford English Dictionary Machiavellianism is defined as "the employment of cunning and duplicity in statecraft or in general conduct", which was derived from the Italian Renaissance diplomat and writer Niccolò Machiavelli, who wrote *the book Principe (The Prince)*, among other works. The term Machiavellianism is a term used by social and personality psychologists to describe a person's tendency to be emotionally cool and detached.

The word Machiavellian used in modern psychology to describe one of the "dark triad" personalities, along with narcissism and psychopathy.[14] It is characterized by a person having a deceitful interpersonal style associated with cynical beliefs and pragmatic morality. It is felt that people with this tendency tend to be more able to detach from conventional morality and

218

to deceive and manipulate others. Some psychologists have considered Machiavellianism to be essentially a subclinical form of psychopathy, although recent research suggests that while Machiavellianism and psychopathy overlap, they are distinct personality constructs.[15] I believe that those 'personality constructs' are staxes in the gyroscopic model.

Machiavellianism has also been located within the circumplex, which consists of the two independent dimensions of agency and communion. Agency refers to motivation to succeed and to individuate the self, whereas communion refers to motivation to merge with others and to support group interests. Machiavellianism lies in the quadrant of the circumplex defined by high agency and low communion. Machiavellianism has been found to lie diagonally opposite from a circumplex construct called *self-construal*, a tendency to prefer communion over agency. This suggests that people identified as High Mach: do not simply wish to achieve they wish to do so at the expense of, or at least without regard for, others.[16]

During the 1960s, Richard Christie and Florence L. Geis developed a test for measuring a person's level of "Machiavellianism". Their MACH-IV test, a twenty-statement personality survey, became the standard self-assessment tool to measure Machiavellianism.[17] People scoring high on the scale 'high Machs' tended to endorse statements such as, "Never tell anyone the real reason you did something unless it is useful to do so" (No. 1), but not to endorse statements like: "Most people are basically good and kind" (No. 4), "There is no excuse for lying to someone else" (No. 7), or "Most people who get ahead in the world lead clean, moral lives" (No. 11). Machiavellianism has been found to be negatively correlated with the Agreeableness and Conscientiousness dimensions on the Neuroticism-Extraversion-Openness Personality Inventory - Revised (NEO-PI-R).

The NEO-PI-R was developed by Paul T. Costa, Jr. and Robert R. McCrae for use with adult men and women at least 17 years of age without any overt psychopathology.[18, 19] It is based on the Big Five personality model. The acronym OCEAN is used to remember the big five elements: Openness, Conscientiousness, Extraversion, Agreeableness, and Neuroticism. This is an area of study worth pursuing when attempting to understand the subject of personality organization.

Very often following a tragic event such as a school shooting, most of the emphasis is put on how to help the many victims of the shooting.

Focus on security and what led up to the incident are of prime concern. Subsequently, focus is put on what can be done to prevent such future tragedies. Unfortunately, little time is spent on examining the culture of violence in which we live and possible ways of changing it. For, until we have a cultural change towards a society of inclusiveness and peace, we will always witness such tragic events.

Using their scale, Christie and Geis conducted multiple screens and experiments that revealed the interpersonal strategies and behaviors of "High Machs" versus "Low Machs". The results of their studies have been widely replicated over subsequent years. Measured on the Mach-IV scale, males on the average are slightly more Machiavellian than females.

We live in a society rich in High Mach types. You know them well. The: type A 'dog-eat-dog' types. You run across them every day, they are the ones engaged in cut-throat business tactics, thinking: 'I've got to out-do the next guy', 'get them before they get you', or alternatively they engage us in road rage. This type of mentality is truly ingrained in our society. Our nation was born in violence and has lived by such a credo for quite some time.

Just prior to many of the episodes of mass murder it has often been reported, in retrospect, that the perpetrators had become withdrawn and more distant from the people with whom they were connected. When they reach this level, they lose their emotional connection to people and they begin to see people as 'things' rather than as people. It is easier to kill a 'thing' than to kill a person. People become just objects to deal with.

During 2002, the Machiavellianism scale of Christie and Geis was applied by behavioral game theorists Anna Gunnthorsdottir, Kevin McCabe and Vernon L. Smith in their search for explanations for the variance of observed behaviors in experimental games.[20] They examined the individual choices which did not correspond to assumptions of material self-interest captured by the standard Nash equilibrium prediction. They found that in a trust game, those with high MACH-IV scores tended to follow 'homo economicus' equilibrium strategies while those with low MACH-IV scores tended to deviate from the equilibrium and instead made choices that reflected widely accepted moral standards and social preferences.

So, what happens to these children when they begin to develop a distorted view of themselves, the world, and of right and wrong? Parents with children such as these usually end up feeling angry and frustrated with their children's failure to respond to the attempts that are made to control their negative behaviors. Their child is always in trouble and doesn't seem to learn from their mistakes. As a result of their bad behaviors, these children are often spoken to or reprimanded by their parents, other family members, teachers, principals, coaches, neighbors, clergy, and even by the police and judges. However, even with episodic interventions they frequently fail to learn and fail to change.

In cases like this, parents sometimes resort to emotional and even physical punishment and abuse. They have them placed in institutions to deal with their destructive behaviors. Such abuse has the potential for creating 'monsters' as those tortured children build resentment and begin to justify their hatred of people. What these children really need is support, guidance, clear instructions, emotional training, clear concrete choices, early humane behavioral consequences for their negative behaviors, and supervision.

Severe and repeated punishment in isolation is the worst thing that can be done. It serves as an impetus for the development of narcissistic, antisocial, and Machiavellian perspectives. Letting children like this run the streets unsupervised with other antisocial and potentially violent children is a disaster waiting to happen. Again, child abuse, especially severe emotional, physical and/or sexual abuse is a sure way to create a social misfit and an outright sociopathic monster.

Digging deeper I had to ask myself the question: Where did this all start? When did violence become a way of dealing with issues in America?

As I began to re-examine the literature regarding the many things I had been taught, in my numerous history classes over the years. Multiple inconsistencies became blatantly apparent. Those many inconsistencies I uncovered gave rise to many more critical questions. Questions that I felt compelled to find the answers to. For instance, as a child I had been taught that when European explorers first settled this land that it was done in a peaceful manner. That they were friendly and even altruistic towards Native Americans. This, as they sought a new place to live as a free people. Thanksgiving dinner was portrayed as an enchanting ubiquitous sign that all was peaceful, collaborative, and congenial between the settlers and Native Americans.

However, after closer scrutiny of the facts, I soon learned that America's story began quite differently. It had begun with the explorers pilfering this land from Native Americans. Christopher Columbus, who is now celebrated by a holiday was quite a brutal monster. Spanish explorer Columbus took the title 'Admiral of the Ocean Sea' and proceeded to unleash a reign of terror unlike anything seen before in history. When he was done, eight million Arawak Indians, virtually the entire native population of Hispaniola, the original Native people of the West Indies; had systematically been exterminated. They suffered torture, rape, murder, slavery, starvation, and/or disease at the hands of Christopher Columbus.

A Spanish missionary, Bartolome de las Casas, described eye-witness accounts of mass murder, torture and rape. Author, Barry Lopez[21], summarizing Las Casas' report wrote the following:

"One day, in front of Las Casas the Spanish dismembered, beheaded, or raped 3,000 people. 'Such inhumanities and barbarisms were committed in my sight,' he says, 'as no age can parallel....' The Spanish cut off the legs of children who ran from them. They poured people full of boiling soap. They made bets as to who, with one sweep of his sword, could cut a person in half. They loosed dogs that 'devoured an Indian like a hog, at first sight, in less than a moment.' They used nursing infants for dog food."[22]

Those who followed in Columbus's wake continued to commit many unspeakable, historically documented, atrocities against Native Americans. Those atrocious acts included physical violence, psychological trauma, rape, and murder against Native Americans. Andrew Jackson was another brutal monster who inflicted much woe and devastation on Native Americans. Of note, my maternal grandmother was part Arawak, and my paternal grandmother was raised by the Apache tribe. So, discovering this information later in life after having been misled or lied to by multiple educators had a highly significant and personal impact on me. It taught me the power of information. The power of lies and half-truths.

Further, in 1783 George Washington, America's first president, ordered that those Native Americans remaining within the areas of the initial 13 states be "hunted like beasts" and that a "war of extermination" be waged against those preventing access to desired lands, most notably the Ohio River Valley.[23] Washington fought for the British against the Indians, and received thousands of acres of native land as payment for his services.

On May 31, 1779, George Washington wrote to General Sullivan who was leading an expedition against the Iroquois: "The immediate object is their total destruction and devastation and the capture of as many person of every age and sex as possible, …ruin their crops…and prevent their planting more…lay waste all settlements around that the country may not be merely overrun but destroyed." [24]

The previous passages were an awakening for me. It exposed me to the fact of how my thoughts and beliefs had been purposely shaped in such a way as to obscure, distort, and even hide the truth. I was taught that I should respect George Washington, Christopher Columbus, and Andrew Jackson while attending elementary school. Now here's a few questions for you. Should I respect them? Should I be celebrating Columbus Day? Should I be celebrating a monster? Would that be psychologically healthy for me? Would it honor or insult my ancestors? Would this have a propensity to allow for furthering an environment of mistrust and foster anger and hostility?

However, we all know that world-wide there are those with malicious intent; most often driven by their greed and their quest for power. They find their sense of security through the domination and degradation of others. If an individual chose to target a group to serve as a sink for their anger, frustration, and hatred, and followed through with direct action then the origin of a new societal axis of hatred could be fostered. If they were to successfully fill people's heads with negative ideas, beliefs, images, propaganda, and perspectives about the targeted group (i.e., that the targets are bad, despicable, lazy, undesirable, sub-human animals) soon the gyroscopic forces of that individual's society would promote the absorption of the destructive information by that society's members.

Eventually this process would fully evolve to make the targeted hatred come to its full fruition. For once the rest of the members of that society absorb the negative ideas, images, beliefs, and fears they will begin to incorporate them into their own personal perspectives of the world. They will then identify with each other, further enhancing the power of their collective gyroscopic forces and newfound perspective of hatred toward the targeted group. Multiple discussions concerning the targeted group would then begin to emerge.

Negative assumptions and stereotypes would then be applied to the individual members of the targeted group. The individual members of that targeted group would then be placed under a spotlight and expectations of negative behavior from the various members of that targeted group would then emerge. Soon symbols would be developed to condense the hatred and twisted ideas of that society into a convenient portable package. History is replete with such examples: the swastika of the Nazis, the burning cross of the Ku Klux Klan (KKK), the double lightning bolts of Hitler's S.S., to name just a few.

Directly resulting from the open hatred directed at the targeted group, widespread general fear of the targeted group would eventually arise. The fear would then be used to further fuel the hatred felt by that society's members toward the targeted group. There would then be highlighted reporting of any observed negative behaviors by any individual member or members of the targeted group. This reporting would be accomplished by employing all sources of media: word-of-mouth, gossip, newspapers, magazines, books, movies, television programs and news broadcasts. This would serve to reinforce the manufactured negative stereotypes concerning the targeted group.

New laws would then emerge that would target the identified group. One of hatreds' most poisonous derivatives, narcissistic arrogance, would then arise to rear its ugly head. Those who spew their hatred and then espouse to be superior to the targeted group set the stage for the dehumanization of the targeted group. At this point the members of the targeted group are characterized as being sub-human or worse yet just animals. Any ideas or concepts counter to the newly established axis would be swiftly and reflexively rejected. Any person speaking up for the targeted group would immediately become suspect and would be ostracized from that society. Attempts would be made to discredit that person and to make them appear to be: 'misguided', 'crazy', 'disloyal', 'treasonous', 'weak', or simply just a 'sympathizer' of the targeted group.

This derisive approach of systematically targeting groups has been used worldwide for centuries. History is unfortunately filled with multiple clear examples of this form of horrid behavior. The atrocities of the Nazi Regime, African American slavery, the genocide of Native Americans, the Civil the horrific barbaric actions of the K.K.K., the indentured servitude of the Chinese railroad workers, the Mexican-American war, the Japanese internment camps, genocide in Croatia, South African Apartheid, genocide in Rwanda, and countless other worldwide cases of genocide, slavery, and 'ethnic cleansing' serve as examples of such atrocious behavior. The list goes on and on!

Google the term genocide and you will quickly find that history is replete with examples. Those many dark stains that have been left on the soul of humanity are, rightfully so, indelible. They should remain indelible to remind us of our own destructive potential. Perhaps to serve as a monument to the depths of depravity that humanity can reach when such forces of evil arise.

However, even with the lessons of the past to reflect upon, worldwide examples of ethnic cleansing continue to exist. We find ourselves engaged in a daily subliminal war of negative symbols directed at each other. I firmly believe that this unspoken process underlies one of the major sources of stress and suffering for many of the people of our world. At the risk of sounding redundant, we all must face and deal with the true facts of our past. The philosopher George Santayana once stated, "Those who cannot remember the past are condemned to repeat it."

Throughout the Millenia, in their quest for power, countless rulers and dictators have used gyroscopic forces to their advantage. Alexander the Great, Napoleon, Hannibal, Attila the Hun, Hitler, Mussolini, Hirohito, Mao, Lenin, Ide Amin Dada, Saddam Hussein, and Ivan the Terrible: just to name a few. All of them with their desire for absolute power channeled their aggressive and sexual drives through their self-developed staxis of evil. They attached their desires to various purposes and goals and then asserted their wills through a clear structure of command. Their method, which follows, is still in use today.

First, identify major problems in one's society and a group of people to serve as a target for hatred. One can use either an internal or an external group of people to serve as the identified target. Proceed to make the identified group: the identified cause of the major problems in one's society. Then, fill the masses heads with information, beliefs, propaganda, and perspectives that support one's goals and platform of hatred against the identified group.

Then attach the ideas, beliefs, and perspectives to emotions, such as anger or fear. Hitler was particularly masterful with this aspect. As people absorb and incorporate these elements into their mind's inner wheel, they will begin to align themselves with the axis of that ruler or dictator. Not

225

only will they begin to identify themselves as agreeing with the major axis platform, but also as an integral part of that dictator's new regime.

Next, all rulers and dictators employ the use of symbols and stereotypes to unify the members of their regime. The symbols are used to market small packages of hatred to individuals and groups. Those symbols become both feared by the targets of the hatred, while being revered by the perpetrators of the hatred. As things proceed, the dictator's masses begin to feel a newfound sense of power and a greater sense of stability. A rise in their self-esteem to the point of overt arrogance.

Eventually a core group forms that establishes themselves as the elite members of that society. At this point things are well on the way towards the establishment of a new sustained axis of power. As the elite group begins to make arbitrary statements, rules, and decisions they start to disenfranchise some of the general members of the group. Attempts are made to keep 'those people' who would speak counter to the axis power's perspective in 'their place'. This serves to protect the elite members of that society, by weaving, a protective shroud of fear to control the behaviors of the general members.

As gyroscopic forces take a stronger hold the members of that regime will begin to reject any ideas or beliefs that run counter to the new regime's axis. Historically speaking, when any person has dared to question or to counter their axis power's dictums with ideas and perspectives of their own; they have been dealt with swiftly and harshly. Most often this has been accomplished through their public humiliation, intimidation, torture, and/or execution. Whatever its form, the punishment has most often been both swift, complete and effective.

Most of the loyal members of the new axis would feel fully justified in protecting their regime by carrying out such punitive actions, no matter how horrific. This appalling behavior is mostly reflexive in nature and is fueled and guided by the natural laws of gyrotropism. Thus, it is always the expected outcome in any society driven by fear, sadistic intent, greed, or simply by the love of power. The expected use of punishment to counter public dissention is known by most people at an intuitive level. Thus, people have learned through the ages to be quite wary of directly confronting any established regime, form of government, or axis power.

It is this fear of retaliation by the governing members of the major axis that silences the masses, and unfortunately this can thereby inhibit them from participating in the active prevention of corrupt, evil, and immoral governments. However, people's ability to tolerate a corrupt and abusive government for extended periods is thankfully time limited. It is inevitable that when people are placed under an unjust and abusive government that rebellion will eventually arise.

Should rebellion occur, violence would very likely be associated with that rebellion. That violence would be directed at the rigidity fostered by the inherent gyroscopic forces of the regime in question. There would also be an intellectual process pursued by the leaders of the revolt. This process often begins by analyzing what information has been used to manipulate the masses of people. Using that information, a set counter-information (counterintelligence) is then developed to add to the 'inner wheels' of their supporters to combat the brainwashing of the regime. This would initially lead to cognitive dissonance which would then have to be processed by everyone.

As the new axis continues to recruit members and evolve into a new structure, it begins to strengthen itself as an axis that is directly counter to the force of the pre-existing abusive regime. The new axis almost always asserts the edict that they plan to totally abolish the previous existing abusive regime. This dynamic has been played-out repeatedly throughout history. It lies at the core of the cycling of governments over time.

Another far reaching example of the development of an evil oppressive system, with all its sinister outcomes, occurred right here in American with the formation of the eugenics movement. Few people realize how highly developed, wide-spread, and entrenched the eugenics movement became in the U.S. during the early 1900's. The eugenics movement supported the idea of forced sterilization of selected U.S. citizens and believed in selective breeding of citizens to ensure the eventual perfection of the white race.[25]

In fact, the eugenics movement ideology was very heavily embedded in American culture during the 1920's and 1930's; many years before Hitler's rise to power. For instance, high school students would go to their cinemas to see the film "Stork" which supported the idea of forced sterilizations.[26] People were introduced to the idea that there was a need to guard the pure white American gene pool. In reality that pool was already quite diverse, with whites having come from multiple regions of the world (England, Europe, etc.).

A 'scientific approach' was taken by many 'experts' who attempted to put in place systems that ensured the preservation of the 'pure' white race. More than just providing the scientific roadmap for Hitler's monstrous oppression, America funded Germany's eugenic institutions. By 1926, Rockefeller had donated some $410,000 (almost $4 million in today's money) to hundreds of German scientists engaged in eugenics research. In May 1926, Rockefeller awarded $250,000 toward creation of the Kaiser Wilhelm Institute for Psychiatry. Among the leading psychiatrists at the German Psychiatric Institute was Ernst Ridin, who became director and eventually a co-architect of Hitler's system of medical oppression.[27, 28]

A branch of the Kaiser Wilhelm Institute's complex of eugenics institutions was the Institute for Brain Research. Since 1915, it had operated out of a single room. Everything changed when Rockefeller money arrived in 1929. A grant of $317,000 allowed the institute to construct a major building and take center stage in German race biology. The institute received additional grants from the Rockefeller Foundation during the next several years.

Eighteen solutions were explored in a Carnegie-supported, 1911, Preliminary Report of the Committee of the Eugenic Section of the American Breeder's Association, to Study and to Report on the Best Practical Means for Cutting-Off the "Defective Germ Plasm" in the Human Population. Point No. 8 was euthanasia. The most commonly suggested method of 'eugenicide' in the United States was a lethal chamber, or public, locally operated gas chambers.[29]

Cold Spring Harbor Laboratory, Long Island, was a eugenics center founded by the Carnegie Institution. Among its activities was the stockpiling of millions of index cards on ordinary Americans, as researchers carefully plotted the removal of families, bloodlines, and whole populations. From Cold Spring Harbor, eugenics advocates agitated in the legislatures of America, as well as the nation's social service agencies and associations. Several organizations in the United States were prominent in organizing and enforcing eugenics research: the Eugenics Record Office (ERO), the American Breeders Association (ABA), the Race Betterment Foundation, and the American Eugenics Society (AES).[30, 31]

The ERO, established in 1910 at Cold Spring Harbor, New York, probably did the most to promote eugenics research. ERO founder Charles

Davenport published several influential booklets that helped standardize nomenclature for pedigree studies. Budding eugenics researchers convened at Cold Spring Harbor each summer to learn how to conduct "field work": interviewing subjects. While some eugenicists privately supported practices such as euthanasia or even genocide, legally-mandated sterilization was the most radical policy supported by the American eugenics movement.[32]

A number of American physicians performed sterilizations even before the surgery was legally approved, though no reliable accounting of the practice exists prior to passage of sterilization laws. Indiana enacted the first law allowing sterilization on eugenic grounds in 1907, with Connecticut following soon after. Despite these early statutes, sterilization did not gain widespread popular approval until the late 1920s.

After 1914, courses on eugenics were being offered at some of America's leading universities. Harvard, Columbia, Cornell, and Brown Universities were among those who listed courses that included eugenics. In the 1920s, the National Association's Committee on Racial Well-Being sponsored programs to help college teachers integrate eugenic content into their courses. By 1928, eugenics was a topic in 376 separate college courses, which enrolled approximately 20,000 students.

A content analysis of high school science texts published between 1914 and 1948 indicates that a majority presented eugenics as a legitimate science. These texts embraced Galton's concept of differential birthrates between the biological "fit" and "unfit", training high school students that immigration restriction, segregation, and sterilization were worthy policies to maintain in American culture.[33]

Advocacy in favor of sterilization was one of Harry Laughlin's first major projects at the Eugenics Record Office. In 1914, he published a Model Eugenical Sterilization Law that proposed to authorize sterilization of the "socially inadequate"; those people supported in institutions or "maintained wholly or in part by public expense". The law encompassed the "feebleminded, insane, criminalistic, epileptic, inebriate, diseased, blind, deaf, deformed and dependent...including orphans, near-do-wells, tramps, the homeless and paupers".[34]

By the time the Model Law was published in 1914, twelve states had enacted sterilization laws. By 1924, approximately 3,000 people had been involuntarily sterilized in America; the vast majority (2,500) in California.

David S. Arnold, M.D.

That year Virginia passed a Eugenical Sterilization Act based on Laughlin's Model Law. It was adopted as part of a cost-saving strategy to relieve the tax burden in a state where public facilities for the "insane" and "feebleminded" had experienced rapid growth.

The law was also written to protect physicians who performed sterilizing operations from malpractice lawsuits. Virginia's law asserted that "heredity plays an important part in the transmission of insanity, idiocy, imbecility, epilepsy and crime." It focused on "defective persons" whose reproduction represented "a menace to society".[35]

Borrowing from Laughlin's Model Law, the German Nazi government adopted a law in 1933 that provided the legal basis for sterilizing more than 350,000 people. Laughlin proudly published a translation of the German Law for the Prevention of Defective Progeny in "The Eugenical News". A copy of the Model Law is provided in Appendix B. It is worth reading.

On June 30, 1936 the University of Heidelberg, in Germany, awarded several 550th Anniversary honorary degrees to 43 foreigners. Among the honored group of foreigners were six Americans: three of whom were: Professor Kirsopp Lake, of Harvard University, Professor Harry H. Laughlin, of the Carnegie Institution, Cold Spring Harbor, and Ferdinand Thun of Redding.[36] Laughlin was awarded an honorary degree from the University of Heidelberg as a tribute for his work in "the science of racial cleansing".[30]

In 1918, Paul Popenoe, the Army venereal disease specialist during World War I, co-wrote with Roswell Hill Johnson the widely used textbook, "Applied Eugenics", which argued, that "from an historical point of view, the first method which presents itself is execution . . . Its value in keeping up the standard of the race should not be underestimated". In the U.S., during 1933 alone, at least 1,278 coercive sterilizations were performed, 700 on women.

California's two leading sterilization mills in 1933 were: Sonoma State Home with 388 operations and Patton State Hospital with 363 operations. Other sterilization centers included: the Agnew's, Mendocino, Napa, Norwalk, Stockton, and Pacific Colony state hospitals.

Carrie Buck, a seventeen-year-old girl from Charlottesville, Virginia, was picked as the first person to be sterilized. Carrie had a child, but was not married. Her mother Emma was already a resident at an asylum, the Virginia Colony for the Epileptic and the Feebleminded. Officials at the

230

Virginia Colony stated that Carrie and her mother shared the hereditary traits of "feeblemindedness" and "sexual promiscuity".

To those who believed that such traits were genetically transmitted, Carrie fit the law's description as a "probable potential parent of socially inadequate offspring". A legal challenge was arranged on Carrie's behalf to test the constitutional validity of the law.[34, 35]

At her trial, several witnesses offered evidence of Carrie's inherited "defects" and those of her mother Emma, Colony Superintendent Dr. Albert Priddy testified that Emma Buck had "a record of immorality, prostitution, untruthfulness and syphilis." His opinion of the Buck family more generally was: "These people belong to the shiftless, ignorant, and worthless class of anti-social whites of the South."

Although Harry Laughlin never met Carrie, he sent a written deposition echoing Priddy's conclusions about Carrie's "feeblemindedness" and "moral delinquency". Sociologist Arthur Estabrook, of the Eugenics Record Office, traveled to Virginia to testify against Carrie. He and a Red Cross nurse examined Carrie's baby Vivian and concluded that she was "below average" and "not quite normal."[34, 35]

Relying on these comments, the judge concluded that Carrie should be sterilized to prevent the birth of other "defective" children. The decision was appealed to United States Supreme Court, Justice Oliver Wendell Holmes Jr., himself a student of eugenics, wrote the formal opinion for the Court in the case of Buck v. Bell (1927). His opinion repeated the "facts" in Carrie's case, concluding that a "deficient" mother, daughter, and granddaughter justified the need for sterilization.

The historic decision included the now infamous words. "It is better for all the world if instead of waiting to execute degenerate offspring for crime, or to let them starve for their imbecility, society can prevent those who are manifestly unfit from continuing their kind...Three generations of imbeciles are enough".[34, 35]

Historical research has revealed that Carrie Buck's sterilization was based on a false "diagnosis" and her defense lawyer conspired with the lawyer for the Virginia Colony to guarantee that the sterilization law would be upheld in court. Carrie's illegitimate child was not the result of promiscuity; she had been raped by a relative of her foster parents.

Ironically, school records also prove that Carrie was not "feebleminded. Her first-grade report card showed that Carrie was a solid "B" student, had received an "A", in deportment, and had been on her school's honor roll. The Buck v. Bell decision supplied a precedent for the eventual sterilization of approximately 8300 Virginians.

The opinion that eventually challenged the sterilization law, in the case of Skinner vs. Oklahoma (1942), was written by Justice William O. Douglas. He highlighted the inequity of Oklahoma's law by noting that "a three-time chicken thief could be sterilized while a three-time embezzler could not". Douglas stated: "We have not the slightest basis for inferring that the inheritability of criminal traits follows the neat legal distinctions which the law has marked between those two offenses." See Appendix B for more details.

The 1942 ruling created an uneasy legal atmosphere regarding existing mass sterilizations and thereby put a heavy damper on sterilization rates which had boomed since the Buck v. Bell ruling of 1927. However, Skinner v. Oklahoma is often erroneously credited with ending all compulsory sterilization in the United States. The only types of sterilization which the Skinner ruling immediately ended were punitive sterilizations. It did not specifically comment on the compulsory sterilization of the mentally disabled or mentally ill. Thus, it was not a strict overturning of the Court's ruling in Buck v. Bell (1927).

After the discovery of Nazi atrocities at the conclusion of WWII, which included the compulsory sterilization of 450,000 people over a ten year period and done in the name of eugenics, eugenics as an ideology lost almost all public favor. The Nazi sterilization law drew heavy inspiration from American statutes; and the close association between eugenics and racism.

Despite the Skinner case, and realization of Nazi atrocities, sterilization of people in institutions for the mentally ill and mentally retarded continued through the mid 1970's. At one time or another, 33 states had statutes under which more than 64,000 Americans endured involuntary sterilization.

Most of the over 64,000 sterilizations performed in the United States that fell under the protection of eugenics legislation were not performed in prisons or performed on convicted criminals; punitive sterilizations made up only negligible amounts of the total operations performed, because most states and prison officials were uneasy about their legal status. The last known forced sterilization in the United States occurred in 1981 in Oregon. The Buck v: Bell precedent allowing sterilization of the so-called "feebleminded" has never been over-ruled.[34-36]

So why did I discuss all of the above? Today we see the formation of various political factions in American politics. They, too, take advantage of rhetoric to build a sustainable political momentum. As time passes, any such entity may eventually gain the critical momentum required to become fully entrenched. This can be quite dangerous in societies where biases are allowed to exist and worse yet are encouraged to grow. It is everyone's responsibility to monitor and prevent such biases from leading to the atrocities we have witnessed in the past. As the human genome project progresses there is room for great evils to arise.[37, 38]

What further compounds the circumstance is that people tend to take the easiest emotional path to follow. I noted earlier that there is a natural human tendency to be emotionally lazy. Thus, we are prone to always take the shortest and easiest emotional path through life. Especially: if that easier path is fully prepared and structured for us. The path of hatred towards people, groups, and systems can be such a path. We tend to lump people into groups based on race, ethnicity, color, religion, creed, occupation, nationality, political affiliation, political ideology, body type, age, gender, sexual preference, hair color, place of residence (neighborhood, city state), abilities, disabilities, likes, dislikes, and on-and-on.

Quite simply, it is easier to hate an entire group than to spend the time and emotional energy that it takes to get to know each member of a particular group on an individual basis. And only then: to decide if and if it is appropriate to be angry with or to be fully accepting of a particular individual. And: to what degree. Take into consideration all the energy that must be expended to do so. In addition to this, as I had mentioned previously, we are strongly gyroscopic for a reason.

We wish to remain 'stable' with our old beliefs, ideas, views of others, and perspectives of the world. This is a lot to overcome when an easier path is presented for us to traverse. Consider the tremendous counter-energy of a person's internal gyroscopic forces that by their very nature tend to resist any attempts made at introspection, flexibility, and change.

When an individual is fed poisonous gossip, ideas, views and information, concerning a particular person, group, doctrine, or event in a manipulative fashion, it can create the emotion of hatred and in turn instigate the creation of a new subordinate staxis of hatred, and Thus, result in the eventual "brainwashing" of that individual. It is the basis for the "mind control" power of cults and of evil empires and entities.

Consider the following perspectives. The generally accepted impetus for the formation of a democracy is that all members of that given society have an equal voice as to how things are to be handled by their given society. There is room for the open expression of ideas, opinions, concepts, and beliefs as people decide how things should be done or handled. As time passes, those core beliefs, ideas, concepts, opinions, mores, perspectives, etc., serve as a foundation for the establishment of general rules and laws, which Thus, in turn lead to a structured set of expected and enforced societal behaviors.

The members of that society then collectively agree to live by the rules and laws imposed. These enforced expectations add to the dynamic forces that power the inner wheel of that government. In keeping with the gyroscopic model, that government by natural law must eventually begin to resist any new ideas or perspectives that attempt to shift its established axis. The system then becomes rigid. When new perspectives arise, particularly when driven by individual needs, this can cause a sense of instability for the governing system.

Wide-spread cognitive dissonance can arise with its accompanying mental discomfort. As people begin to use selective pieces of information to support their views or stand on issues, the cognitive dissonance begins to intensify. As noted previously, there is usually a strong emotional urge to resolve, as soon as possible, the anxiety and stress that result from cognitive dissonance.

Typically, this is done by adding "consonant cognitions" that are consistent with one or the other of the dissonant elements or reducing dissonance by making it a smaller part of the total, or more directly, by changing one of the dissonant cognitions. This leads to self-persuasion with a resultant distortion of objective reality. So strong, can be the distortion of reality, that the person can enter the domain of frank psychosis. As an aside, bigots and racists are psychopathic in this sense. Racists reach a point where their hatred is so ingrained and rigid, that they are incapable of seeing others from a reality-based perspective.

As things progress in this democratic society under question, any new ideas presented are very often reflexively rejected as they counter the force and energy of that government's 'spinning wheel': gyroscopic momentum. Systems can develop tremendous inertia against change. When opposing views arise in the form of direct rebuttals of the new ideas; this leads to a further sense of instability and loss of cohesion. This is often why politicians very often cannot state what they really think or feel concerning a particular topic or subject, as they are restrained by the gyroscopic force of their governing system and that of the voters of their given society. They cannot be seen to talk outside the popular politic. That is, if they wish to be re-elected.

However, after all consideration is given to a specific topic, a final political decision on the topic at hand, pro or con, must be made. Here, there is a natural crossover between business and politics. There is a dictum in business: that one should decide democratically, taking into consideration all the members concerns and ideas, but implement autocratically; in a dictatorial fashion. This without showing concern for any rebuttals that may occur. This then allows for the system's 'gyroscope' to maintain its previously established axis, or to instead, develop a new axis. This approach allows for the formal process and procedures that can be used to establish clear direction.

Though all may not be happy with the final decisions made, most are often happy with the restored sense of stability that often follows the final decision-making process. This sense of stability often brings a greater sense of personal safety and security to the individual members of the group. I noted that all governments by natural law must eventually begin to resist any new ideas or perspectives that attempt to shift their established axis of power. New ideas are reflexively rejected. Thus, begging the golden question as to whether a truly long-term, self-sustaining, form of true democracy is ever possible: given the powerful gyroscopic forces involved.

A university study was performed entitled "Testing Theories of American Politics: Elites, Interest Groups and Average Citizens," where researchers compared 1,800 different U.S. policies that were put in place by politicians between 1981 and 2002 to the type of policies preferred by the average and wealthy American, or to special interest groups. Researchers concluded that U.S. policies are formed more by special interest groups than by politicians properly representing the will of the general people, including the lower-income class: Thus, they concluded that our government should be considered an oligarchy and not a democracy. One finding in the study: The U.S. government now represents the rich and powerful, not the average citizen, United Press International reported.

"The central point that emerges from our research is that economic elites and organized groups representing business interests have substantial independent impacts on U.S. government policy, while mass-based interest groups and average citizens have little or no independent influence," the study found. The study also found: "When a majority of citizens disagrees with economic elites and/or with organized interests, they generally lose." If a truly democratic society is to exist, there must be a powerful counterforce that implores the need for open-mindedness and flexibility.

People who master themselves can reach great heights and achieve great things in our world. However, the gyroscopic effect not only lies at the core formation of great people, but also at the core formation of potentially monstrous ones as well. It can lead to the formation of an individual who's major staxis and/or subordinate staxis is one of apparent pure evil. It is important to understand this, for all it takes is just a cheering warm body, even if completely devoid of any form of intellect, to mindlessly jump-on-board with them. All coups and dictatorships have this manipulation of the gyroscopic process at their core.

Therefore, it is imperative to be careful of what one constructs, for we all will ultimately have to pay the price if things go wrong. It is critical that this process be fully understood by all, to help prevent incidents of such as the historical incidents of inhumanity from occurring in the future. The only way to prevent any or all the devastation and destruction perpetrated by evil individuals or regimes is to prevent them from ever happening in the first place.

So, the question is how can we use the information provided Thus, far to specifically prevent such atrocities in the future? By taking the following steps:

> First: Education is critical. By being ever-aware of the gyroscopic dynamics, people will be less likely to get caught-up in a web of inflexible, short-sighted, divisive, and destructive politics. It requires all citizens to constantly monitor what is being said or proposed for their society

and work towards personal growth. Choosing to ignore or passively accept past lies and distortions of the truth leads to the creation of an environment conducive to the birth and nurturance of oppression.

Second: By being ever vigilant to actively prevent any individual or system that proposes to oppress any person or group through the use of distorted facts and stereotypes. To get children who are evidencing signs of an antisocial or narcissistic personality disorder supportive mental health help early, rather than waiting for tragedy to strike. To help them to build a healthy self-esteem and to be a vital part of society.

Third: By personally taking the responsibility for not seeing people as simply part of a group; but instead as individuals. We tend to be lazy, and it is easier for us to lump people into groups and categories rather than spend the time and energy it takes to get to know each person we meet as an individual.

These three steps would be a great start towards a more balanced, supportive and loving society and indeed world-at-large. But it requires people's buy-in. Whether that will happen or not rests with individuals who care enough to establish such a societal axis of responsibility through education and enlightenment. We truly need to make the welfare of all of humanity our core ethic. Until peace is our true philosophy, we will always have violence.

By reviewing the steps taken by the mass murderers discussed at the beginning of this chapter one can clearly see the steps they took as they added negative elements to their inner wheels to construct their malicious subordinate staxes which were driven by their narcissism and supported by their Sociopathic and Machiavellian attitudes. Elliot Rodger's manifesto should be read by all clinicians, law enforcement agents, teachers, politicians, or anyone who is interested in understanding and preventing such violence in the future.

I feel that if children and adolescents who are in psychological trouble are identified very early on during their development, *and there are always warning signs*, then responsible adults can intervene. If responsible adults were to take an active role, via mentorship, in re-integrating these children into the school population, while seeking effective therapy to work on their self-esteem; such horrific events would be much less likely.

If we were to recognize children who feel ostracized, bullied, isolated and take the responsibility to take them under their wing and ensure that the child felt an important part of the fabric of their community this would go a very long way in reducing the probability of such tragic events. The process of re-integration through active listening, guidance, participation, and support would ideally disrupt and counter the formation of a pathologic staxis in those children identified.

Today, we hand our children violent video games and movies to fill their hearts and minds with distorted ideas of humanity and justice. The video games treat people as objects where the goal is to, coldly, devoid of any compassion or emotion, shoot and kill them. This approach to rearing our children will lead only to future horrific atrocities, gloom, and doom for us all. For it creates an environment: that provides the destructive elements necessary for the development of a staxis of inhumanity and evil. Once formed that evil staxis can not only go unchecked, but it can be nurtured by such an environment. This breeding ground must be shut down! This requires a massive cultural change towards peace and co-existence.

We can control the number of illegal guns on our streets, we can increase the security levels at our schools, and we can be more vigilant at identifying potential perpetrators of violence, but it will not stop the violence. What has the greatest potential for stopping such acts of violence is for responsible individuals to deal with each child on an individual basis to promote the formation of a healthy staxis as opposed to an unhealthy pathologic staxis. This takes time, caring, guidance, and love. Also, what is needed is a cultural overhaul towards a society of peace instead of one that nurtures a 'dog-eat-dog'...'go ahead...make my day' mentality of violence. Whenever I am told that one person, or group, or religion, or society is responsible for all of the world's violence, my reply is that psychopathy is an equal opportunity employer.

The sixties movement's mantras of "peace" and "love that were touted by the young as desirable traits for our society to fully adopt. Somehow that sentiment has fallen to the wayside. Perhaps that peace movement fell victim to the entrenched negative gyroscopic forces of a self-serving violence prone American society. Tragically, we lost a movement which might have transformed our society for the better. Hopefully: we will regain the perspective of love and peace someday. Hopefully, we will see love and caring as a source of strength, rather than as a source of weakness or vulnerability. Every time I see a young person driving their car with a peace symbol affixed to their bumper, I feel a sense of hope.

Again, this chapter serves purely as an introduction to a subject matter which deserves deep study and several books in its own right!

23

Application to the Community

ON THE EVENING OF APRIL 4, 1968, MY MOTHER ENTERED THE ROOM crying profusely after hearing a tragic news report. It was the day that Rev. Martin Luther King, Jr. was assassinated. Being a child at the time I failed to fully comprehend the full personal and historical significance of that moment. Nor did I fully appreciate my mother's reaction to the news. However, I felt the gravity of what had just happened through my mother's emotions. Her reaction greatly unsettled me. It proved to be a truly sad day for all of mankind. My limited life experiences had helped to shape me for many assorted things, but nothing had prepared me for my mother's reaction. Her reaction most certainly sharpened my ambition to explore and understand the things that affect us all.

I felt compelled to search for the underlying order that could explain why things exist and happen as they do. I desired a deeper understanding of the people and systems that surrounded me. This, if not simply just for clarity's sake alone: for mental growth and greater peace of mind. As I soon discovered, historical review and analysis can often provide some of the groundwork required for the development of greater clarity. This chapter presents a very brief exploration of the possible application of the gyroscopic theory to better understand ourselves and our society. Having been raised as a member of the African American community, of which I am most familiar, I will focus on that community. My hope here is to show a practical application of my gyroscopic model and the utility it has to offer.

Members of the African American community live in a post-slavery, post-segregation, post-civil-rights atmosphere. It is quite important to understand the impact that past events have had on African Americans as a people. There are many who suffer from the damage done by the disruption of our basic family units and our traditional community support systems. There are those who suffer the after-effects of inter-generational post-traumatic stress disorder (P.T.S.D.) and depression. There are those who live with a sustained pattern of repetitive trauma. They are never able to enter the "post" phase of P.T.S.D., as the occurrence of traumatic events never ceases.

There are those of us who exist with a "plantation mentality" as if they are still living in slavery. They live with a staxis of feeling inferior and are always wondering what might offend the majority (i.e., 'descendent slave masters', 'bigots'). They continue the behaviors ingrained by slavery while thinking that they are living as "free" men and women. They live in total blindness of themselves and of the world-at-large. When confronted with their maladaptive behaviors, they may be prone to justify their behaviors in a dismissive, angry, and/or hostile fashion.

It can be helpful to understand some of the effects of trauma from an impact on the brain perspective. Through the process of evolution, our brains have developed from the earlier core basic structures located deep within our brains. Those structures contain our *limbic system* which controls our sexual and aggressive drives. The more advanced parts of our brains (the outer cortex) contain our intellectual functions: concentration, language ability, orientation to the environment, judgment, future planning, memory, reading, writing, and mathematic abilities, among many others.

The goal of slavery was to remove people's ability for free thought. For the surest and most powerful way to oppress any person or people is to suppress or obliterate their higher levels of cortical function. To regress them to an animalistic state of being left only with their core sexual and aggressive drives. If you can prevent people from being cerebral, and then restrict them to act only as their base-selves, then you can treat them like animals. By shutting down the cerebral function, the individual is stuck with only their base (sexual and aggressive) drives to work with. At this point they can easily be completely separated from their history and their culture. Families can be disrupted. Entire communities can be fragmented with the underlying goal being to divide and conquer.

Unfortunately, today we see evidence of such a process with some of our young men and women. Particularly with respect to some of our young African American men and women. This subgroup of our youth's focus is predominantly on sex and violence with no comprehensive view of the future. This focus is reflected and broadcast through current day music videos. Rap music videos, in particular. This complex subject will be covered in further depth in the next chapter. In that pursuit many of our young have abandoned their pursuit of diverse cerebral mastery. They have abandoned the pursuit of total self-perfection.

So, the obvious question here is how can we use this information to deal with this problem?

First: Effective quality education is vital! By being made aware of the intended effects of past oppression individuals can become cognizant of their situation and can begin to heal from damage already done. We must teach our children from an early age to be more cerebral: in counter distinction to becoming more sexual and/or aggressive. Several groups who have faced past oppression (i.e., portions of the African American community, the Jewish community, the Islamic community, the Asian community, the post-WWII Japanese community, the LGBQT community, etc.) have responded to their oppression by raising their children to be cerebral. They teach them to master (suppress) their sexual and aggressive drives through education, religion and/or culture to succeed in this world. All our children must be taught the great value and long-term benefits of education and of being intellectuals, while keeping it in balance with their spirituality and their ability to form intimate relationships with their eventual partners.

Second: By being ever attentive to our children's thoughts, feelings and needs. By being actively involved and fully participatory. We must provide structure, guidance, proper role-modeling, and mentorship for our children.

Third: By instilling in our children, the concept of taking personal responsibility for their own actions and eventually their own self-creation: they can grow to become independent, self-sufficient, self-reliant, and family and community oriented and connected individuals.

These three steps would be a great start towards a more balanced, supportive and loving society. But it requires many people's buy-in. It rests with individuals who care enough to establish such an enlightened environment for our children.

In view of my newfound insights and with my having been raised in the Catholic Church, I felt it was necessary to explore how information might have been used to shape and impact my spiritual beliefs and practices as well. In order to do so, I had to re-examine the foundations of the Catholic Church. Indeed, I had to examine several of the many religious groups and organizations of our country and of the world at large to gain a greater comparative perspective.

It was a tremendous internal struggle to allow myself to think the unthinkable as I examined the information before me. It was considered somewhat taboo to do so. Truly unholy. Even sacrilegious! As an act of abject evil to think in such disrespectful ways. I had discovered during my search a historical parallel that was used during slavery. Fear had been used to draw a line that should not be crossed. No questions should be asked. No thinking was allowed. No one should ever dare to question the slave master.

Having been raised to be a devout Catholic, I had to force myself to ask some very powerful and difficult questions. Some of those questions I am quite certain would have been considered to be Anti-American by some. Some might consider my words to be blasphemous or evil. But the questions had to be asked for the sake of truth. For instance: How can one build churches, synagogues, temples, or mosques on stolen ground and then call them sacred houses of God? If the very physical foundation of a church was literally stolen (through sinful violence, torture, and rape), what type of God would be worshipped in such a place? What type of God would have allowed for such horrific acts of inhumanity?

Where was this God while hundreds of thousands of innocent people were being raped, beaten, dismembered, monstrously fed to animals, and slaughtered? Many more questions arose. I knew early on, however, that this was certainly not a God that I would ever want to worship. I know that these questions and their answers employ harsh words, but those words lie in the harsh truths of the past. In fact, these observations and realizations had the effect of propelling me on my quest for even greater truth.

They opened my eyes to how brainwashed we all are and how avidly we cling to our own world of fantasy for a sense of security. Indeed, it is deeply appalling how fundamentally unsound and inherently flawed and untrue our various perspectives can be even when presented with evidence of such past acts of depravity. Are you one who can view and deal with the truth? If so, the information and insights presented in this book can clear the way for you to make needed changes in your thinking, your perspectives, your personal life, and in your community.

Of course, the information have I just cited, has a propensity to induce in those who read it intense feelings of anger, guilt, disbelief, and hatred among others. Especially for the descendants of both the victims and perpetrators of the horrific past acts of violence and injustice previously mentioned. The anger and hatred that results can be quite crippling and destructive. I was once told that such talk just incites racial tensions and hatred. Should I then just stop and ignore the truth? To let the gross distortions of the truth we have all been brainwashed with persist? Those lies set the stage for deep racial divides in America and for the mental anguish experienced by all of those they touch.

I now wish to repeat a section from my earlier chapter concerning "mood gone wrong" (chapter 5). I have italicized two paragraphs which highlight some of the consequences of not dealing with anger.

Expressing your anger in an assertive manner, and not in an aggressive or hostile manner; is the healthiest way to express your anger. To do this, you have to learn how to make clear what your concerns, feelings and needs are, express how they can be met, and do so without hurting others in the process. Being assertive does not mean being pushy or demanding; it means being respectful of yourself and others as you express your feelings and needs in an honest and non-threatening manner. It means being an adult.

Anger can be suppressed, and then through focused rational thought converted into more constructive and positive behavior. A potential problem with this method of dealing with anger is when the anger is turned inward on the self and never dealt with. Anger turned inward and not dealt with can lead to high blood pressure, fatigue, lowered immunity, and/or depression. Holding on to anger and hatred is like drinking a cup of poison and hoping that other, person, gets sick! It only makes the angry person sick. Like actual poison, anger and hatred can lead to a person's premature demise.

We must not take the path of being non-intellectual or lose touch with our true spiritual natures. African Americans and Native Americans must not lose sight of our natural cultural and spiritual tendency to be inclusive of others. And if you are truly spiritual or believe in God, to love all of our human brothers and sisters because we recognize that we are all true children of our world and of our universe.

Many of our communities need effective corrective action to deal with the multitude of problems that plague them. It would help if there were a structured model that could be used to assess, understand, and communicate the problems requiring one's attention and action. The gyroscopic model can be employed to better understand our communities. With a clear understanding of the needs of a given community in mind, one can begin to lay the foundation for effective change. One can develop goals and an effective vision for a given community and see it to its fruition.

I will now share some information from my personal life experience to illustrate how the gyroscopic theory can be used to analyze, understand, and impact our world. Having grown-up in the Crown Heights community of Brooklyn, New York, I was exposed to many diverse cultures and interesting experiences. I was one of three children, born to a City of New York Social Service Worker and a former World War II Army Sergeant.

By the time I reached five years of age, my parents had divorced. I often wonder if the fact that my father was dark skinned, and my mother could have passed for white affected their marriage at a time when segregation was at its peak. My father re-married and began raising another family. He subsequently had nothing to do with us in terms of time or financial support. Thus, my mother was abandoned to the tasks of serving as the single parent of three children while working for a meager wage in a very stressful full-time job as a Social Worker helping others. She also had to care for the needs of her ailing mother who lived with us. She selflessly walked a very long path of painful self-sacrifice; never making a single complaint about her plight, while thanking God for his blessings daily. Hers became a life of duty to her children, her mother, her community, and to being a devoted follower of our local church.

Having been raised under such circumstances, I am no stranger to the adversity that millions of single moms face each day. I lived among people that struggled to put food on the table and to gain the right to be considered as human beings by our society. That fought for the right to have an education and to have the right to vote for their elected officials. Injustices were blatant. I sat in fear as I watched people being hosed down on the news and dogs being let loose on them. Those were the things that fueled my passion to learn and to seek truth.

The gyroscopic model and method have the potential for a wide range of practical applications. The gyroscopic model can be applied not only to individuals, but to systems and communities as well. In fact, it can be used as a guide to examine, understand, and to fix broken or disrupted systems and communities. I will now describe how the gyroscopic model and method can be used to explore, understand, and then to address some of the many problems of our troubled communities.

This chapter intentionally covers a wide range of topics to show the breadth of matters that this type of exploration using the gyroscopic theory can address. I will first examine some of the more prominent problems that have plagued our communities over the years. We will explore some things that have worked to help our communities and things that have tended to make them worse. I will offer possible solutions for addressing some of the core underlying problems we face.

It is no secret that today broad segments of our lower-income African American, Native American, Latino, and white communities are in a state of dire emergency. Gangs, violence, domestic abuse, child abuse, bullying, guns, high rates of homicide, scholastic failure, alcohol abuse, substance abuse, poverty, obesity, teen pregnancy, HIV and other sexually transmitted diseases, poor nutrition, poor access to healthcare, exposure to environmental toxins, and higher rates of infant mortality than the national average, are but few of the many problems that plague our more troubled communities.

Before delving into a discussion of the problems I would first like to examine the impact that our general media has on our daily lives. For today the general media serves as a focal point for the expression of ideas and perspectives, and indeed, it has a role in shaping our ideas and perspectives as well. I have chosen to begin by examining the impact that the media has on our children, because our children are the most vulnerable.

It is quite noteworthy that most of our children start their lives watching television. I feel that the psychological impact of television and the media on our children's early mental life has not been taken seriously enough. Studies reveal that some infants start watching television as early as two months of age! As, television, is often used as an electronic babysitter and source

246

of entertainment and comfort for caretakers. Television has quite literally entered the cradle.

Early childhood is a period when children are absorbing information at an accelerated rate. Unfortunately, children lack the more developed ego defenses of adults and Thus, are mostly defenseless against the ideas, beliefs and perspectives that are planted in their conscious and unconscious minds. Aside from not having the ego defenses of adults, they lack the benefit of experience and the level of cognitive processing that is required to effectively filter the material being rapidly hurled at them. They are not able to choose what is truly healthy or culturally appropriate for them to incorporate, or to exclude from, their psyches.

What then do our children see on those T.V. screens?

First, here are some interesting facts you should know:

The average American pre-school child watches 3 1/2 hours of television per day.

By the age of eight, most children are watching four hours per day.

The average kindergarten student has watched 5,000 hours of television.

That is more time than he or she will spend in an elementary school classroom.

Most children spend more time watching television than they will spend on any other waking activity; including going to school.[39]

The average child sees more than 20,000 commercials in one year. More than 9 out of 10 food ads on Saturday-morning television are for high sugar cereals, candy bars, salty canned foods, fat-filled fast foods, chips, and other nutritionally flawed foods.[40]

247

While the level of violence on prime-time television is about 5 violent acts per hour, the level of violence in children's Saturday-morning programming is about 32 violent acts per hour.[41]

By the time a child reaches 6th grade, he or she will have witnessed at least 8,000 murders and over 100,000 other acts of violence on TV.[41]

According to the A.C. Nielsen Company, the average American watches 4 hours and 48 minutes of TV each day. This equals 20% of each day. That is more than 72 days of non-stop TV-watching per year. By age 65 the average American will have spent nearly 13 years watching TV. Americans spend more than 33 hours per week watching videos across screens.[41]

Children who watch a large number of aggressive programs also tend to hold attitudes and values that favor the use of aggression to resolve conflicts.[40,41]

The TV is, on, in the average U.S. home for 7 hours, 12 minutes per day.

66% percent of Americans regularly watch television while eating dinner.

According to Neilson, "90 percent of purchasing decisions are made subconsciously". For more information: go to the following website (http://nielsen.com/us/en/measurement/consumer-neuroscience.html).

I truly guarantee you will be amazed!

So, again, what do they see on those screens?

It is very important to note that nearly eighty-five percent of the television programs and advertising shown at any given moment involve images of 'the majority': i.e., of white Americans. You can check the validity of my statement for yourself by flipping through all of the channels, at any given time, and on any given day. Take note of the percentage of white vs. non-white faces you witness and you will come to see my point. This has become increasingly true of primetime television in recent years.

The small percentage of black images on television and all but absent images of Native Americans, Asians, Hispanics and Latinos portrayed against a background of mostly white images teaches our children that they are all second-class citizens by birth. It teaches them that they are not the most important part or focus of American society. That they are not considered the "majority" in this society. That they are quite simply: all just "minorities". This directly instructs, and clarifies for our African American, Native American, Hispanic, Latino, and Asian children that they are simply an after-thought of American society.

Most of the African American, Native American, Latino, and Asian images shown on television and in movies are blatantly negative and stereotyped. Unfortunately, the media industry has been able to successfully recruit those who are eager and willing to engage in self-deprecating acts of buffoonery for fame and profit. They are willing to portray negative images of their own people while elevating the images of the majority. They portray negative images of Black and Latino men and do nothing to advance their own local communities. The very few positive African American, Native American, Asian, and Latino images that we do see on television and in movies hardly undoes the damage caused by the overwhelming backdrop of negative images fired at our children daily.

If an individual absorbs the images and perspectives presented by the "majority" and at the same time rejects their own heritage out of feeling that it is inherently negative; they can become culturally "whitewashed". As a result, one can lose their sense of cultural identity. In some cases, they may never have developed a sense of their cultural identity and tragically may strongly reject their own culture altogether. Even as a child watching "Cowboy and Indian" movies on television I wondered how Native American children felt watching the cavalry slaughter their people as non-Native Americans people around them cheered. Only to have the authors and directors of the movie attempt to glorify and justify the actions of the cavalry as each episode concluded. What damage to Native Americans! What damage to us all!

This subject hit home for me personally when as a child I was told that I was one-quarter Apache and part Arawak. My father's mother (my grandmother!) was supposedly a full-blooded Apache woman, but later I discovered that she was raised by the Apache! My mother's mother was part Arawak. To think that as a child I had several times rooted for the cavalry! This as they were killing my Native American ancestors! What damage to me personally! The continuance of blatant or most often subtle programing of this type serves to ensure the perpetuation of a foundation for a hostile and hateful world for our children. Unchanged and unchecked it is destined to deliver such a world to their children as well.

It is not only what is present on television that has such a damaging impact, but also what is absent. The absence of people of color from most television programs and major motion picture productions is an atrocity to all people regardless of their race. It serves to support and perpetuate a highly distorted view of our world. It serves as a monument to non-inclusivity. I further believe that it delivers a direct assault on the early formation of our children's psyches and leads to many of the personal and social problems that arise later in their lives.

The blatant omission by most television programs and movies of the literally thousands of contributions made by African Americans, Native Americans, Asians, Hispanics and Latinos and all other ethnic groups in every area of science, technology, medicine, industry, and the arts has a destructive impact by creating what I term absentee nullification. That is, the creation of the illusion of the non-existence of people of color in any area of endeavor which might be noteworthy, other than in sports or the performing arts of course. These are truly worthy areas of endeavor. However, they are not all that we are.

This mental assault has a tremendously negative impact on the early formation of our children's self-esteem. Not only do non-whites have this problem, but so do poor and low-income whites. Poor whites also get negatively cast on television and in the media. With the ever-increasing number of new television programs that depict depraved behavior involving lower income people, we now get to witness negative stereotypes of poor whites as well.

However, poor whites still have access to many positive images of whites on television with which they can attempt to identify and Thus, counteract

250

the malicious attack on their self-esteem. While this is a significant advantage it does not serve to fully erase the negative impact on the psyches of children of low-income white families who very often incorporate the negative self-images projected their way and who too are relegated to a second-class status.

As our children continue to grow these negative images are further reinforced by daily news and other media reports that reveal how dangerous and despicable African American, Native American, and Latino youths are. Young black men tend to be negatively highlighted. They are portrayed as being angry and should be feared and avoided! Look at your daily televised morning news shows. I guarantee you will see at least one report of a black male involved with committing some form of crime.

This serves to further erode the already damaged self-esteem of our children and sometimes that of their own parents as well. It demoralizes us all. As a result of this, many of our youths feel that they are undesirable and that they truly are unwanted parts of this society. Unable to fully identify with mainstream America and the "American Dream", some of our young look elsewhere to deal with their sense of rejection and to heal their damaged self-esteem. They look for a place where they can find a source of love, growth and support.

In some cases, this involves entering a gang where they are fully accepted and valued for their intelligence, loyalty, bravery, daring, risk taking skills, ingenuity, cleverness, special talents, wisdom, and tenacity. Sometimes they may choose to join the military as they search for acceptance. In other cases, it involves taking on difficult adult responsibilities, such as by becoming a teen parent. By becoming a parent, they can increase their self-esteem and sense of self-worth by creating a human being who is totally reliant on their care and love. Taking care of a baby has many associated goals which can serve as building blocks for the bolstering of a parent's self-esteem: as those goals are completed. This makes them feel good about themselves and that they are needed.

However, for teenagers, it often dooms them by causing them to take on too many difficult and overwhelming adult responsibilities, too early in their lives. These circumstances may then prevent them from pursuing the higher education required to obtain higher paying jobs. Thus, they become entangled in a cycle of poverty and develop a general unhappiness with the course of their lives. They may eventually become bitter and entrenched in depression.

The need for African Americans to challenge instilled perspectives was borne-out in the following quote by James Baldwin.

> **Quote:** The power of the white world is threatened whenever a black man refuses to accept the white world's definitions.
>
> James Baldwin

The impact of the media on our beliefs and perspectives was borne-out in the following quote by Malcolm-X.

> **Quote:** "The media's the most powerful entity on earth. They have the power to make the innocent guilty and to make the guilty innocent, and that's the power. Because: they control the minds of the masses."
>
> Malcolm X

During the summer of 1977, following my sophomore year as a Biology Major at Syracuse University, I was hired to be a live-in residential advisor and biology teaching assistant by the highly successful Brooklyn Model Cities Summer Program. I had attended that same summer program as a student during my latter elementary school days while growing up in Brooklyn, New York. The program was designed to take African American middle and high school students from inner city environments and introduce them to the college environment in the hope of encouraging them to eventually pursue higher education by attending college.

The administration, teachers, and general staff were predominantly African American. They provided for an educational environment that not only afforded positive academic role models, but also taught students about themselves and their value to our community. It allowed for the development of the student's self-esteem and their belief in their abilities. It was made clear to the students, from day one, that they were *very* important. The experience also exposed them to African American local and world history, and to their culture in a positive and supportive environment.

In retrospect, it provided the positive elements the students could then incorporate into their inner wheels, in order to re-define their major staxes. This effectively served to challenge their existing major staxes which by then had been heavily polluted with negative self-images, ideas, and stereotypes. Many academic, athletic, and artistic goals were set and individual accomplishments were recognized and were rewarded. This very clearly led to self-esteem building for all of the students involved. These are the type of programs that our communities need! Yet, as clearly as they are successful and needed, they remain in a constant desperate struggle for funding; year-after-year.

During that summer, I had the pleasure to work with a student named Larry who had been assigned to the Biology class where I served as an assistant teacher. He had a terrific sense of humor, and having to serve as a role model, I often found myself fighting to suppress my own laughter at his various antics in the classroom. He had a big "afro" hairstyle and wore tie-dyed tee shirts. Often while crossing the campus, he would run up from behind me, place his arm around my shoulder and say in a comical voice "Hi, Daaaveey...how are you dooooing toooday". I can recall his face and the sound of his voice like it was yesterday. I was only four years older than Larry and he appeared to get a charge out of the fact that I could appreciate his sense of humor.

Another example of his humor was when he was photographed for his meal card. He kept his mouth wide-open with his tongue sticking out and had a finger pointing to his mouth as if to say 'feed me...I'm starving'. He was a very likable and pleasant teenager. One day as we were walking across the college campus, I had a serious discussion with him about his antics in the classroom. I stated that I thought he was a very bright student. That while he had a wonderful sense of humor, that if he joked with people all of the time, he would never be taken seriously when he needed to be taken seriously. That it is necessary to have a balance between being humorous and being serious. I also stated that no matter where you go in life, you will need to know something about science and math.

As part of the biology course, several experiments were presented for the students to complete. One such experiment involved planaria, which are flatworms that have the power to regenerate their body parts that are severed. For the experiment we were going to cut the planaria in half and allow them to regenerate. However, due to improper storage, the planaria didn't survive and Thus, we were unable to complete the experiment. I remember that this greatly upset and disappointed Larry. But at that very moment, I got to see in his eyes the intensity of his interest in science. I knew he would go far in anything he did and that it would somehow involve science.

At that point in his life, Larry was actively working on building a future career in acting. Well, "Larry", as it turns out, was Laurence Fishburne the actor. Unknown to me at that time, he had already starred in the film "Cornbread Earl and Me". That summer he left for a few days to attend a screen test for the film "Apocalypse Now". The rest of course is history. Since that time, I have followed his acting career and movies closely. He has become a very positive role model for young African Americans everywhere. In particular: for young African American men.

He has starred in a very wide-range of movies and television shows from his earlier role of "Cowboy Bob" on the Pee Wee Herman T.V. show to Othello. His many plays, movies, and appearances are truly too numerous to mention here. He has truly become the consummate actor and star. I must admit that I had to smile when he began appearing in several science-based movies and shows, such as: "The Matrix", "Fantastic Four" (he provided the voice of the Silver Surfer), "Predator", the recent forensic science based T.V. show Crime Scene Investigators (C.S.I.).

I smiled because it reminded me of my telling him that he will always need to know about science. I am not telling this story out of some misguided sense of my own importance in his life. I was one of a multitude of people who had the chance to influence Larry during his early growth. It's because of the sense of reward I felt, caring about a young black man who was immersed in the same often negative world that I was. I developed a sense of purpose to help others like me. I felt my brief connection with him during his youth enhanced my life as well. This is why we all must get involved with our youth.

As I remember it, his mother was a math and science teacher and his father was a corrections officer. Their roles were much greater than all others combined. They had already raised Larry to be a very likable and well-adjusted adolescent. I am telling this story to point out how all of our lives can unexpectedly intersect and present us with opportunities to support and influence the growth and potential of others; especially with our children. We should never underestimate the impact we can have on a person's development.

It is important to help build their self-esteem and to help rid them of any negative self-images that they have been indoctrinated with. To find those positive elements that help to build their self-esteem, rather than to destroy it. It takes little time to provide positive supportive guidance to our youth and it doesn't cost anything but a few minutes or hours of our time each week. It is important to provide them with an accurate and unbiased view of our world from which to work and grow. Many of the students who attended the summer program went on to enter college and have made positive contributions to society through their many successes.

Unfortunately, some of the negative paths that our African American, Native American, and Latino youths choose to take; very often land them in jail or prison. The following passages outline some important facts from the Sentencing Project Group Report and the Bureau of Justice Statistics:

Since the early 1970s the prison and jail population in the United States has increased at an unprecedented rate. During 1970 there were approximately 200,000 inmates in state and federal prisons.[42, 43] By June 2005 the U.S. had 2.2 million people behind bars, and we became home to the world's largest prison population. More than a 500% increase! During the year 1980, the total jail and prison population was approximately 540,000, about one-quarter of the size it is today. During that same year, drug offenders accounted for 6% of all prisoners.

Today drug offenders account for nearly 25%. During 2005, 1-in-37 Americans had spent time in jail; up from 1-in-53 during 1974.[42] White males born during 2001 currently have a 1-in-17 chance of going to prison. For Hispanic males born during 2001 the odds are a 1-in-6 chance of going to prison. For black males born during 2001 the odds are a 1-in-3 chance of going to prison. 1 of every 6 African American men, are current or former prisoners, compared with only 1-in-38 white men.[44, 45]

One out-of-every eight black men in their twenties are in prison or jail on any given day of the week. In 2005, Hispanics comprised 20% of the state and federal prison population, a rise of 43% since 1990. As a result of these trends, one-of-every six Hispanic males and one-of- every 45 Hispanic females born today can expect to go to prison in his or her lifetime. The 'three strikes and you're out' legislation adopted in 1994, which provides for a 25-years-to-life sentence, has led to a huge increase in the prison population.

The Sentencing Project Group reports that 70-percent of those sentenced to state prisons in 1998 were convicted of non-violent crimes; drug offenders made up 57-percent of federal prison inmates in 1999.[39] U.S. government statistics reveal that thirteen percent of people who admit to using drugs are black. But blacks account for 35-percent of those arrested for drug possession, and 74-percent of those who are imprisoned for it. There is a major disparity in sentencing for crack cocaine users (used more by blacks and Hispanics) and powder cocaine users (used more by whites). The current law states that possession of 5 grams of crack cocaine nets the same mandatory five-year sentence as possession of 500 grams of powder cocaine.[46, 47]

Drunk drivers kill 22,000 people annually. While deaths from overdoses, disease, and violence associated with illicit drug use is approximately 21,000 annually. However, almost all U.S. cases of driving while intoxicated are dealt with as misdemeanors, and are usually punished by fines, loss of one's driver's license, or mandatory community service. While the usual punishment for possession of drugs is up to five years in jail for the first offense. It is worthy to note that drunk drivers are predominantly white males.[48]

A new report released by the Sentencing Project reveals a record 140,610 individuals are now serving life sentences in federal and state prisons. Of those, 6,807 were juveniles at the time of their crime. Of those serving life sentences, 29% have no possibility of parole. Sixty-six percent of those serving life sentences are non-white, and seventy-seven percent of the juveniles serving life sentences are non-white.[48]

As a psychiatrist, I must make note of the tremendous role that mental illness plays here. Just one diagnosis alone, ADHD, apparently has a huge impact. Studies show that at least 25% of prisoners in the United States have ADHD.[49] The rate of recidivism among all felons is very high. With an estimated two thirds of felons being re-arrested within about 3 years of their release. These statistics have important implications for society at large.

Research evidence suggests that the diagnosis and treatment of ADHD could have a huge positive impact on crime rates. During 2009, the National Bureau of Economic Research sought an explanation for the decline in violent crimes starting during the 1990s. They hypothesized that there was a relationship between the increase in prescribing of newer-generation antidepressants and stimulants for ADHD, and the observed decline in violent crimes.[49]

The researchers compared the rates of prescriptions for these psychiatric medications to rates of violent crimes in the United States from 1997-2004, using a statistical regression analysis to interpret their data. They found a significant inverse correlation between medication prescribing and violent crime rates. In other words, as prescriptions went up, violent crimes came down. As a comparison, control group, the authors looked at the prescription rate of medications for cholesterol treatment and found no relationship between the number of prescriptions for those medications and the crime rate.

At the conclusion of their study, the researchers stated, "Our evidence suggests that, in particular, sales of new-generation antidepressants and stimulants used to treat ADHD are negatively associated with rates of violent crime." They added, "To put this in perspective, doubling the prescription rate (of antidepressants) would reduce violent crimes by 6%, or by 27 crimes per 100,000, at the average rate of 446.5 crimes per 100,000: population. A similar calculation with stimulants would decrease crimes by a range of 30-38 crimes per 100,000. While doubling the prescription rates seems like a large change, it has been estimated that 28% of the US adult population in any year has a diagnosable mental or addictive disorder, yet only 8% seeks treatment."[50]

The researchers also reported that the crime rate in Canada fell during the same period. As with the United States, Canada was also among the world leaders in treatment with the newer psychiatric medications. This finding supports the concept that identifying and treating ADHD alone, can lead to a win-win situation for all involved. Individuals with the condition will experience the benefit of proper treatment, and the public will benefit by becoming less likely to become victims of crime.[51-55]

If we truly were to focus on treating all manner of mental illness (i.e., Depression, Bipolar Disorder, Schizophrenia, Substance Abuse, etc.) affecting inmates, it would have a profound impact on crime in our country. If we were to reach those affected by mental illness early in life, i.e., during their elementary school years, we would likely prevent them from having to enter the prison system altogether. However, this would mean having to overcome the existing societal gyroscopic forces that want things to remain as they are. The gyroscopic model can be used as a guiding platform for developing the methods to be used to affect needed changes.

Be aware that the gyroscopic model can also be used as a tool for the manipulative misuse of information. It can be used to intentionally sway people's opinions towards a particular end. Now let's experiment with attempting to shift your perspective in two different directions by employing two disparate scenarios. By doing so, perhaps you can get a sense of how one's axes (perspectives) can be shaped and shifted.

Scenario one:

For a moment, try to forget your previous beliefs and perspectives concerning people's use of illegal drugs. Consider the fact that a tremendous amount of our tax revenues and public resources are expended for the enforcement of the legal statutes directed at stopping the users and distributors of illegal substances. However, drug enforcement policies appear to have failed in several respects.

These failures include: minimal reduction of illicit substance consumption; little reduction of violent crime; failure to significantly reduce illegal drug importation, failure to prevent individuals from becoming involved in the drug trade; failure to prevent street-level drug sales and their widespread availability to potential users; failure to impact upon the huge profits and financial opportunity available to drug dealers and members of organized crime; failure to provide adequate substance abuse treatment and other needed assistance to illicit substance users and their families.

Some supporters of illicit substance decriminalization note that both the financial and social costs of law enforcement directed at fighting illicit substance use far exceed the damage that illegal substances themselves cause. For example, during 1999 approximately 60,000 prisoners (nearly 3.3% of the total prison population) who were convicted of violating U.S. marijuana laws were kept behind bars at a cost to taxpayers of $ 1.2 billion per year. During the year 1980, the total jail and prison population was approximately 540,000, about one-quarter of the size it is today. During that same year, drug offenders accounted for 6% of all prisoners. Today drug offenders account for nearly 25% of prisoners.

Futile efforts at enforcing the prohibition of illegal substances have been pursued even more vigorously during the years 1980 through 2000 than they were during the 1920s. However, as was the case with Prohibition, all the arrests and incarcerations have not stopped the use and abuse of the prohibited target substance, or its trade for that matter. Cocaine and heroin supplies are up and the cost of those substances has fallen due to increased supply.

The failure of drug prohibition explains why more and more people from former Baltimore mayor Kurt Schmoke to Nobel Laureate Milton Friedman, to conservative columnist William F. Buckley Jr., and former secretary of state George Shultz; have all argued that drug prohibition causes more crime and harm than it prevents. This occurs while three major killers in our society, namely alcohol, tobacco, and guns have a federal agency the ATF (Alcohol, Tobacco, and Firearms) that protects and helps regulate tax revenues from the sales associated with these items.

Let's suppose that our society decided to make illegal drugs legal, and they were to be supplied and regulated for free by the government. With no available market, the illegal drug trade would die within a few days. This has been experimented with in other countries, and some promising results have been reported Thus, far. There have been reports of up to a 60% decrease in crime rates (burglary, thefts, violent crimes, etc.) that is felt to be due to a decreased need for negative drug-related acquisition behaviors, and this is felt to be directly due to the previously illegal drugs being made available free of charge.

Also, reports of fewer overdoses have been made, attributed to government regulation and standardization of the purity of the drugs (less contamination), less spread of HIV, Hepatitis B, and Hepatitis C, and more people freed up to seek substance abuse treatment. It is generally felt that with less time spent on the negative time-consuming behaviors such as stealing and connecting with drug dealers used to acquire the illegal drugs, the drug users have more time to be recruited into treatment centers and to regain contact with their support systems.

While drugs such as marijuana, cocaine, and heroin are illegal: it is generally accepted by many that the U.S. "war on drugs" has been an abysmal failure. Much like the national prohibition of alcohol was. The current approach to the drug problem has inadvertently led to an increase in the street value of illicit drugs, which in turn has attracted more unscrupulous people and organized crime, who are anxious to make a huge profit by getting in on the illegal drug trade. The drug money used to fund paramilitary groups, who protect cocaine crops and poppy fields and guard the illegal transport of drugs into the U.S., eventually is used to fund the oppression and terrorism perpetrated by those same groups.

Aside from the crime directly associated with the drug trade, there is an extension to other areas of illegal activity such as: prostitution, gambling, child pornography, slave trafficking, and other forms of organized crime through the channeling of the ill-gotten money. This is a global problem and involves not only the criminals, but many governments, and the 'legal' banking industry as well.

Interestingly, the U.S. has a revenue generating government agency; the Alcohol, Tobacco, and Firearms Agency (ATF), which regulates the sale and distribution of our three most worrisome problems: alcohol, tobacco and firearms. All of which have caused more deaths and impairment than all illegal drugs combined. It has been estimated that if the U.S. government legalized marijuana, it would save U.S. taxpayers 7.7 billion dollars per year on the costs associated with the enforcement of prohibition.

Aside from this it has been estimated that marijuana legalization would yield tax revenues of 2.4 billion dollars annually if it were to be taxed like all other general goods such as alcohol and tobacco. If it were to be taxed at rates comparable to those of alcohol and tobacco it would yield a whopping $6.2 billion annually in tax revenues. "Medical marijuana" brings tax revenues to several states as of the printing of this book. Also, two states Colorado and Washington have recently legalized marijuana for recreational use. If people wish to use illicit substances, no one can stop them. If one drug becomes illegal, then they will simply move on to something else to abuse. It is not the substances, but the people who use them that is the problem. It ultimately requires a cultural change to stop drug abuse, not ineffective regulation. Now let's look at things from the opposite perspective.

Scenario two:

Many arguments have been made for the wide-spread legalization of illicit substances such as cocaine, heroin, marijuana, methamphetamine, ecstasy, and LSD. The rationale for such a stance is often based on the argument that prohibition of those drugs doesn't work and leads to more crime and worse health conditions (such as the transmission of HIV and Hepatitis C by addicts who share needles). However, there is much data to support the well-founded argument that illicit substances should not be made legal. For instance, if we were to focus on marijuana use and its ill health effects it's not as harmless a drug as some would have us believe.

According to a statement made by the National Institute on Drug Abuse: "Studies show that someone who smokes five joints per week may be taking in as many cancer-causing chemicals as someone who smokes a full pack of cigarettes per day." Smoking just one joint, deposits about four times more tar into the lungs than does a filtered cigarette. Marijuana has many other harmful effects such as: distorted perception, memory impairment, difficulties with thinking clearly, impaired ability to problem solve, decreased muscle strength, an increased heart rate, a distorted sense of time, decreased motivation, paranoia, and anxiety.

Harvard University researchers report that the risk of a heart attack is five times greater than usual during the first hour after smoking marijuana. Yet proponents of for its legalization often present marijuana as a harmless "natural" drug. The many negative health and social effects of heroin, cocaine, LSD, methamphetamine, and ecstasy are well known. With time the healthcare costs associated with legalization of illicit substances would far out-weigh the current costs associated with keeping them illegal.

Often the pro drug-legalization group uses the argument that since the 'war on drugs' can never be won, that the approach is of no real value. However, with that same line of logic in mind, no one would ever suggest we should legalize theft because it has never been eradicated from our society. An argument has been made that legalization of drugs would put criminals out of business. It has been suggested that by making drugs cheaper it reduces the profit incentive for criminals. Legalizing illicit drugs would likely cause their cost to go down. However, their use would likely increase as has been the experience with cheaper crack cocaine and heroin in the U.S.

David S. Arnold, M.D.

The most vulnerable population to be pulled into drug use, the 12- to 18-year-old age group, would still be prohibited from buying drugs even in a regulated system. Criminals would simply intensify their targeting of that age group to make-up for losses elsewhere. With legalization of illicit drugs, one would see a rise in the rate of violent crimes such as assaults, driving under the influence, domestic violence, rape, and child abuse. One would also see a rise in work-related injuries as well.

The US Drug Enforcement Administration reports having made significant progress in fighting drug use in America. In a document entitled "Speaking Out, Against Drug Legalization" published in May 2003. An excerpt from that document follows:

> 'Now is not the time to abandon our efforts. The Legalization Lobby claims that the fight against drugs cannot be won. However, overall drug use is down by more than a third in the last twenty years, while cocaine use has dropped by an astounding 70 percent. Ninety-five percent of Americans do not use drugs. This is success by any standards.'

Discussion:

Notice that both camps can offer very persuasive arguments that at least superficially seem to make good sense. There are multiple topics I could have chosen to serve as the topic for debate. The central point being that just about anyone can make a persuasive argument for just about anything. Hearing both arguments can leave one feeling perplexed and confused as to which approach is the right one. My reason for presenting these examples is only to illustrate how information can be used to shape our perspectives. If we are fed only one perspective for extended periods of time, especially when charged with conviction, we likely will begin to incorporate that perspective and make it our own. That will then influence the choices we make.

The gyroscopic theory can be used as a guide to understand people's beliefs, perspectives, and their methods of influence. It sheds light on how gyroscopic forces can be manipulated to create a platform for the formation or malformation of new perspectives. It explains how people can be swayed by large amounts of information. As more orchestrated information is directed their way, it serves to strengthen their newly manufactured perspective. Thus, causing them to become even more convinced of the legitimacy of their newfound perspective: and more rigid in terms of their thinking regarding the subject at hand. This phenomenon directly affects the structure of our society and our body of laws and regulations.

Statistics tied to information are frequently used to sway people's opinions and perspectives. Statistics can be manipulated to convincingly support just about any platform or perspective there is. There is an old joke that a statistician is someone who can place your feet into a hot oven and your head into a freezer, while they convince you that your body is at room temperature. Thus, the statistics used to support an argument, or perspective should always be viewed with a critical eye. Aside from serving as an easy target for the previous joke, statistics can be very helpful when used as a tool to uncover entrenched untrue perspectives by exposing the actual facts involved.

The fact that gyroscopic forces can be manipulated has endless social implications. For instance, the generally unspoken negative perspectives and stereotypes that have been deliberately programmed into people, serves to further reinforce the existence of racial profiling in the U.S. In one study, which took place in the state of Maryland, a section of the I-95 highway was evaluated for racial profiling perpetrated by police. It was estimated that only 17 percent of all drivers were black, while 73 percent of those who were pulled over and searched were black. In many cars searched in this manner, no drugs or contraband items were found. When those items were found, they were just as likely to be found in cars driven by whites. The term DWB 'driving while black' was adopted by the black community to highlight the issue of racial profiling and the open bias conducted by law enforcement agencies.[52]

According to the Sentencing Project Group report, black women are more likely to end up in prison than white women. In 1980 there were 12,300 women held in state and federal prisons; and by 2002 there were 96,000. The number of incarcerated mothers rose 131 percent from 1991 to 2007. The number of fathers incarcerated rose 77 percent during the same time period. Approximately 1.7 million children have a parent in prison.[56,57]

Sixty-five percent of women in prison have families. Their children are often denied visits on the grounds that their mothers are 'too unfit' to allow for such privileges. Many states have laws that allow them to pursue termination of a woman's parental rights on the grounds of incarceration. Seventy-five percent of women in prison were regular illicit drug users prior to their incarceration. According to the Project Group reports, nearly 40 percent had monthly incomes of less than $600.34.[56,57]

Historically, women have always gotten the 'short-end-of-the-stick' when it comes to earned income. More than half of imprisoned women have a past history of physical or sexual abuse. Forty-six of our fifty U.S. states have disenfranchisement laws which take away the voting rights of anyone serving time for a felony. Some states take away voting rights permanently. Felony disenfranchisement laws effectively strip the freedoms guaranteed by the Fifteenth Amendment to the U.S. Constitution: which first gave black people the legal right to vote in U.S. elections. Today 1.4 million black men, approximately 13 percent of the black male population, can't vote due to their past felony convictions. In the states of Alabama and Florida, 31 percent of black men are permanently banned from voting. Interestingly, Florida has played a pivotal role in several recent key elections.[56,57]

The destructive nature of drug abuse and dependence in our communities is quite clear. Drug abuse often begins with an attempt to control one's own emotions and state of mind. Drugs are used either escape bad feelings or to induce good ones. Drugs are often used to get rid of negative feelings such as stress, worry, anxiety, anger, hopelessness, helplessness, depression, despair, loneliness, psychological pain, low self-esteem, etc. Sometimes, it starts with an attempt to 'fit in' with peers; or simply for the purpose of novel excitement and thrill seeking. Drugs can create the illusion that one feels 'good', and that one is 'powerful and in control'. The additional use of aggression and violence can also give one a sense of power and control. Any action moviegoer can verify this observation. Incarceration often leads to unintended consequences for those imprisoned and for our society at large.[58-63]

We live in a country with a long history of violence that is often glorified by our media. We indulge in celebrating war heroes and the past acts of the destruction of our foes. Great efforts are made to justify that violence. There are many 'nostalgic' films of the old west depicting violence against Native Americans. There are war documentaries which tend to directly or indirectly glorify even Fascists such as Hitler, Stalin, Lenin, Hirohito, and

Mussolini depending on the viewer. There are groups who make a hobby of re-enacting past battles and wars. Our youth, born with no prior knowledge of such things, simply absorb the information thrown their way and then follow that lead. If our society continues to openly or subliminally embrace aggression and violence as a way of life; we will forever incorporate it in our children and bring violence to its ugly fruition.

A major portion of the solution to our problem lies in the protection of our children from the onslaught of negative images and information thrown their way. These images can become a permanent part of our children's unconscious minds and serve to weaken the very foundation of their self-esteem. It is important to understand that we are engaged in a daily symbolic war. It is a war of words, symbols, ideas, perceptions, and perspectives.

We must recognize that we are all products of this system, and that we must protect ourselves from negative ideas and images as well. We must actively expunge such poisons from our own minds because they power the gyroscopic forces that most often lead us to failure and a self-destructive lifestyle. We must create a positive counter-literature and counter-media to protect our children. We must employ a defensive strategy of counter-symbols.

Parents must aggressively work to strengthen their children's self-esteem. Refer to other sections of this book concerning self-esteem. We must set clear attainable goals for our children to allow for them to build and maintain their self-esteem. If we fail to act, we will be doomed to become hopelessly cynical about our future and that of our children. This may seem to be a difficult task, but by no means is it an impossible one.

The following passages reveal how information presented to us can be distorted.

Regarding the topic of, who is "the father of medicine"?

The Merriam-Webster Dictionary states:

Hip·poc·ra·tes \hi-ˈpä-krə-ˌtēz\

ca 460–*ca* 377 B.C. ***father of medicine*** Greek physician (born *c.* 460 BC, island of Cos, Greece—died *c.* 375, Larissa, Thessaly)

Greek physician regarded as the father of medicine. During his lifetime, he was admired as a physician and teacher. PLATO and ARISTOTLE mention him in several of their own works, and Aristotle's student Meno recounts his ideas about the causes of disease. The Hippocratic Collection (*Corpus Hippocraticum*) was assembled for the LIBRARY OF ALEXANDRIA in Egypt. About 60 medical writings have survived that bear Hippocrates' name, most of which were not written by him. The collection deals with ANATOMY, clinical subjects, diseases of women and children, prognosis, treatment, SURGERY, and medical ethics. The Hippocratic Oath (suspected not to have been written by Hippocrates), also part of the Hippocratic Collection, dictates the obligations of the physician to students of medicine and the duties of pupil to teacher. In the oath, the physician pledges to prescribe only beneficial treatments, to refrain from causing harm or hurt, and to live an exemplary life.

The On-line Wikipedia Encyclopedia states:

"Hippocrates (hih POK ruh teez) lived 400 years before the birth of Christ. He is known as the father of medicine because many of the things he discovered are still practiced today...During the time when Hippocrates lived, people were very superstitious. They believed there were four fluids in the body which matched four elements: air, earth, fire and water. They would carry sick people to the temple because they thought the god of medicine, Aesculapius (es kyoo LAY pe us) could heal them. They would say magic words over the patient to try and heal them."

But the real question is: Was Hippocrates really 'the Father of Medicine'? Take note that in the Hippocratic Oath of Physicians, Hippocrates refers to Asclepius.

The Hippocratic Oath:

I swear by Apollo the Physician and **Asclepius** and Hygieia and Panaceia and all the gods and goddesses, making them my witnesses, that I will fulfill according to my ability and judgment this oath and this covenant:

To hold him who has taught me this art as equal to my parents and to live my life in partnership with him, and if he is in need of money to give him a share of mine, and to regard his offspring as equal to my brothers in male lineage and to teach them this art - if they desire to learn it - without fee and covenant; to give a share of precepts and oral instruction and all the other learning to my sons and to the sons of him who has instructed me and to pupils who have signed the covenant and have taken an oath according to the medical law, but no one else.

I will apply dietetic measures for the benefit of the sick according to my ability and judgment; I will keep them from harm and injustice.

I will neither give a deadly drug to anybody who asked for it, nor will I make a suggestion to this effect. Similarly, I will not give to a woman an abortive remedy. In purity and holiness, I will guard my life and my art.

I will not use the knife, not even on sufferers from stone, but will withdraw in favor of such men as are engaged in this work.

Whatever houses I may visit, I will come for the benefit of the sick, remaining free of all intentional injustice, of all mischief and in particular of sexual relations with both female and male persons, be they free or slaves.

What I may see or hear in the course of the treatment or even outside of the treatment in regard to the life of men, which on no account one must spread abroad, I will keep to myself, holding such things shameful to be spoken about.

If I fulfil this oath and do not violate it, may it be granted to me to enjoy life and art, being honored with fame among all men for all time to come; if I transgress it and swear falsely, may the opposite of all this be my lot.

Translation: from the Greek by Ludwig Edelstein. From The Hippocratic Oath: Text, Translation, and Interpretation, by Ludwig Edelstein. Baltimore: Johns Hopkins Press, 1943.

Question: Who was Asclepius?

Egypt became a unified country five thousand years ago, and until the arrival of Alexander the Great in 332 BC, it had remained a fiercely independent land with its own very distinctive art, religion and culture. The Egyptian Imhotep (**Asclepius**) was called the "God of Medicine" and the "Prince of Peace". Imhotep was worshipped as a god and healer from approximately 2850 B.C. to 525 B.C., and as a full deity from 525 B.C. to 550 A.D.

He had become a God of Medicine, in whom the Greeks, who also called him Imouthes, recognized him as Æsculapius (Asclepius). Asclepius: of the Hippocratic Oath. For 3000 years he was worshipped as a god in Greece and Rome. Early Christians worshipped him as the "Prince of Peace." He was the world's first named architect who built Egypt's first pyramid. Even kings and queens felt compelled to bow at his throne. Imhotep lived during the Third Dynasty at the court of King Zoser.

Imhotep has been recognized as: the world's first doctor, a priest, a scribe, a chief lector, a sage, a poet, an architect, an astrologer, an astronomer, a vizier (a civil officer in ancient Egypt having vice-regal powers), a magician (as medicine and magic were often used together).and as a chief minister, though Djoser, the second king of Egypt's third dynasty (who reigned from 2630–2611 BC).

He may have lived under as many as four kings. An inscription on one of that king's statues gives us Imhotep's titles as the "chancellor of the king of lower Egypt", the "first one under the king", the "administrator of the great mansion", the "hereditary Noble", the "high priest of Heliopolis", the "chief sculptor", and finally the "chief carpenter".

Imhotep's best-known writings were medical texts. As a physician, Imhotep is believed to have been the author of the "Edwin Smith" Papyrus in which more than 90 anatomical terms and 48 injuries are described. He founded a school of medicine in Memphis, a part of his center was known as "Asklepion", which remained famous for two thousand years. This all occurred some 2,200 years before the Western "Father of Medicine" Hippocrates was born.

Imhotep was also a philosopher. He urged contentment and preached cheerfulness. His proverbs contained a "philosophy of life." Imhotep coined the saying: "Eat, drink and be merry, for tomorrow we shall die." When the Ancient Egyptians crossed the Mediterranean, they laid a large portion of the foundation for Greek culture. Imhotep's teachings were absorbed there.

Yet, Greek culture, at that time, was such that they asserted that they were the originators of all things, and Imhotep was forgotten for thousands of years. Thus, a legendary figure, Hippocrates, who came more than 2000 years after Imhotep, came to be known as the "Father of Medicine".

Sir William Osler (July 12, 1849 – December 29, 1919) was a Canadian physician and one of the four founding professors of Johns Hopkins Hospital. Osler created the first residency program for specialty training of physicians, and he was the first to bring medical students out of the lecture hall for bedside clinical training ('rounds'). He has frequently been described as the "Father of Modern Medicine". "It is Imhotep, who was the real Father of Medicine", says Sir William Osler, Imhotep was "The first figure of a physician to stand out clearly from the mists of antiquity." Imhotep diagnosed and treated over 200 diseases, 15 diseases of the abdomen, 11 of the bladder, 10 of the rectum, 29 of the eyes, and 18 of the skin, hair, nails and tongue. Imhotep treated tuberculosis, gallstones, appendicitis, gout and arthritis. He also performed surgery and practiced some dentistry.

Imhotep extracted medicine from plants. He also knew the position and function of the vital organs and circulation of the blood system. The Encyclopedia Britannica states: "The evidence afforded by Egyptian and

Greek texts support the view that Imhotep's reputation was very (well) respected in early times...His prestige increased with the lapse of centuries and his temples in Greek times were the centers of medical teachings."

Yet, even today, no medical school or university in the United States openly teaches this truth. We are led away from Imhotep, and taught that Hippocrates is the father of medicine, with not a mention of Imhotep. This is a clear distortion of the facts and of reality itself. Thus, any tie to the early ownership of medicine is essentially stripped from black culture.

Do you think that if the children of our African American communities were raised to be fully aware of things such as the history of Imhotep, that they would feel a greater sense of self-worth and ownership of the field of Medicine? Instead of feeling as they currently do. As insignificant outsiders? That they just might pursue careers in Medicine out of a sense of pride? Is it our responsibility to explore and learn such things to help ensure that such things get taught in our communities? I think so!

Note: The eye of the Egyptian God Horus was an ancient symbol of protection and healing and is thought by some to be the source of the sign Rx used by modern physicians on prescriptions. When alchemy (or chemistry), which had its cradle in Egypt and derived its name from Khami (an old title for Egypt), was passed to the hands of the Greeks and then later to the Arabs, this sign passed with it. It was also adopted by the Gnostics of the early Christian church in Egypt.

In a cursive form it is found in medieval translations of the works of Ptolemy the astrologer (as the sign of the planet Jupiter). As such it was placed upon horoscopes and upon formulae containing drugs made for administration to the body, so that the harmful properties of these drugs might be removed under the influence of the lucky planet. At present, in a slightly modified form, it still figures at the top of prescriptions written by doctors daily (Rx). Rx became the symbol for reaction in chemistry and stood for "reaction drugs" at pharmacies. There is a famous saying that the victor gets to write history. A critical analysis of just what history has been written for us to blindly accept, that has been re-written to mislead, must be done. This is solely our responsibility.

24

Conclusion

I HAVE COVERED MANY TOPICS IN THIS WORK. A LOT OF THINGS TO THINK about and consider. One of the goals of this book was to expose how strongly influenced we are by socially imposed ideas, beliefs and perspectives. It reveals how the invisible, yet powerful gyroscopic forces greatly impact our lives daily. This book presented a model and method that can be used to expose and explore the gyroscopic forces. It explores how the gyroscopic theory and method can be used to change one's state of being through the process of guided self-creation.

Together, the gyroscopic model and method hold great promise in helping us to understand ourselves, others, and our world. They can be used by individuals to obtain greater mental flexibility, power, and stability through the attainment of a clearer understanding of the things which impact them. As individuals grow and change for the better perhaps all will gain greater joy and happiness from their lives and from their dealings with each other. The ultimate long-term goal is continuous personal growth and change.

This book also attempts to lay a foundation for how the gyroscopic model and method can be applied to better understand and solve many life issues and problems. It points out how profoundly influential and conflicted the information we absorb can be. It attempts to show how we are forced to balance and justify these forces daily to maintain our own sense of stability.

With only one world to live in, and our collective need to survive it, we should feel compelled to grow and change in a collaborative and supportive fashion with all our fellow human beings. However, unfortunately, not everyone believes this. They prefer to remain blind to our world, while being fully trapped by their own gyroscopic forces. Yet despite this, there remain those who dedicate their lives to personal growth through self-discovery. So, there is reason to hope.

Many tough questions present themselves for us to answer. For instance: If we feel fully comfortable with our station in life? Should we choose to remain blind to the rest of the world? Do we seek the truth, or do we find contentment with distortions of the truth given us? Are we comfortable even with outright lies? Do we remain stagnant, or do we grow emotionally? Surely, some choose emotional stagnation and blindness. However, it is important that we all know that there is a way to avoid such an undesirable state of being.

No one born before or after you will ever be you. You have the ultimate power to direct the conditions of your own existence and your fate. Never let anyone define who or what you are. Strive to keep actively aware of your own beliefs and perspectives and how they influence your daily behavior. Try to keep aware of your use of ego defenses that can sometimes blind you to what is clearly right in front of you. Or cause you to act in ways that would be best to modify.

My hope is that by using the model and method presented here you will be better prepared to make positive changes in your own life. Having done so, hopefully you will have a positive influence on the lives of others and on the many systems of our world. Clear focus and consistent practice are essential for lasting change, continuous growth, and sustained success.

I would like to leave you with a very powerful poem that has had a profound impact on my life. It has gotten me through difficult times. It is a poem entitled Invictus, written by William Ernest Henley (1849-1903): [64, 65]

> Out of the night that coverts me,
> Black as a pit from pole to pole.
> I thank whatever gods may be,
> For my unconquerable soul.
>
> In the fell clutch of circumstance,
> I have not winced nor cried aloud.

Under the bludgeoning of chance,
My head is bloodied, but unbowed.

Beyond this place of wrath and tears,
Looms but the horror of the shade.
And yet the menace of the years,
Finds and shall find me unafraid.

It matters not how straight the gait.
How charged with punishment the scroll.
I am the master of my fate.
I am the captain of my soul.

A few words about the author of Invictus. The word Invictus is Latin for "unconquered". It was first published in 1888 in Henley's *Book of Verses*, where it was the fourth in a series of poems entitled *Life and Death (Echoes)*. At the age of 12 years old, Henley fell victim to tuberculosis which invaded his bones. A few years later the disease had progressed to his foot and his physicians announced that the only way to save his life was to amputate his lower leg directly below the knee. It was amputated when he was 25 years old. In 1867, he successfully passed the Oxford local examination as a senior student. In 1875, he wrote the "Invictus" poem from his hospital bed. Despite his disability he survived with one foot intact and led an active life until his death at the age of 53-years. Memorize this poem for strength when you need it. You are the master of your fate. You are the captain of your soul. Watch your choices.

I wish you much peace, love and happiness on your life's journey!

Appendix A

Some common examples of how ego defense mechanisms are put into operation are presented for further clarification.

LISTING OF EGO DEFENSE MECHANISMS AND THEIR DEFINITIONS:

ACTING OUT – The individual deals with emotional conflict through actions rather than by using reflections or feelings.

Example: A person throws a book at a wall, slams a door, or knocks over a chair rather than verbalizing their feelings of anger and frustration in a clear and coherent manner.

AFFILIATION – The individual deals with emotional conflict by turning to others for their help or support. This involves sharing one's problems with others, but does not imply that the individual is trying to make someone else responsible for their problems.

Example: Support groups such as Alcoholic Anonymous meetings, Narcotics Anonymous meetings, bereavement groups, weight loss groups, diabetes groups, etc.

AIM INHIBITION – Placing a limitation on instinctual demands by accepting partial or modified fulfillment of the original desires.

Examples: A person is conscious of their sexual desire for another, but finding it too frustrating to get their desires met "decides" that all they really need is friendship with the person they desire. A student who originally deeply desired to become an astronaut "decides" to become an aerospace mechanic or a flight control assistant instead.

ANTICIPATION – The individual deals with emotional conflict by experiencing imagined emotional reactions in advance of actual events. By anticipating the possible consequences of future events, and by considering several realistic possible responses or solutions, they hope to deal with life events with less stress while achieving better outcomes.

Example: 'If I were to tell them this: then they would probably say or do that; then I would do so-and-so; and then everything would be okay.'

ALTRUISM – The individual deals with emotional conflict by a dedication to meet the needs of others. Unlike self-sacrifice, which is sometimes characteristic of reaction formation where the person does the opposite of what they truly feel unconsciously. The individual receives gratification either vicariously or from the positive response and regard of others.

AUTISTIC FANTASY – The individual deals with emotional conflict by excessive daydreaming as a substitute for true human relationships, taking more effective actions, or active problem solving.

Example: An excellent example can be found in the movie "The Secret Life of Walter Mitty" featuring Danny Kaye. See it. You'll understand. Kerplukita, kerplukita! ☺

AVOIDANCE – A defense mechanism consisting of refusal to encounter situations, objects, or activities because they represent unconscious sexual or aggressive impulses (with accompanying anxiety and stress) and carry the possibility of punishment for those impulses.

Example: A high school student avoids going to a school dance because she 'just doesn't feel like going'. When she is fighting her unconscious sexual impulses and her fear of acting on them and the possibility of being punished for doing so.

COMPENSATION – Encountering failure or frustration in some sphere of activity, one over-emphasizes another area of activity. The term is also applied to the process of over-correcting for a handicap or limitation.

Examples: A physically unattractive adolescent becomes an expert pianist. A person born with a clubbed foot becomes a star athlete in track and field competitions.

CONVERSION – Conflicts are transformed into physical symptoms involving portions of the body innervated by sensory or motor nerves. Conversion and Somatization are the only defenses that are always pathological.

Examples: A man's arm becomes paralyzed after having strong impulses to strike his co-worker. A woman develops hysterical blindness, after she learns a loved one has died, and that their body needs to be identified at the local morgue.

DEFLECTION – A defense mechanism whereby the individual diverts attention away from themselves by redirecting the audience's focus and attention to another person.

Examples: "I know I need to improve a portion of my work, but Frank has been doing this project entirely the wrong way!"

DENIAL – The individual completely rejects a thought or feeling.

Examples: Visibly angry, following a negative interaction with a woman, a person states: "I'm not angry with her!" A person having severe chest pain denies any possibility that they are having a heart attack. People living near a major fault dismiss the tremors they feel as being indicative of a major earthquake.

DEVALUATION – The individual deals with emotional conflict by attributing exaggerated negative qualities to themselves or to others.

Examples: "She's just a slave driver and a real witch!", "I have to face it: I'm the worst tennis player in the whole world!"

DISPLACEMENT – The individual takes their feelings connected to the original target and redirects them to another target.

Examples: You get mad at your boss and then go home and kick your dog. A woman who is abandoned by her boyfriend, then quickly finds another man for whom she immediately develops the "same" feelings of "love". Actually, she transfers her original feelings to the second man.

DISSOCIATION – Splitting-off a group of thoughts or activities from the main portion of one's consciousness: compartmentalization.

Examples: A politician works vigorously for integrity in government, but at the same time engages in business ventures that involve severe conflicts of interest. He does so without being consciously aware of the hypocrisy involved; and without seeing any connection between the two activities. Note: Some dissociation is helpful in keeping one portion of our life from interfering with another (i.e., not bringing problems home from the office).

FIXATION – The halting of the process of development of the personality at a stage short of complete and uniform mature independence.

Example: A 30-year-old man who behaves in a childlike manner and still needs his mother to remind him to bathe for personal hygiene.

HELP REJECTING COMPLAINING – The individual deals with emotional conflict by complaining frequently, or by making repetitious requests for help. The requests for help disguise deep negative feelings, feelings of hostility, or deeply felt criticism of others. The person's hostile feelings are then expressed by rejecting the very suggestions, advice, and/ or help that others offer. The actual complaints or requests may involve physical or psychological symptoms or general life problems.

HUMOR – The individual deals with emotional conflict or external stressors by emphasizing the amusing, humorous, or ironic aspects of the conflict or stressors at hand.

278

Example: A customer says to a waiter, "I'm sure this orange juice would taste pretty good, if it weren't for the coffee grounds!" (Then he laughs) "If I break one more dish, I'll set a new world record!"

IDEALIZATION – Overestimating the desirable qualities and benefits of a desired object, while underestimating its limitations and pitfalls.

Examples: A lover speaks in glowing terms of the beauty and intelligence of his average looking girlfriend who is obviously not very bright. A purchaser, having finally decided between two items, over-emphasizes the advantages of the one chosen.

IDENTIFICATION – The unconscious modeling of oneself after another person. One may also identify with the values and attitudes of a group as well.

Examples: Without being aware that he is copying his teacher, a student assumes a similar mode of dress and manner and grows a moustache just like his teacher's. A business student dresses and behaves like the 'Wall Street type'.

IDENTIFICATION WITH THE AGGRESSOR – The individual deals with emotional conflict by identifying with their aggressor, Thus, taking on the attributes, beliefs, and behaviors of their aggressor.

Example: A prisoner begins to identify with an aggressive prison guard, and starts to enforce prison rules against other prisoners, as if he was a guard.

INCORPORATION – The assimilation of external objects (i.e., people) into one's own psyche, ego and/or superego. This is one of the earliest defense mechanisms utilized. The parent becomes almost quite literally a part of the child. Parental values, preferences, and attitudes are acquired and incorporated by the child.

Example: "One should always be honest when doing business. My dad would be proud if he could see this deal."

INTELLECTUALIZATION – A more intellectualized form of rationalization often with jargon thrown in. The individual deals with emotional conflict by the excessive use of abstract thinking or the making of generalizations to control or minimize disturbing feelings of tension and anxiety.

Example: After losing the race to a political opponent, the former candidate states: 'This political situation reminds me of how important it is for one to recognize the essentially transient nature of our existence, the true meaning of life, and those intangible things that are truly important to us as individuals.'

INTROJECTION – The process of assimilation of a picture of an object (as the individual conceives that object to be, i.e., the gestalt) into one's psyche.

Example: We have our own picture in our mind, of who our mother is, who our father is, who our sister is, who our brother is, who our aunt Margaret is, who our supervisor is, etc.

ISOLATION OF AFFECT – The splitting-off of the emotional components from our thoughts. One **thinks** the feeling, rather than **feels** the feeling.

Examples: 'That should make a person feel quite angry.' This: while the individual ignores their own true feelings of intense anger. 'The sight of blood might be upsetting to some people.' This, while ignoring their own inner feelings of upset.

Isolation may only be temporary (i.e., affect postponement). Example: A bank teller appears strong, calm and cool while experiencing and helping to foil a bank robbery, but afterwards feels weak, is tearful and appears visibly shaken by the experience.

OMNIPOTENCE – The individual deals with emotional conflict or with internal or external stressors, by feeling or acting as if they possess special powers or abilities and Thus, are superior to others.

Example: A politician states: 'I know and understand all problems in this community and can fix them all; therefore, I'm the best person for the job.'

PASSIVE AGGRESSION – The individual deals with emotional conflict by indirectly, passively, expressing aggression toward others. There is a lot of overt compliance masking covert resistance, resentment, and/or hostility.

Example: An unobstructed motorist, travels at 30 miles per hour on a 55 mile per hour speed limit highway during rush hour traffic. A person sitting closest to a work phone lets it ring endlessly without answering it.

PROJECTION – The individual believes that someone else has the thought or feeling that they, themselves, actually harbor.

Examples: 'My boss hates me'. When, actually, the individual hates their boss. 'That secretary has a crush on the new guy'. This: as stated by a clerk who actually harbors unconscious romantic feelings towards the new guy on the job. A woman, who has unconscious sexual feelings about a co-worker, accuses him without basis of being a 'wolf'.

PROJECTIVE IDENTIFICATION – As with projection, the individual in question deals with emotional conflict by falsely attributing to another, his or her own unacceptable feelings, impulses, **or thoughts. Unlike simple projection, the individual does not fully deny h**aving the feelings that are projected. Instead, the individual remains aware of his or her own feelings or impulses, but erroneously justifies them by attributing them to the other person's thoughts or feelings. Ironically, this individual may induce the very feelings in others, that were first mistakenly believed to be there, making it difficult to clarify who did what, to whom and when in the first place.

RATIONALIZATION – The individual offers a socially acceptable and somewhat apparently logical explanation for an act, or a decision, that was produced by unconscious impulses. You come up with various explanations to justify the situation, while you are denying your true feelings. The person rationalizing is not intentionally inventing a story to lie or fool someone else, but instead is misleading themselves as well as the listeners.

Examples: "They're being so critical of us because they really think we're the best." A man buys a new car having convinced himself that his older car won't make it through the winter. A woman, with a closet full of unused clothes, buys a new dress because she doesn't have anything else to wear.

REACTION FORMATION – An individual's feeling gets turned into its extreme opposite; this is an over-compensation for unacceptable impulses.

Examples: A man strongly dislikes an employee, and without being aware of doing so, he 'bends over backwards' not to criticize the employee and gives him special privileges and job advances. A person with strong antisocial impulses to harm animals leads a crusade against animal cruelty. A married woman, who is disturbed by her feelings of attraction to one of her husband's friends, treats him rudely. The opposite of this situation can also occur, "I think he's a lovely person" – though really unconsciously she hates the person.

REGRESSION – The individual reverts to old, usually immature behaviors.

Example: 'Let's play hooky from the staff meeting today!' 'Let's throw wet paper towels at the bathroom ceiling!'

REPRESSION – The unconscious, involuntary exclusion of a painful or conflicted thought, impulse, or memory from awareness. This is the primary ego defense mechanism; all others tend to reinforce it.

RESISTANCE – This defense mechanism produces a powerful opposition to the bringing forward of repressed (unconscious) thoughts and feelings to the individuals awareness. Through its operation, the individual strongly seeks to avoid memories or insights that would arouse tension or anxiety.

RESTITUTION – The individual relieves their feelings of guilt by making up or reparation (paying-up) with some interest added: overpaying.

Example: "Thank you for the cup of coffee. I'll mow your lawn for a month to repay you."

SELF-ASSERTION – The individual deals with emotional conflict (or with internal or external stressors) by expressing their feelings and thoughts directly, in such a way that it is not coercive or manipulative of others.

SOMATIZATION – Conflicts are represented by physical symptoms involving parts of the body that are innervated by the sympathetic and parasympathetic nervous systems.

Example: A student who is very worried about failing an exam develops a 'stomach ache' which prevents them from having to take the exam that day.

SUBLIMATION – Redirecting and often reducing the force of an instinctual drive by using the energy in other socially productive and acceptable activities.

Examples: Playing football: 'We're going to kill the other football team in this game!' 'I'm going to write a song about anger.'

SUBSTITUTION – An individual secures an alternative or substitutive gratification that is comparable to one that would have been obtained had frustration not occurred.

Example: When a long planned for steak dinner, is suddenly cancelled by their co-workers, an employee buys and eats several hot dogs and a pint of ice cream.

SUPRESSION – An individual is aware of a feeling they are experiencing, but consciously pushes it under the surface to hide it. Usually presented as an ego defense mechanism, but actually it is the conscious analog of repression. It is an intentional exclusion of material from consciousness. Suppression may lead to subsequent repression.

Examples: Upset by their guests, a person thinks to themselves: 'I'm going to overlook their rudeness and drive it from my mind; and I'll be nice to them anyway.' A student goes on vacation worried that he may be failing a course; he then decides not to spoil his holiday by thinking about school.

SYMBOLIZATION – An object or act, represents a complex group of objects and acts, some of which may be conflicted in design and/or unacceptable to the ego.

Examples: A soldier, when asked why he volunteered for the army, states: "To defend the flag." He rejects, as being irrelevant, a subsequent question about the overall purpose of the war.

UNDOING – The individual attempts to reverse or undo their feeling by doing something that indicates the opposite feeling.

Examples: You give a 'warm and friendly' present to someone you intensely dislike.

I would like to add one that I have observed:

MANIPULATIVE THOUGHT INSERTION – An individual inserts thoughts or beliefs into the minds of others in an attempt to induce a desired reaction or outcome, thereby reducing their own inner anxiety and stress. This is often accomplished through the use of obfuscation; which is the intentional clouding of issues to evade the truth of a matter. It makes use of a proverbial "smoke screen" to warp the truth in order to defend one's position or perspective and is quite common place.

Examples:

> The "bad" parent, teacher, clergy member, or coach who fills an individual's head with: self-doubt and negative thoughts about themselves, in an attempt to control that person's behavior. It often leads a person not to pursue a particular goal or interest of theirs. When anxious about an undesirable long ride to attend an event, a person strongly informs others that the event is very likely to be cancelled due to inclement weather; this with the hope that people will become fearful and wish to cancel the trip.

Worried that his main competitor will appear more confident at a sales meeting a salesman tells his competitor that he heard that the product she is selling is defective and was likely recalled by her company that very morning. This in an attempt to shake her confidence and to simultaneously quell his own anxiety. Interestingly, he might actually convince himself that he had previously witnessed a news report stating that there was a recall of the product (use of false memories) in order to deal with his own guilt over having been deceptive.

Appendix B

Eugenical Sterilization
in the
United States

By
HARRY HAMILTON LAUGHLIN, D. Sc.
Assistant Director of the Eugenics Record Office,
Carnegie Institution of Washington,
Cold Spring Harbor, Long Island, New York,
and
Eugenics Associate of the Psychopathic Laboratory
of the Municipal Court of Chicago.

Published by the
PSYCHOPATHIC LABORATORY OF THE MUNICIPAL COURT
OF CHICAGO
DECEMBER, 1922

CHAPTER XV.
MODEL EUGENICAL STERILIZATION LAW.

A. PRINCIPLES SUGGESTED FOR A STANDARD STATE LAW.

It may be safely stated that the experimental period for eugenical sterilization legislation has been passed so that it is now possible to enact a just and eugenically effective statute on this subject. The following outline sets forth the underlying principles which should guide such a law.

Persons Subject. All persons in the State who, because of degenerate or defective hereditary qualities are potential parents of socially inadequate offspring, regardless of whether such persons be in the population at large or inmates of custodial institutions, regardless also of the personality, sex, age, marital condition, race, or possessions of such person. Standards established and terms defined by the statute.

Executive Agencies Provided. State Eugenicist who shall devote his entire time and attention to his office, aided by an ample corps of assistants, selected by appointment or civil service according to the customs of the particular state.

Basis of Selection: Procedure. 1. Investigation by State Eugenicist upon his own initiative or upon complaints lodged or information given by an official, an organization or a citizen. 2. Opinion concerning a particular individual in reference to "potential parenthood of socially inadequate offspring" rendered after scientific investigation, by State Eugenicist to Court of Record. 3. Early date set by court for hearing case. 4. Court to notify and summon interested parties. 5. Due provision for legal counsel for the defendant and for trial by jury. 6. Judgment: Order for eugenical sterilization if the contention of the State Eugenicist is upheld 7. Execution of the order under the supervision and responsibility of the State Eugenicist. 8. In case of inmates of institutions, execution of order may be suspended until inmate is about to be released, allowing ample time for convalescence. 9.

Provision for the study of mental, moral, physiological, social and economic effects of different types of sterilization.

Type of Operation Authorized. 1. "Surgical operation upon or medical treatment of the reproductive organs of the human male or female in consequence of which the power to procreate offspring is permanently nullified." 2. Specific type of operation or treatment in each case to be determined by the State Eugenicist upon the advice of duly qualified physicians and surgeons. 3. Due provision for safe, skillful and humane operation and treatment.

State's Motive. Purely eugenic, that is, to prevent certain degenerate human stock from reproducing its kind. Absolutely no punitive element.

Appropriations Available for Enforcing the Act. Ample appropriations for the maintenance of the activities of the State Eugenicist as a permanent and effective institution.

B. FULL TEXT FOR A MODEL STATE LAW.

AN ACT to prevent the procreation of persons socially inadequate from defective inheritance, by authorizing and providing for the eugenical sterilization of certain potential parents carrying degenerate hereditary qualities.

Be It Enacted By The People Of The State of . . . . . that:

Section 1. Short Title. This Act shall be known as the "Eugenical Sterilization Law."

Section 2. Definitions. For the purpose of this Act, the terms (a) socially inadequate person, (b) socially inadequate classes, (c) heredity, (d) potential parent, (e) to procreate, (f) potential parent of socially inadequate offspring, (g) cacogenic person, (h) custodial institution, (i) inmate, and (j) eugenical sterilization, are hereby defined as follows:

(a) A socially inadequate person is one who by his or her own effort, regardless of etiology or prognosis, fails chronically in comparison

290

with normal persons, to maintain himself or herself as a useful member of the organized social life of the state; provided that the term socially inadequate shall not be applied to any person whose individual or social ineffectiveness is due to the normally expected exigencies of youth, old age, curable injuries, or temporary physical or mental illness, in case such ineffectiveness is adequately taken care of by the particular family in which it occurs.

(b) The socially inadequate classes, regardless of etiology or prognosis, are the following: (1) Feeble-minded; (2) Insane, (including the psychopathic); (3) Criminalistic (including the delinquent and wayward); (4) Epileptic; (5) Inebriate (including drug-habitués); (6) Diseased (including the tuberculous, the syphilitic, the leprous, and others with chronic, infectious and legally segregable diseases); (7) Blind (including those with seriously impaired vision); (8) Deaf (including those with seriously impaired hearing); (9) Deformed (including the crippled); and (10) Dependent (including orphans, ne'er-do-wells, the homeless, tramps and paupers).

(c) Heredity in the human species is the transmission, through spermatozoön and ovum, of physical, physiological and psychological qualities, from parents to offspring; by extension it shall be interpreted in this Act to include also the transmission post-conceptionally and ante-natally of physiological weakness, poisons or infections from parent or parents to offspring.

(d) A potential parent is a person who now, or in the future course of development, may reasonably by expected to be able to procreate offspring.

(e) To procreate means to beget or to conceive offspring, and applies equally to males and females.

(f) A potential parent of socially inadequate offspring is a person who, regardless of his or her own physical, physiological or psychological personality, and of the nature of the germ-plasm of such person's co-parent, is a potential parent at least one-fourth of whose possible offspring, because of the certain inheritance from said parent of one or more inferior or degenerate physical, physiological or psychological qualities would, on the average, according to the demonstrated laws of heredity, most probably function as socially inadequate persons; or at least one-half of whose possible offspring would receive from said parent, and would carry in the germ-plasm but would not necessarily show in the personality, the genes or genes-complex for one or more inferior or degenerate physical, physiological or psychological qualities, the appearance of which quality or qualities in the personality would cause the possessor thereof to function as a socially inadequate person, under the normal environment of the state.

(g) The term cacogenic person, as herein used, is a purely legal expression, and shall be applied only to persons declared, under the legal procedure provided by this Act, to be potential parents of socially inadequate offspring.

(h) A custodial institution is a habitation which, regardless of whether its authority or support be public or private, provides (1) food and lodging, and (2) restraint, treatment, training, care or residence for one or more socially inadequate inmates; provided that the term custodial institution shall not apply to a private household in which the socially inadequate member or members are close blood-kin or marriage relations to, or legally adopted by, an immediate member of the care-taking family.

(i) An inmate is a socially inadequate person who is a prisoner, patient, pupil, or member of, or who is otherwise held, treated, trained, cared for, or resident within a custodial institution, regardless of whether the relation of such person to such institution be voluntary or involuntary, or that of pay or charity.

(j) Eugenical Sterilization is a surgical operation upon or the medical treatment of the reproductive organs of the human male or female, in consequence of which the power to procreate offspring is surely and permanently nullified; provided, that as used in this

292

Act the term eugenical sterilization shall imply skillful, safe and humane medical and surgical treatment of the least radical nature necessary to achieve permanent sexual sterility and the highest possible therapeutic benefits depending upon the exigencies of each particular case.

Section 3. Office of State Eugenicist. There is hereby established for the State of......the office of State Eugenicist, the function of which shall be to protect the state against the procreation of persons socially inadequate from degenerate or defective physical, physiological or psychological inheritance.

Section 4. Qualifications of State Eugenicist. The State Eugenicist shall be a trained student of human heredity, and shall be skilled in the modern practice of securing and analyzing human pedigrees; and he shall be required to devote his entire time and attention to the duties of his office as herein contemplated.

Section 5. Term of Office, Appointment, and Responsibility. The State Eugenicist shall be appointed by the Governor, with the consent of the Senate, shall be responsible directly to the Governor, and shall hold office until removed by death, resignation, or until his successor shall have been duly appointed.

Section 6. Seal. The Governor of the State shall cause a seal to be fashioned and made for the Office of the State Eugenicist, which seal shall be duly entrusted to the State Eugenicist and shall constitute the evidence of authority under this Act.

Section 7. Duties of State Eugenicist. It shall be the duty of the State Eugenicist:

(a) To conduct field-surveys seeking firsthand data concerning the hereditary constitution of all persons in the State who are socially inadequate personally or who, although normal personally, carry degenerate or defective hereditary qualities of a socially inadequating nature, and to cooperate with, to hear the complaints of, and to seek information from individuals and public and private

293

social-welfare, charitable and scientific organizations possessing special acquaintance with and knowledge of such persons, to the end that the State shall possess equally accurate data in reference to the personal and family histories of all persons existing in the State, who are potential parents of socially inadequate offspring, regardless of whether such potential parents be members of the population at large or inmates of custodial institutions, regardless also of the personality, sex, age, marital condition, race or possessions of such persons.

(b) To examine further into the natural physical, physiological and psychological traits, the environment, the personal histories, and the family-pedigrees of all persons existing in the State, whether in the population at large or as inmates of custodial institutions, who reasonably appear to be potential parents of socially inadequate offspring, with the view to determining more definitely whether in each particular case the individual is a cacogenic person within the meaning of this Act.

(c) To maintain a roster of all public and private custodial institutions in the state, and to require from the responsible head of each such institution, a record by full names and addresses, social and medical diagnosis and other pertinent data in reference to all accessions and losses of inmates as such occur from time to time; the said State Eugenicist may require a copy of any record which the particular institution may possess in reference to the case, family or institutional histories of any inmate which the State Eugenicist may name.

(d) To follow up, so far as possible, the case-histories of persons eugenically sterilized under this Act, with special reference to their social, economic, marital and health records, and to investigate the specific effects of eugenical sterilization.

(e) To preserve as property of the State complete records of all investigations and transactions of the office of State Eugenicist, and annually to render to the Governor in writing a true and complete report thereof.

(f) To perform such other duties as are enumerated elsewhere in this Act.

Section 8. Coöperation by Custodial Institutions. For the purpose of securing the facts essential to the determination required by this Act, the responsible head of any public or private custodial institution within the State shall, on demand, render promptly to the State Eugenicist all reports herein contemplated, and shall extend to said Officer and his duly appointed agents ready access to all records and inmates of the particular institution.

Section 9. Power to Administer Oaths and to Make Arrests. The State Eugenicist and his assistants appointed in writing by him for the purpose, shall have power to administer oaths, to subpoena and to examine witnesses under oath, and to make arrests.

Section 10. Opinion of State Eugenicist. If, after an investigation contemplated by this Act, the State Eugenicist is of the opinion that a particular subject of such investigation, which such subject is hereinafter called the propositus, is a potential parent of socially inadequate offspring, it shall be the duty of said State Eugenicist to present such opinion in writing, to a court of record in the County wherein the particular propositus resides, sojourns, is held or is apprehended; provided that such opinion shall be accompanied by the historical and biological evidence upon which such opinion is based, and by a petition to said court praying for the legal determination of the question of fact, whether the particular propositus is, as held in the opinion, a potential parent of socially inadequate offspring; provided that in case of apparent over-sight or dereliction by the State Eugenicist, any citizen of the state over twenty-one years of age, of sound mind and respected character, may institute proceedings for the legal determination of the question in fact, whether a particular named person is, as such complaining citizen may allege, a potential parent of socially inadequate offspring, by presenting to the court of record in the county in which the particular propositus lives or sojourns, a statement duly sworn to relating the evidence upon which the

295

particular allegation is based, and praying for a legal determination of the above-stated question of fact, whereupon within thirty days of the filing of such petition, such court shall consider the adequacy of such evidence and, in its discretion, shall dismiss the case or shall command the State Eugenicist to make the eugenical investigation provided for by this Act in reference to the particular propositus, and to return his findings back to the court issuing such command, which findings shall be returned within ninety days of the issuing of such command and shall contain an opinion by the State Eugenicist as to whether the particular propositus is in fact a potential parent of socially inadequate offspring; provided that if such report presents the opinion that the particular propositus is a potential parent of socially inadequate offspring, the legal and eugenical processes in the case shall proceed as in other cases as provided by this Act; provided that if such report presents the opinion that the particular propositus is not a potential parent of socially inadequate offspring, the court may, in its discretion, dismiss the case or may order the legal and eugenical processes to proceed as in other cases provided by this Act.

Section 11. Appointment of Date for Hearing. Within ten days after the presentation of the written opinion by the State Eugenicist holding a particular propositus to be a potential parent of socially inadequate offspring, or the presentation of a negative opinion by the State Eugenicist contrarily to which opinion the court determines to proceed, it shall be the duty of the court to which such opinion is presented to appoint a time for hearing the case, which appointed time shall be within thirty days of the appointing day if the court receiving the opinion is in continuous session, and not later than the next regular session, if said court is held periodically.

Section 12. Notification of Parties Concerned. It shall be the further duty of said court to notify the propositus or the legal guardian, custodian, or next friend of said propositus, the Attorney-General of the State, and the State Eugenicist, concerning the time, place and nature of the contemplated hearing; to summon the propositus to such hearing, or if said propositus be under legal guardianship, in custody, or if, in the opinion of said court, said propositus be incapable of understanding the nature of a summons, to command the legal guardian, or custodian of said propositus, or an executive officer of said court, to present the person of said propositus before said court at the appointed time and place; to subpoena witnesses; if need be, to appoint legal counsel at the expense of the State to represent the propositus; and to institute such other processes as may be necessary according to the statutes of the state and customs of the particular court, in order to insure a prompt, just and legal decision in the matter.

Section 13. The State's Legal Counsel. In all legal actions growing out of this Act, it shall be the duty of the Attorney-General of the State, assisted by the prosecuting attorney of the county in which the particular court is seated, to represent the State.

Section 14. Determination by Jury. On demand of either party to a hearing as herein contemplated, the question of fact shall be decided by a majority vote of a jury of six, summoned and conducted in accordance with the laws of the State governing trials by jury, but in case no such demand be made, the judge presiding over the court shall decide the case.

Section 15. Judgment. If, after the case has been duly heard and tried, it is the opinion of the court or the jury, as the case may be, that the particular propositus is a potential parent of socially inadequate offspring within the meaning of this Act, it shall be the duty of said court to declare the particular propositus to be a cacogenic person, and to command the State Eugenicist to arrest, if need be, such particular cacogenic person, and to cause such person to be eugenically sterilized in a skillful, safe and humane manner, and with due regard to the possible therapeutical benefits of such treatment of operation; securing, if possible, the consent and cooperation of said cacogenic person, and, if such there be, of the legal guardian, custodian or next friend of said cacogenic person; and such court shall further command that the particular cacogenic person shall not be released from the custody of the State Eugenicist until said order has been duly executed, but that the said particular cacogenic person be not held in the custody of the State Eugenicist longer than is necessary for the consummation of the eugenical sterilization and convalescence therefrom; and said court shall further command the State Eugenicist to report back, immediately upon the release of the person sterilized, to the court issuing the said command, a sworn statement as to the identity of the person eugenically sterilized and the place, date, nature and outcome of the particular operation or treatment; provided that in case the said cacogenic person be an inmate of a custodial institution, the court shall issue a supplementary order commanding the responsible head of such particular custodial institution to provide access for the State Eugenicist and the physician and surgeon appointed by said State Eugenicist, to the person of the particular cacogenic person in the best-equipped hospital quarters which such custodial institution affords for the consummation of the particular eugenical sterilizing operation or treatment, and to aid and co-operate in such consummation; provided that in case the court is convinced that the conduct or security of said cacogenic person is such that said person will not become a parent, the court may in its discretion suspend the order for eugenical sterilization during the period of such conduct and security.

Section 16. Appeals. In litigation growing out of this Act, appeals from the decision of the court of first instance shall lie as in civil trials de novo at law, as provided by the statutes of the State.

Section 17. Type of Eugenical Sterilization. The particular type of surgical operation or medical treatment for effecting sterilization in each particular case legally ordered in consequence of this Act shall be determined upon by the State Eugenicist, after due consultation with competent medical and surgical advisors.

Section 18. Manner of Consummation. All cases of eugenical sterilization executed in consequence of this Act shall be consummated under the direct supervision and responsibility of the State Eugenicist, in a skillful, safe and humane manner, with due regard to the possible therapeutic benefits to be derived therefrom, and in strict accordance with modern sanitary, hospital, medical and surgical knowledge and practice; provided that the contracts for the hospital, medical and surgical services involved in such consummation shall be entered into for the State by the State Eugenicist, who shall determine the necessary and reasonable fees incident thereto, which fees shall be paid by the State from funds previously appropriated for said purpose; provided that in case the person ordered sterilized be an inmate of a custodial institution, and if in the opinion of the State Eugenicist, the hospital facilities of the particular institution are inadequate, or if time ample for eugenical sterilization and convalescence does not permit the particular -operation or treatment to be consummated before the time previously set for the discharge, release or parole of the particular propositus, the order for eugenical sterilization shall not be consummated in the custodial institution, but that the responsible head of said particular custodial institution shall at the time previously set for the discharge, release or parole of the particular propositus, so discharge, release or parole said person into the custody of the State Eugenicist, who shall then proceed to execute the order for the eugenical sterilization as in cases originating in the population at large.

Section 19. Liability. Neither the State Eugenicist, nor any other person legally participating in the execution of the provisions of this Act, shall be liable either civilly or criminally on account of said participation.

Section 20. Illegal Destruction of Reproductive Functions. Nothing in this Act shall be construed so as to prevent the medical or surgical treatment for sound therapeutic reasons of any person in this State, by a physician or surgeon licensed by this State, which treatment may incidentally involve the nullification or destruction of the reproductive functions; provided that any person in this State, except as duly ordered by the courts of law as contemplated in this Act, who willfully, and without the aforementioned therapeutical necessity, nullifies or destroys or assists in nullifying or destroying, the reproductive functions of any person, shall be guilty of a felony, and shall be punished by not less than — months imprisonment or a fine of — dollars, or both, or by not more than — months imprisonment or a fine of — dollars, or both.

Section 21. Punishment of Responsible Head of Institution for Dereliction. The responsible head of any public or private custodial institution in the State who shall discharge, release or parole from his or her custody or care any inmate who has been duly ordered by a court of this State to be eugenically sterilized, before due consummation of such order as herein contemplated, unless, as herein provided, such particular inmate be discharged, released or paroled into the custody of the State Eugenicist, shall be guilty of a misdemeanor, and shall be punished by not less than

— months imprisonment or — dollars fine, or both; or by not more than — months imprisonment or — dollars fine, or both.

Section 22. Supremacy of this Act. All statutes or portions of statutes of this State contrary to this Act are hereby repealed.

Section 23. When Effective. This Act shall take effect immediately.

C. THE FEDERAL GOVERNMENT AND EUGENICAL STERILIZATION.

a. Principles Suggested for a Federal Statute.

Persons Subject. 1. Immigrants who are personally eligible to admission but who by the standards recommended in the model state law are potential parents of socially inadequate offspring. 2. All persons below the standards of parenthood set in the model state law who are beyond the jurisdiction of state laws, including the inhabitants of the District of Columbia, unorganized and outlying territories, Indian reservations, inmates of federal institutions, and soldiers and sailors.

Executive Agencies Provided. Federal Eugenicist attached to Public Health Service or the Children's Bureau, aided by an ample corps of assistants.

Basis of Selection: Procedure. Same as for model state law, naming in place of state courts of record, Federal Courts of appropriate jurisdiction.

Type of Operation Authorized. Same as for model state law.

United States' Motive. Purely eugenic.

Appropriations Available for Enforcing the Act. Ample appropriations for the maintenance of the activities of the Federal Eugenicist as a permanent and effective institution.

b. Comment.

Up to the present time, the Federal Government has not enacted any legislation bearing either directly or indirectly upon eugenical sterilization. The matter of segregating, sterilizing, or otherwise rendering non-reproductive the degenerate human strains in America is, in accordance with the spirit of our institutions, fundamentally a matter for each state to decide for itself. There is, however, a specialized field in which the Federal Government must cooperate with the several states, if the human breeding stock in our population is to be purged of its defective parenthood.

The relation between the inheritable qualities of our immigrants and the destiny of the American nation is very close. Granting that the fecundity of native and immigrant stock will run evenly, then it is clear that from generation to generation the natural qualities of our present human parenthood will more and more assume the character of the natural qualities of immigrant parents. Thus, if the American nation desires to upbuild or even to maintain its standard of natural qualities, it must forbid the addition through immigration to our human breeding stock of persons of a lower natural hereditary constitution than that which constitutes the desired standard.

If our standard of physical, mental and moral qualities for parenthood strike more heavily against one race than another, then we should be willing to enforce laws which take on the appearance of racial discrimination but which indeed would not be such, because in every race, even the very lowest, there are some individuals who through natural merit could conform to our standards of admission.

The immigration policy of the eugenicist, who has at heart the preservation, upbuilding and specialization of our better family stocks. is to base the criterion for admission of would-be immigrants primarily upon the possession of sterling natural qualities, regardless of race, language, or present social or economic condition.

It is suggested that a Federal Eugenicist, attached to the Public Health Service, or to the Children's Bureau, aided by an ample corps of assistants, would constitute an effective administrative agency for sterilization under federal authority. Some of the assistants of the office of Federal Eugenicist should be delegated to cooperate with the Immigration Service of the Department of Labor, and the Bureaus of Criminal Identification, and of Prisons, of the Department of Justice, and possibly with the Bureau of Education of the Department of the Interior. If the projected plan for examining the admissibility of immigrants in their native homes before their purchase of transportation, or even upon the steamships before landing, were adopted, it would be possible to pass satisfactorily upon the eugenical qualifications of the particular immigrant. This would be effected by attaching eugenicists to the medical and social staff to which would be delegated the task of determining the eugenical qualifications of each candidate for admission.

The Federal Government has exclusive jurisdiction over immigrants, and it controls interstate and foreign quarantine. It has also exclusive jurisdiction, either direct or final, over the socially inadequate, both within and not in custodial institutions, in the District of Columbia, the Indian reservations, and the territories which have not yet been admitted to statehood. It operates and controls the twenty-four federal custodial institutions for various types of the socially inadequate. Thus, a Federal law would be needed in order effectually to cooperate with the eugenical efforts of the states, should the latter generally determine upon sterilization as a means for cutting down the birth rate among degenerates. The office of Federal Eugenicist attached to the Public Health Service or the Children's Bureau would constitute an appropriate executive agent of a federal sterilization statute.

References

1   Freud, Sigmund (1920)," Beyond the Pleasure Principal"

2   Freud, Sigmund (1910), "The Origin and Development of Psychoanalysis", *American Journal of Psychology* 21(2); 196–218.

3   Freud, Sigmund (1923), *Das Ich und das Es*, Internationaler Psycho-analytischer Verlag, Leipzig, Vienna, and Zurich. English translation: The Ego and the Id, Joan Riviere (trans.), Hogarth Press and Institute of Psycho-analysis, London, UK, 1927. Revised for: The Standard Edition of: The Complete Psychological Works of Sigmund Freud, James Strachey (ed.), W.W. Norton and Company, New York, NY, 1961.

4   Freud, Sigmund (1923), "Neurosis and Psychosis". The Standard Edition of the Complete Psychological Works of Sigmund Freud, Volume XIX (1923-1925): The Ego and the Id and Other Works; 147-154

5   Freud, Anna, "The Ego and the Mechanisms of Defense", The Writings of Anna Freud, Vol. 2, 1936

6   Greenwald, A. G., McGhee, D. E., & Schwartz, J. K. L. (1998). Measuring individual differences in implicit cognition: The Implicit Association Test. *Journal of Personality and Social Psychology, 74*, 1464-1480.

7   Nosek, B. A., Banaji, M. R., & Greenwald, A. G. (2002). Harvesting implicit group attitudes and beliefs from a demonstration website. Group Dynamics, 6(1), 101-115.

8   Shariat, Sheryll; Sue Mallonee; Shelli Stephens-Stidham (December 1998). "Summary of Reportable Injuries in Oklahoma". Oklahoma State Department of Health. Archived from the original on January 10, 2008.

9   "Oklahoma City Police Department Alfred P. Murrah Federal Building Bombing After Action Report" (PDF). Terrorism Info. p. 58. Archived from the original on July 3, 2007

10   "Victims of the Oklahoma City bombing". USA Today. Associated Press. June 20, 2001. Archived from the original on February 27, 2011.

11   "Columbine High School Shootings Fast Facts". CNN. September 19, 2013.

12   Lamb, Gina (April 17, 2008). "Columbine High School". The New York Times.

13 Goldberg, Carey. "For Those Who Dress Differently, an Increase in Being Viewed as Abnormal." The New York Times. May 1, 1999

14 Paulhus, D.L. & Williams, K.M. 2002. "The Dark Triad of personality: Narcissism, Machiavellianism, and psychopathy". Journal of Research in Personality 36 (2002) 556–563

15 Paulhus, D.L. & Williams, K.M. 2002. "The Dark Triad of personality: Narcissism, Machiavellianism, and psychopathy". Journal of Research in Personality 36 (2002) 556–563.

16 Christie, R. & Geis, F. (1970) "Studies in Machiavellianism". NY: Academic Press.

17 Christie, R., and F. L. Geis. (1970) "How devious are you? Take the Machiavelli test to find out." *Journal of Management in Engineering* 15.4: 17.

18 Costa, P.T., Jr. & McCrae, R.R. (1992). *Revised NEO Personality Inventory (NEO-PI-R) and NEO Five-Factor Inventory (NEO-FFI) manual.* Odessa, FL: Psychological Assessment Resources.

19 Cattell, R. B.; Marshall, MB; Georgiades, S (1957). "Personality and motivation: Structure and measurement". *Journal of Personality Disorders* **19** (1): 53–6. doi:10.1521/pedi.19.1.53.62180. PMID 15899720.

20 Gunnthorsdottir, Anna & McCabe, Kevin & Smith, Vernon, 2002. "Using the Machiavellianism instrument to predict trustworthiness in a bargaining game," Journal of Economic Psychology, Elsevier, vol. 23(1), pages 49-66, February.

21 Bartolome de las Casas, "The devastation of the Indies: A brief account," Johns Hopkins University Press, (1992).

22 Barry Lopez, "The Rediscovery of North America: The Thomas D. Clark lectures," University Press of Kentucky, (1990).

23 David E. Stannard, "American Holocaust: Columbus and the Conquest of the New World," Oxford University Press, (1992).

24 Hans Koning, "The conquest of America: How the Indian nations lost their continent," Monthly Review Press, (1993).

25 Bender, Daniel E. (2009). American abyss: savagery and civilization in the age of industry. Cornell University.

26 Pernick, Martin S. (1999). The Black Stork: Eugenics and the Death of "Defective" Babies in American Medicine and Motion Pictures since 1915. Oxford University Press.

27 Kühl, Stefan (2001). The Nazi Connection: Eugenics, American Racism, and German National Socialism. Oxford University Press US.

28 Black, Edwin (November 9, 2003). "Eugenics and the Nazis – the California connection". San Francisco Chronicle.

29 Black, Edwin (2003). War Against the Weak: Eugenics and America's Campaign to Create a Master Race. New York / London: Four Walls Eight Windows

30 Engs, Ruth C. (2005). The eugenics movement: an encyclopedia. Greenwood Press.

304

31   Reilly, Philip R. "Laughlin, Harry Hamilton." American National Biography. New York: Oxford University Press, 1999, 13:252.

32   Lombardo, Paul A. (2011). A Century of Eugenics in America: From the Indiana Experiment to the Human Genome Era. Indiana University Press.

33   Popenoe, Paul & Johnson, Roswell H. (1918). Applied Eugenics, New York, Macmillan Company.

34   Lombardo, Paul A. (2008). Three generations, no imbeciles: eugenics, the Supreme Court, and Buck v. Bell. JHU Press.

35   Skinner v. Oklahoma, 316 U.S. 535 (1942).

36   Kevles, Daniel J. (1986). In the Name of Eugenics: genetics and the uses of human heredity. Harvard University Press.

37   Murphy, Timothy F. & Lappé, Marc, ed. (1994). Justice and the human genome project. University of California Press.

38   Ordover, Nancy (2003). American eugenics: race, queer anatomy, and the science of nationalism. University of Minnesota Press.

39   Nielsen Media Research, 1998.

40   Mediaweek, April 20, 1998; p.8.

41   Senate Judiciary Committee Staff Report, "Children, Violence, and the Media." 1999; p.2.

42   The Sentencing Project, 'Facts About Prisons and Prisoners', www.sentencingproject.org/df/1035.pdf.

43   Bonczar, Thomas P.: Prevalence of Imprisonment in the U.S. Population, 1974-2001, Bureau of Justice Statistics, 2003; p. 8.

44   The Sentencing Project, 'Facts About Prisons and Prisoners', ibid

45   Bureau of Justice Statistics, Sourcebook of Criminal Justice Statistics, 2001, www.albany.edu/sourcebook.

46   The Sentencing Project, ibid

47   ACLU, 'Drugs and race', 17 December 2001

48   The Sentencing Project, 'Does the Punishment Fit the Crime? Drug Users and Drunk Drivers, Questions of Race and Class', www.sentencingproject.org/pdfs/9040smy.pdf.

49   Eme, R.: Attention-deficit hyperactivity disorder and correctional health care. J. Correctional Health Care.2009;15:5-18.

50   Marcotte DE, Markowitz S: A Cure for Crime?: Psycho-Pharmaceuticals and Crime Trends. Cambridge, Mass: National Bureau of Economic Research; 2009. Available at: http://www.nber.org/papers/215354 Accessed February 15, 2010.

51   Harrison Paige M., Beck, Allen J.: Prisoners in 2005, Bureau of Justice Statistics, 2006; p. 8.

52   Blumstein, Alfred: "Racial Disproportionality of U.S. Prison Populations Revisited," University of Colorado Law Review, Vol. 64, No. 3, 1993.

[53] Tonry, Michael: "Racial Disproportions in US Prisons," British Journal of Criminology, Vol. 34, 1994.

[54] Jankowski, Louis W.: Correctional Populations in the United States, 1990, Bureau of Justice Statistics, 1992; p. 86;

[55] Bureau of Justice Statistics, 'Prevalence of Imprisonment in the US Population, 1974-2001', August, 2003.

[56] The Sentencing Project, Women in the Criminal Justice System, May 2007.

[57] Sentencing Project, 'Fact Sheet: Women in Prison', op.cit.

[58] King, Ryan S., Mauer, Marc, Young, Malcolm C.: Incarceration and Crime: A Complex Relationship, The Sentencing Project, 2005.

[59] Mauer, Marc: "Intended and Unintended Consequences: State Racial Disparities in Imprisonment," The Sentencing Project, January 1997.

[60] Human Rights Watch/ The Sentencing Project, 'Losing the Vote', 1998.

[61] Fellner, Jamie: "Punishment and Prejudice: The Racial Costs in the War on Drugs," Human Rights Watch, May 2000.

[62] Harrison Paige M., Beck, Allen J.: Prison and Jail Inmates at Midyear 2005, Bureau of Justice Statistics, 2006; p. 11

[63] Sabol, William J., Minton, Todd D., Harrison, Paige M.: Prison and Jail Inmates at Midyear 2006, Bureau of Justice Statistics, 2007; p. 9

[64] Brownell, W. C. (1963). American prose masters: Cooper, Hawthorne, Emerson, Poe, Lowell, Henry James. Harvard University Press. p. 283.

[65] Henley, William Ernest (1888). A book of verses. London: D. Nutt.

Printed in the United States
by Baker & Taylor Publisher Services